Arthur Henry Brown

The Anglican Psalter and canticles

The Psalms and canticles newly adapted to Anglican etc.

Arthur Henry Brown

The Anglican Psalter and canticles
The Psalms and canticles newly adapted to Anglican etc.

ISBN/EAN: 9783337043131

Printed in Europe, USA, Canada, Australia, Japan

Cover: Foto ©ninafisch / pixelio.de

More available books at **www.hansebooks.com**

The Anglican Psalter and Canticles.

THE

PSALMS AND CANTICLES

NEWLY ADAPTED TO ANGLICAN

CHANTS OF ECCLESIASTICAL

CHARACTER,

BY

ARTHUR HENRY BROWN.

LONDON:

THOMAS BOSWORTH, 198, HIGH HOLBORN.

1878.

CRERAR AND SMITH,
TYPE MUSIC AND GENERAL PRINTERS, 3, FEATHERSTONE BUILDINGS, HOLBORN, LONDON.

CONTENTS.

	PAGE
PREFACE	vii
EXPLANATION OF THE MARKS	x
TABLE OF PROPER PSALMS ON CERTAIN DAYS, AND FOR SPECIAL OCCASIONS	xi
DIRECTIONS AS TO THE USE OF THE CANTICLES	xiii
TE DEUM, AMERICAN VERSION	xiv
VENITE, EXULTEMUS DOMINO	1
PASCHA NOSTRUM (SPECIAL SETTING)	2
PASCHA NOSTRUM (EASTER ANTHEMS)	3
TE DEUM LAUDAMUS	4
BENEDICITE, OMNIA OPERA	6
BENEDICITE, OMNIA OPERA (SPECIAL SETTINGS)	8
BENEDICTUS	10
JUBILATE DEO	11
QUICUNQUE VULT	12
MAGNIFICAT ANIMA MEA	14
CANTATE DOMINO	15
NUNC DIMITTIS	16
DEUS MISEREATUR	17
VARIED ORGAN HARMONIES FOR MONOTONIC RECITATION OF CANTICLES OR PSALMS ON ASH WEDNESDAY AND GOOD FRIDAY	18

PSALTER, PROPER PSALMS AND MISERERE.

| INDEX OF COMPOSERS ... ... | 215 |

PREFACE.

NOTWITHSTANDING the large number of English Psalters set to Anglican Chants which are now before the public, the present work is really an attempt to supply a *desideratum*. During late years a taste for sound Church music has spread very widely throughout the Anglican Churches. The works of our early Church composers have been increasingly appreciated, and Chant Tunes upon their models have been multiplied, until a collection has been found, which, for richness, for variety, and for power of devotional expression, is unsurpassed in any part of Christendom.

The Editor of the Anglican Psalter has endeavoured to utilise this large body of material. Limiting himself to compositions of strictly Ecclesiastical character, he has adapted four different series of chants to each group of the Psalms in their daily course, the selection being made with the most careful regard to the sentiment of each Psalm. These series are numbered 1, 2, 3, and 4, and are set respectively in the same or allied keys, to ensure easy transition. Those in the upper line, Nos. 1 and 2, have been selected as intrinsically the most appropriate to the spirit of the Psalm to which they are appropriated. Series 3 are jubilant in character, and are therefore adapted to festival seasons. The fourth series are plaintive, and suited for more *triste* or penitential occasions. In no case is the same melody used to more than one group of Psalms throughout the same course. By this means a variety and freshness have been aimed at which have not hitherto been attained. In selecting the chants, care has been taken to avoid those with too high a reciting note.

A melody has also been selected for the *Venite* for each morning in the month, having special regard to the character of the Psalms which it precedes. The Proper Psalms, with their music, are printed again at large at the end of the book.

PREFACE.

That this work may be more generally useful to the Church, provision is made for those verses of the *Te Deum* in which the American version differs from our own.

Simultaneously with the spread of a sounder taste in Ecclesiastical melody, has been developed the means of producing printed music at a price within the reach of all, even the poorest worshippers. In the production of the *Anglican Psalter* these opportunities have been fully used, and it is accordingly issued at an unprecedentedly low price.

The system of pointing here adopted is one which the Editor believes to be grounded upon true principles; its essential plan being to apportion, so far as is consistent with correct English accent, one syllable to each musical beat, and to avoid a dissyllable for the final note of both mediation and cadence.* Thus, wherever either of these has the penultimate or ante-penultimate accent in its last word, the two, or three, final syllables have been spread over the last two measures, instead of appropriating them to the last measure only. For example :—

(Penultimate Accent.)	(Ante-penultimate Accent.)
For behôld from hĕnce-forth :	That we should be sâved from our é-ne-mies :
In glôry év-er-läst-ing.	And to remêmber His hó-ly co-ve-nant.

INSTEAD OF—

Fôr behóld from henceforth :	That we should be sâved fróm our enemies :
În gló-ry ev-er-lasting.	Ând to remémber His ho-ly covenant.

By no other means can a smooth and pleasant method of English chanting be obtained. What, for instance, can be more objectionable and unmusical than to hear words of from two to five or six syllables jumbled together upon one final note, such as "wilderness," "tabernacle," "uncharitableness?" In Gregorian chanting, by the varying lengths of the musical cadences, and the alternative notes of some of the Mediations, these difficulties are easily disposed of; but, owing to the inflexible nature of the Anglican Chant, commonly so-

---

* It has been found absolutely necessary in a few instances to treat the following words as monosyllables when occurring as the finals of either Mediation or Cadence :—"Doer," "doers," "doest," "doing," "going," "goings," "heaven," "heavens," "iron," "liars," "Peor," "power," "prayer.";

called, another mode of treatment must be used to ensure smoothness; and that here adopted seems to meet all requirements.

Some seven or eight years ago the Editor published in his *Matin and Vesper Canticles of Holy Church*, a chant of new form, having an alternative note in the Mediation, to suit final words of more than one syllable (which form has lately been adopted in the recently published *Psalter, Ancient and Modern);* but it has been rejected here on account of the impossibility of combining both forms with the system of pointing advocated above.

The pointing marks are those which the Editor has used in his other Church works, in preference to the division of the words by change of type, or by bars, which are found to induce a habit of "jibbing" at the first word after the recitation; a practice fatal to good chanting.

The Editor's best thanks are due to those gentlemen whose names are attached to their respective chants, for the use of their compositions; also to the Rev. T. Helmore and Mr. Masters, for that in F by the late W. Dyce; to Messrs. Novello, for Mr. J. Barnby's Chants in D and E, for two others by Mr. Turle, from the *Westminster Chant Book*, and for the two Chants by Dr. Stainer, Organist of St. Paul's Cathedral; to Mr. Blakeley for his Chants from the *Canticle Chant Book;* to Mr. Joule for those from his Collection; and to the Lord Bishop of Lincoln for his Table of the Proper Psalms for Special Occasions.

BRENTWOOD,
Trinity, 1878.

Non vox, sed votum; non musica chordula, sed cor,
Non clamans, sed amans, psallit in aure Dei.

EXPLANATION OF THE MARKS.

1. (^) The Circumflex implies a slight emphasis on the word or syllable so marked, before leaving the reciting note, except when it is on a word of one syllable which takes also the acute accent (*e.g.* verses 7, 8, 9, of *Te Deum*, p. 4, prâi̇́se Thee; also Ps. xix. 15); or the first syllable of a word having the acute accent on the second (*e.g.* verses 4 and 26 of *Te Deum*, pp. 4, 5, côntín-ual-ly; voûchsáfe; also Ps. civ. 23, ûntíl); in these cases it is simply a guide to the accented syllable. See also Ps. lii. 5; Ps. lxxxvi. 10.

2. (´) The Acute Accent corresponds with the first minim, or beat, in the chant after the reciting note.

3. (˙), (˙˙), or (¨) The Dot or Dots after the Acute Accent, or Dots only, indicate a corresponding number of beats in either the Mediation or Cadence; the accent itself being reckoned as one beat. Thus :—

   Thê Fá-ther : Thê Cóm̈-fort-er.
   Eschew êvil and dô good. (Ps. xxxiv. 14.)

4. (⁀) Two syllables, or short words, joined by a Tie, are to be sung to one beat; or to two short notes of the value of one beat. Thus :—

   Unto whôm I swáre in⁀My wrath. *(Venite.)*
   And gíveth lĭ́ght un-to⁀the eyes. (Ps. xix. 8.)
   The heavens decláre the gló-ry⁀of God. (Ps. xix. 1.)

5. (-) Syllables separated by a Hyphen are to be sung to separate notes. Thus :—

   Lôrd Gód of Sa-ba-oth. *(Te Deum.)*
   Thêy will be ál-way prais-ing Thee. (Ps. lxxxiv. 4.)

All complete words, whether of one or more syllables, in either the Mediation or Cadence, are to be sung to separate notes. Thus :— .

   For His Name only is excellent, * and Hís praíse above heaven and earth. (Ps. cxlviii. 12.)

N.B.—Portions of words like -tion, -tient, -iour, -nion, -ower, &c., are treated as one syllable.

6. (*) The Asterisk marks the breathing places : all other punctuation marks in the Recitation may be disregarded.

7. *Can.* (Cantoris), or the Precentor's, is the Gospel, or north side of the choir.

Dec. (Decani), or the Dean's, is the Epistle, or south side.

The Cantoris should sing the uneven, the Decani the even verses.

Full, signifies that both sides of the choir are to sing together, not necessarily *f*, or *ff*.

Any mark of expression, *f*, *p*, *mf*, &c., continues its influence until contradicted, whether marked *full* or not. (See vv. 7, 8, 9, of *Te Deum.)*

The first verse of a Psalm, and the *Gloria Patri*, should always be sung full ; the latter slightly *rallentando* towards the close.

Changeable Chants (Major and Minor), are always to be used as they stand, unless notice to the contrary be given in the margin, as No. 2, Psalm 30. This continues until contradicted.

✱ The Psalms at Mattins and Evensong should not be separated from the *Venite*, or the Response, "The Lord's Name be praised," by any announcement whatever. [People ought to know the Day of the Month, and whether it is Morning or Evening, before they enter the church.] In the cases of those Feasts, Fasts, or Services, for which special Psalms are, or may be, appointed, notice to that effect should be placed at the entrance to the church for the information of the Laity, so that the music of the Office may be continuous and uninterrupted.

PROPER PSALMS ON CERTAIN DAYS.

	Mattins.	Evensong.
Christmas Day	19, 45, 85.	89, 110, 132.
Easter Day	2, 57, 111.	113, 114, 118.
Ascension Day	8, 15, 21.	24, 47, 108.
Whitsun Day	48, 68.	104, 145.
Ash Wednesday	6, 32, 38.	102, 130, 143.
Good Friday	22, 40, 54.	69, 88.
Solemnization of Matrimony	128, 67.	
Burial of the Dead . . .	39, 90.	
Commination	51.	

PROPER PSALMS FOR SPECIAL OCCASIONS.

As put forth by the Ordinary, in the Synod held at Lincoln, Sept. 20, 1871.

TABLE I.

PROPER PSALMS FOR SPECIAL OCCASIONS.

For Advent Sunday—All, or any of the following may be used :—

Mattins—Psalm 18, 82, 96. | Evensong—Psalm 97, 98, 110, 143.

See also below, in Table II., Psalms for the Third Service on Sundays in Advent. These may be used also at Morning Prayer, or Evensong, on those Sundays.

For the Festival of Circumcision, or New Year's Day.

Mattins--Psalm 1, 20, 103. | Evensong—Psalm 40, 113, 144.

Any of these Psalms may be used on *New Year's Eve*, and Psalm 90.

For the Festival of the Epiphany.

Mattins— Psalm 2, 19, or 29, 45. | Evensong—72, 87, 96.

For the Purification of the Blessed Virgin Mary, or the Presentation of Christ in the Temple.

Mattins— Psalm 15, 24, 40. | Evensong—Psalm 48, 131, 134.

For the Annunciation of the Blessed Virgin Mary.
Mattins—Psalm 8, 19, 89. | Evensong—Psalm 110, 131, 132, 138.
For Palm Sunday, or Sunday before Easter.*
Any of the following may be used :—
Mattins—Psalm 5, 20, 21, 118. | Evensong—Psalm 40, 110, 112, 113, 114.
For Thursday before Easter.
Mattins—Psalm 23, 26, 41. | Evensong—Psalm 42, 43, 116.
For Easter Even.
Mattins—Psalm 4, 16, 31, 49, 142. | Evensong—Psalm 17, 30, 76, 91.
For Monday after Easter.*
Mattins—Psalm 54, 72, 81. | Evensong—Psalm 98, 99, 100.
For Tuesday after Easter.*
Mattins—Psalm 103, 108, 111. | Evensong—Psalm 114, 115, 116, 117.
For Monday in Whitsun Week.*
Mattins—Psalm 8, 19, 27, 29. | Evensong—Psalm 33, 46, 47, 48.
For Tuesday in Whitsun Week.*
Mattins—Psalm 65, 76, 77. | Evensong—Psalm 96, 97, 98, 103.
For Trinity Sunday.
Mattins—Psalm 8, 29, 33, 67. | Evensong—Psalm 93, 96, 97, 99.
For the Festival of St. Michael and All Angels, September 29.
Mattins—Psalm 8, 24, 34, 91. | Evensong—Psalm 97, 103, 148.
All Saints' Day, November 1.*
Any of the following may be used :—
Mattins—Psalm 1, 11, 15, 16, 20, 30, 33, 34, 61, 79, 84.
Evensong—Psalm 92, 97, 112, 138, 141, 147, 148, 149.

On Days of Apostles and other Festivals ;
When the Psalms in the Daily order are less appropriate, any of the following may be used, at the discretion of the Minister :—
Psalm 19, 34, 45, 46, 61, 64, 68, 75, 97, 98, 99, 110, 113, 116, 126.
For the Consecration of Churches ; or Anniversaries of their Consecration, and for the Re-opening of Churches after Restoration.
Any of the following may be used :—
Psalm 24, 27, 45, 46, 47, 48, 84, 87, 100, 118, 122, 132, 133, 134, 150.
For the Consecration of Churchyards—Psalm 39, 90.
For Harvest Festivals—Any of the following may be used :—
Psalm 65, 67, 81, 103, 104, 126, 127, 128, 144, 145, 147.
For School Festivals—Psalm 8, 23, 34, 119 (v. 1 to 17), 148.
For Choral Festivals—Psalm 33, 47, 81, 92, 96, 98, 108, 142, 147, 150.
For Ember Days—Psalm 121, 122, 123, 125, 126, 130, 131, 132, 133, 134.
For Rogation Days—Psalm 61, 62, 63, 64, 65, 66, 67.
For Missionary Services—Psalm 19, 72, 117. Also any of the Psalms appointed above for the Festival of the *Epiphany.*
For Diocesan Synods, Visitations, or Ruridecanal Chapters—Psalm 68, 84, 87, 122, 133.
For Annual Festivals of Benefit Societies—Psalm 112, 133, 145.
At Confirmation—Psalm 15, 19, 20, 23, 24, 26, 27, 34, 84, 116, 119, 148.

TABLE II.

PSALMS WHICH MAY BE USED AT A THIRD SERVICE ON SUNDAYS AND SOME HOLIDAYS.

Sundays in Advent.
I. Psalm 45, 46.   II. Psalm 9, 10, 11.   III. Psalm 49, 50.   IV. Psalm 96, 97, 98.
Christmas Day—Psalm 2, 8, 84.   *Sunday after Christmas*—Psalm 87, 96, 98.

---

* The Psalms for *Palm Sunday, Monday and Tuesday in Easter Week and in Whitsun Week, and All Saints' Day,* have been put forth by the Ordinary since the Synod.

Sundays after Epiphany.

I. Psalm 46, 47, 48.	III. Psalm 83, 84, 85.	V. Psalm 95, 96, 97.
II. ,, 65, 66, 67.	IV. ,, 91, 92, 93.	VI. ,, 98, 99, 100.

Septuagesima—Psalm 104.   *Sexagesima*—Psalm 49, 90.   *Quinquagesima*—Psalm 28, 77.

Sundays in Lent.

I. Psalm 6, 25, 32.	III. Psalm 102, 130.	V. Psalm 22.
II. ,, 38, 51.	IV. ,, 141, 142, 143.	VI. ,, 40, 45.

Easter Day—Psalm 3, 30, 76, 93.

Sundays after Easter.

I. Psalm 117, 118.	III. Psalm 98, 99, 100.	V. Psalm 80, 81.
II. ,, 19, 20, 21.	IV. ,, 111, 112, 113.	

Ascension Day—Psalm 2, 57, 110.   *Sunday after Ascension*—Psalm 93, 132.
Whitsun-Day—Psalm 84, 85, 133.   *Trinity Sunday*—Psalm 33, 97, or 148, 149, 150.

Sundays after Trinity.

I. Psalm 1, 2, 3.	XI. Psalm 62, 63, 64.	XXI. Psalm 114, 115, 116.
II. ,, 4, 6, 7.	XII. ,, 71.	XXII. ,, 120, 121, 123, 124.
III. ,, 11, 12, 13, 14.	XIII. ,, 73.	
IV. ,, 25, 26.	XIV. ,, 74, 75.	XXIII. ,, 125, 126, 127, 128, 129.
V. ,, 33, 34.	XV. ,, 79, 80, 81.	
VI. ,, 37.	XVI. ,, 82, 83, 84.	XXIV. ,, 133, 134, 135.
VII. ,, 44.	XVII. ,, 92, 93, 94.	XXV. ,, 136, 137.
VIII. ,, 52, 53, 54.	XVIII. ,, 105.	XXVI. ,, 144, 145.
IX. ,, 56, 57, 58.	XIX. ,, 107.	XXVII. ,, 146, 147.
X. ,, 59, 60, 61.	XX. ,, 109.	

DIRECTIONS AS TO THE USE OF THE CANTICLES.

Venite should not be used on the following days :—19th day of the month ; or on Easter Day, for which special anthems are appointed.
[The Rubric preceding the *Venite* is somewhat vague as to the use of this canticle on certain days which will fall upon the 19th day of the month. For instance, the following Fasts and Feasts will come upon this date in the years named below, on which days the *Venite* will not occur " in the ordinary course of the Psalms," the Psalms being special.
Ash Wednesday will fall upon the 19th day of the month in the years 1890, 1896, 1974, 1958, and 1969.
Good Friday, in 1889, 1935, 1946, and 1957.
Ascension Day, in 1887, 1898, 1955, 1966, and 1977.
Whitsun Day, in 1907, 1918, 1929, and 1991 ; beyond which we need not trouble ourselves.]

TE DEUM, should not be used during Advent ; on Septuagesima Sunday ; on the 19th Sunday after Trinity (if the Old Lessons are used); or the 21st Sunday after Trinity (if the New Lessons are used).

Benedicite, should be sung on the days above mentioned, when the TE DEUM is not used.

Benedictus, should be sung daily, except on February 18th ; June 17th ; Feast of the Nativity of St. John Baptist ; and October 5th (if the Old Lessons are used) ; and daily, except on the Feasts of the Annunciation, and the Nativity of St. John Baptist (if the New Lessons are used).

Jubilate, to be sung on the days above mentioned, when the *Benedictus* is not used.

Quicunque Vult, to be sung at Mattins, instead of the Apostles' Creed, upon these feasts :—Christmas Day, the Epiphany, Saint Matthias, Easter Day, Ascension Day, Whitsun Day, Saint John Baptist, Saint James, Saint Bartholomew, Saint Matthew, Saint Simon and Saint Jude, Saint Andrew, and Trinity Sunday.

Magnificat, should be sung daily, except on the 23rd September (if the New Lessons are used).

Cantate Domino, must not be sung on the 19th evening of the month. If the New Lessons are used, it must be sung on the 23rd September.

Nunc Dimittis, should be sung daily, except on the 26th September (if the New Lessons are used).

Deus Misereatur, must not be sung on the 12th evening of the month. If the New Lessons are used, it must be sung on the 26th September.

All the Chants in this work marked thus * are copyright. In the Index they are marked thus * and thus †; the former being the property of the Editor, the latter that of the Composer. Application for permission to print any of the Editor's copyrights (*) in this collection for Choral Festivals, &c., should be made to Mr. Arthur H. Brown, Brentwood, Essex.

TE DEUM LAUDAMUS.

For the American Version.

12 Thĭne adó-rable, true :
16 Thou didst humble Thysêlf to be bórn of ͡ a Vïr-gin.
28 O Lord, let Thy mêrcy bé upon ͜ us :

Venite, exultemus Domino.—PSALM XCV.

f O COME,* let us sĭng ŭn-to͡
the Lord : let us heartily
rejoice in the strêngth of our sal-
vā-tion.
  2 Let us come before His prêsence
with thanksgĭv-ing : and shêw ourselves glắd in Him with Psalms.
  3 For the Lôrd is a grêat God :
and a grêat Kíng above ắll gods.
  4 In His hand are all the côrners
óf the earth : and the strength of
the hĭlls is Hĭ́s ăl-so.
  5 The sea is Hĭ́s, and He māde
it : and His hânds prepắr-ed͡the
drÿ land.
  p 6 O come,* let us wôrship and
fắll down : and knêel before the
Lórd our Mä-ker.
  7 For Hê is the Lórd our God :
and we are the people of His pâsture, and the shĕep of Hĭ̈s hand.

mf 8 To-day if ye will hear His
voice,* hârden nót your hearts : as
in the provocation,* and as in the
day of temptâtion ĭn the wil-der-
ness ;
  9 When your fâthers témpt-ed
Me : prôved Mé, and saw My
works.
  10 Forty years long * was I
grieved with thĭs gencrắ-tion,͡and
said : It is a people that do err in
their hêarts, for they hắve not known
My ways.
  11 Unto whôm I swáre in͡My
wrath : that they shôuld not én-ter
into My rest.
  f Glory be to the Fâther, ắnd to͡
the Son : ând tó the Ho-ly Ghost ;
  As it was in the beginning, * is
nôw, and éver shall be : wôrld
without énd. 'A'-men.

Pascha Nostrum immolatus est Christus.

17. Adapted by A. H. Brown.

f CHRIST our passover is sácri-fíced for us : thêrefore lét us keep the feast ;

mf 2 Not with the old leaven,✶ nor with the leaven of mâlice and wíck-ed-ness : but with the unleavened brêad of sincé-ri-ty and truth.

f CHRIST being raised from the dêad díeth no more : death hath nô more domín-ion o-ver Him.

p 4 For in that He died,✶ He diéd únto sin once : *f* but in that He líveth, He lív-eth un-to God.

p 5 Likewise reckon ye also yourselves ✶ to be dêad indéed unto sin : *f* but alive unto Gôd through Jé-sus Christ our Lord.

(Full)f CHRIST is rísen fróm the dead : and becôme the fírst-fruits of them that slept.

(Can.) p 7 For sínce by mán came death : *f* by man came also the rê-surréc-tion of the dead.

p 8 For as in Âdam âll die : *f* even so in Chrîst shall áll be made a-live.

✶ F is preferred for 1st Treble.

f Glory be to the Fâther, ánd to the Son : ånd tó the Ho-ly Ghost ;
  As it was in the beginning,✶ is nôw, and éver shall be : wôrld without ênd. 'A'-men.

✶ The above Anthems are set to Pelham Humphrey's Grand Chant, which appears in one or other of the vocal parts throughout.

Pascha Nostrum immolatus est Christus.

f **C**HRIST our Passover ∗ is sacri-
ficed for us : therefore let us
keep the feast ;
mf 2 Not with the old leaven, ∗
nor with the leaven of malice and
wick-ed-ness : but with the unleavened bread of since-ri-ty and
truth.   [1 Cor. v. 7.

f **C**HRIST being raised from the
dead dieth no more : death
hath no more domin-ion o-ver Him.
p 4 For in that He died, ∗ He
died unto sin once : *f* but in that
He liveth, He liv-eth un-to God.
p 5 Likewise reckon ye also yourselves ∗ to be dead indeed unto sin :

f but alive unto God through Je-sus
Christ our Lord.   [Rom. vi. 9.

(Full) f **C**HRIST is risen from the
dead : and become the
first-fruits of them that slept.
(Can.) p 7 For since by man came
death : *f* by man came also the
resurrec-tion of the dead.
p 8 For as in Adam all die :
f even so in Christ shall all be
made a-live.   [1 Cor. xv. 20.
f Glo-ry be to the Father, and to
the Son : and to the Ho-ly Ghost ;
As it was in the beginning, ∗ is
now, and ever shall be : world
without end. A-men.

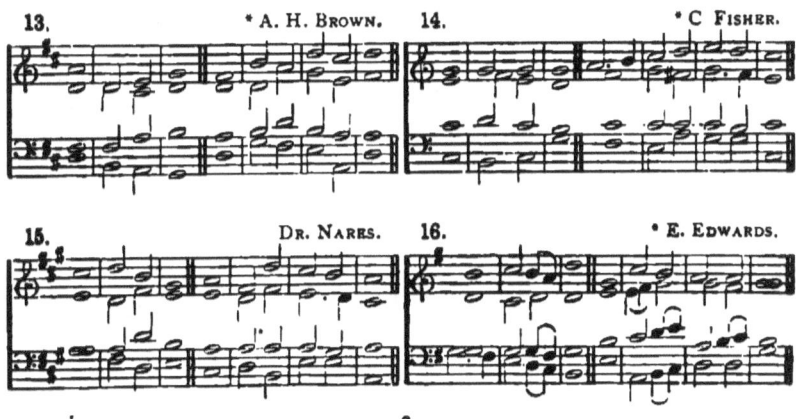

18. *J. Turle.   19. *A. H. Brown.

20. *A. H. Brown.   21. *H. Wicks.

f WE prâise Thée, O God : we
acknôwledge Thée to be
the Lord.
2 All the eârth doth wór-ship
Thee : the Fâther ̭év-er-läst-ing.
3 To Thee all Ángels crý a-loud :
the Hêavens, and áll the powers
there-in.
4 To Thee, Chêrubin, and Sé-ra-
phin : côntín-ual-ly do cry,
(*Full*) *p* 5 Holy,* Hôly, Hô-ly :
Lôrd Gód of Sa-ba-oth ;
(*Full*) *f* 6 Heaven and earth are
fûll of the Má-jes-ty : ôf Thy Glö-ry.
(*Can.*) *mf* 7 The glorious cômpany of the Apôs-tles : (*full*) pŕáïse
Thee.

(*Dec.*) *mf* 8 The goodly fêllowship
of the Prö-phets : (*full*) pŕáïse Thee.
(*Can.*) *mf* 9 The noble ârmy of
Mãr-tyrs : (*full*) pŕáïse Thee.
(*Dec.*) *f* 10 The holy Chûrch
throughout áll the world : dôth ac-
know-ledge Thee,
mf 11 Thê Fä-ther : ôf an ín-finite
Ma-jes-ty ;
12 Thíne hónoura-ble, true : ând
ôn-ly Son ;
13 Also the Hó-ly Ghost : *p* thê
Côm-for-ter.
(*Full*) *f* 14 Thou art the Kíng
of Glö-ry : Ô⁓ Christ.
(*Full*) *f* 15 Thou art the êverlást-
ing Son : ôf the Fä-ther.

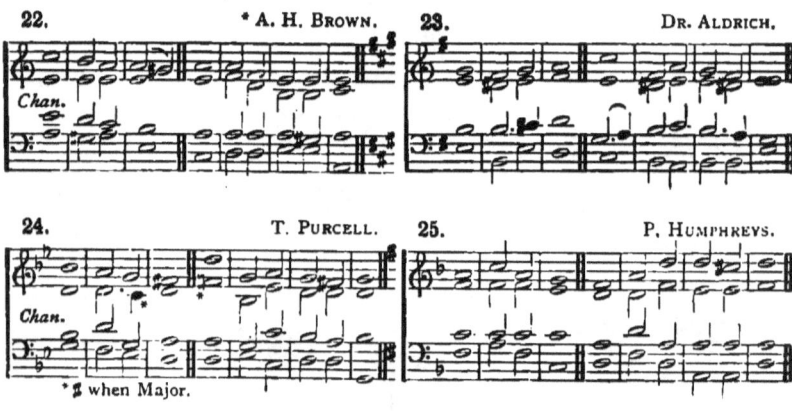

22.   *A. H. Brown.   23.   Dr. Aldrich.

24.   T. Purcell.   25.   P. Humphreys.

* ♯ when Major.

TE DEUM LAUDAMUS.

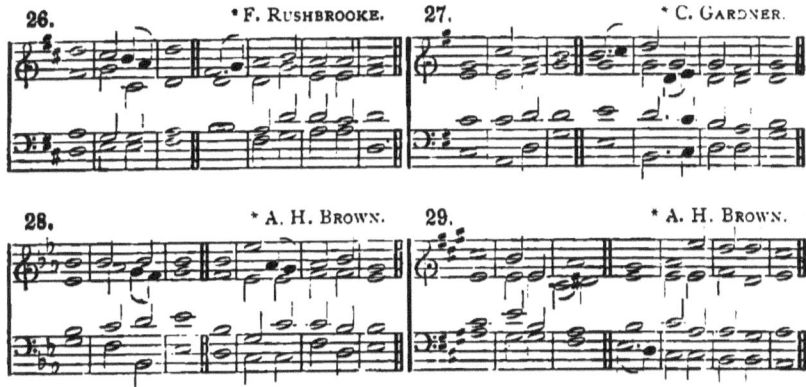

Minor.
(*Dec.*) *pp* 16 When Thou tookest upon Thêe to delív-er man : Thou didst nôt abhór the Vir-gin's womb.
p 17 When Thou hadst overcôme the shárp-ness ͡of death : Thou didst open the Kingdom of Hêaven to áll be-líev-ers.
Major.
f 18 Thou sittest at the ríght hánd of God : in the Glôry óf the Fä-ther.
Minor.
pp 19 We beliêve that Thóu shalt come : tô bê oür Judge.
20 We therefore pray Thee,* hêlp Thy sêr-vants : whom Thou hast redeêmed wíth Thy pre-cious blood.
mf 21 Make them to be nûmbered wíth Thy Saints : in glôry év-er-läst-ing.

p 22 O Lord, sâve Thy pêo-ple : ȃnd bléss Thine he-ri-tage.
23 Gô ͡-vern them : and lîft them úp for ëv-er.
Major.
(*Full*) *f* 24 Dây by day : wê mág-ni-fÿ Thee ;
(*Full*) 25 Ând we wórship Thy Name : êver wórld with-oüt end.
(*Dec.*) *p* 26 Vôuchsáfe, O Lord : to kêep us this dáy with-oüt sin.
27 O Lord, have mêrcy upôn us : hâve mér-cy ͡up-ön us.
28 O Lord, let Thy mercy líghten upôn us : ȃs our trûst is in Thee.
(*Full*) *p* 29 O Lord, in Thêe have I trûst-ed : let me nêver bé con-foünd-ed.

34. * A. H. Brown. 35. * Dr. E. G. Monk.
36. * Dr. Stainer. 37. * L. J. Turrell.

f O ALL ye Works of the Lôrd, bléss ye⁀the Lord : praise Him, and mâgnify Hím for ëv-er.
2 O ye Angels of the Lôrd, bléss ye⁀the Lord : praise Him, and mâgnify Hím for ëv-er.
mf 3 O ye Heâvens, bléss ye⁀the Lord : praise Him, and mâgnify Hím for ëv-er.
4 O ye Waters that be above the Fírmament, bléss ye⁀the Lord : praise Him, and mâgnify Hím for ëv-er.
5 O all ye Powers of the Lôrd, bléss ye⁀the Lord : praise Him, and mâgnify Hím for ëv-er.
6 O ye Sun and Môon, bléss ye⁀ the Lord : praise Him, and mâgnify Hím for ëv-er.
7 O ye Stars of Heaven, bléss ye⁀the Lord : praise Him, and mâgnify Hím for ëv-er.
8 O ye Showers and Dêw, bléss ye⁀the Lord : praise Him, and mâgnify Hím for ëv-er.
9 O ye Winds of Gôd, bléss ye⁀ the Lord : praise Him, and mâgnify Hím for ëv-er.
10 O ye Fire and Hêat, bléss ye⁀ the Lord : praise Him, and mâgnify Hím for ëv-er.
11 O ye Winter and Sûmmer, bléss ye⁀the Lord : praise Him, and mâgnify Hím for ëv-er.
12 O ye Dews and Frôsts, bléss ye⁀the Lord : praise Him, and mâgnify Hím for ëv-er.
13 O ye Frost and Côld, bléss ye⁀ the Lord : praise Him, and mâgnify Hím for ëv-er.
14 O ye Ice and Snôw, bléss ye⁀ the Lord : praise Him, and mâgnify Hím for ëv-er.
15 O ye Nights, and Dâys, bléss ye⁀the Lord : praise Him, and mâgnify Hím for ëv-er.
16 O ye Light and Dârkness, bléss ye⁀the Lord : praise Him, and mâgnify Hím for ëv-er.
17 O ye Lightnings and Clôuds, bléss ye⁀the Lord : praise Him, and mâgnify Hím for ëv-er.

38. * L. J. Turrell. 39. * L. Barcroft.

BENEDICITE, OMNIA OPERA.

(Change here if a second Chant be used.)

f 18 O let the Eârth bléss the Lord : yea, let it praise Him,* and mâgnify Hím for ëv-er.

mf 19 O ye Mountains and Hîlls, bléss ye^the Lord : praise Him, and mâgnify Hím for ëv-er.

20 O all ye Green Things upon the Eârth, bléss ye^the Lord : praise Him, and mâgnify Hím for ëv-er.

21 O ye Wêlls, bléss ye^the Lord : praise Him, and mâgnify Hím for ëv-er.

22 O ye Seas and Flôods, bléss ye^the Lord : praise Him, and mâgnify Hím for ëv-er.

23 O ye Whales, and all that move in the Wâters, bléss ye^the Lord : praise Him, and mâgnify Hím for ëv-er.

24 O all ye Fowls of the Aîr, bléss ye^the Lord : praise Him, and mâgnify Hím for ëv-er.

25 O all ye Beasts and Câttle, bléss ye^the Lord : praise Him, and mâgnify Hím for ëv-er.

(Return to first Chant.)

f 26 O ye Children of Mên, bléss ye^the Lord : praise Him, and mâgnify Hím for ëv-er.

27 O let Israel bléss the Lord : praise Him, and mâgnify Hím for ëv-er.

28 O ye Priests of the Lôrd, bléss ye^the Lord : praise Him, and mâgnify Hím for ëv-er.

29 O ye Servants of the Lôrd, bléss ye^the Lord : praise Him, and mâgnify Hím for ëv-er.

p 30 O ye Spirits and Souls of the Rfghteous, bléss ye^the Lord : praise Him, and mâgnify Hím for ëv-er.

31 O ye holy and humble Men of heârt, bléss ye^the Lord : praise Him, and mâgnify Hím for ëv-er.

32 O Ananias, Azarias, and Mîsael, bléss ye^the Lord : praise Him, and mâgnify Hím for ëv-er.

f Glory be to the Fâther, ánd to^the Son : ánd tó the Ho-ly Ghost ;

As it was in the beginning,* is nôw, and éver shall be : wôrld without ênd. A-men.

Benedicite, Omnia Opera.

46. Ver. 18 only. Dr. P. Hayes.

Gloria Patri.

f O ALL ye Wŏrks of the Lórd,✻ bléss ye the Lord : praíse Him, and ͵mag-ni-fy Him for ĕv-er.
 2 O ye Ângels of the Lórd,✻ bléss ye the L͡ord : praíse Him, &c.
 mf 3 O ye Heávens,✻ bléss ye the Lord : praíse Him, &c.
 4 O ye Wâters that be above the Fírmament, ✻ bléss ye the Lord : praíse Him, &c.
 5 O all ye Pôwers of the Lórd,✻ bléss ye the Lord : praíse Him, &c.
 6 O ye Sûn and Móon,✻ bléss ye the Lord : praíse Him, &c.
 7 O ye Stârs of Heáven,✻ bléss ye the Lord : praíse Him, &c.
 8 O ye Shôwers and Déw,✻ bléss ye the Lord : praíse Him, &c.
 9 O ye Wínds of Gód,✻ bléss ye the Lord : praíse Him, &c.
 10 O ye Fîre and Héat,✻ bléss ye the Lord : praíse Him, &c.
 11 O ye Wínter and Súmmer,✻ bléss ye the Lord : praíse Him, &c.
 12 O ye Dêws and Frósts,✻ bléss ye the Lord : praíse Him, &c.
 13 O ye Frôst and Cóld,✻ bléss ye the Lord : pṛaíse Him, &c.
 14 O ye Íce and Snów,✻ bléss ye the Lord : praíse Him, &c.
 15 O ye Nîghts, and Dáys,✻ bléss ye the Lord : praíse Him, &c.
 16 O ye Lîght and Dárkness,✻ bléss ye the Lord : praíse Him, &c.
 17 O ye Lîghtnings and Clóuds,✻ bléss ye the Lord : praíse Him, &c.
 ✻ *f* 18 O let the Eárth ✻ bléss the Lord : yêa, let it praíse Him, &c.

 mf 19 O ye Móuntains and Hílls,✻ bléss ye the Lord : praíse Him, &c.
 20 O all ye Green Thíngs upon the Eárth,✻ bléss ye the Lord : praíse Him, ͵&c.
 21 O ye Wélls,✻ bléss ye the Lord : praíse Him, &c.
 22 O ye Sêas and Flóods,✻ bléss ye the Lord : praíse Him, &c.
 23 O ye Whales,✻ and all that môve in the Wáters,✻ bléss ye the Lord : praíse Him, &c.
 24 O all ye Fôwls of the Aír,✻ bléss ye the Lord : praíse Him, &c.
 25 O all ye Bêasts and Cáttle,✻ bléss ye the Lord : praíse Him, &c.
 ✻ *f* 26 O ye Chíldren of Mén,✻ bléss y͡e the Lord : praíse Him, &c.
 27 O let Iſrael✻ bléss the Lord :✻ praíse Him, &c.
 28 O ye Priêsts of the Lórd,✻ bléss ye the Lord : praíse Him, &c.
 29 O ye Sêrvants of the Lórd,✻ bléss ye the Lord : praíse Him, &c.
 p 30 O ye Spirits and Sôuls of the Ríghteous,✻ bléss ye the Lord : praíse Him, &c.
 31 O ye holy and humble Mên of héart,✻ bléss ye the Lord : praíse Him, &c.
 32 *mf* O Ananias, Azarías, and Mísael,✻ bléss ye the Lord : praíse Him, &c.
 f Glory be to the Fâther, ánd to⁀ the Son : ánd tó the Ho-ly Ghost ; As it was in the beginning, ✻ is nôw, and éver shall be : wôrld without énd. A-men.

47. BENEDICITE, OMNIA OPERA.

* A. H. Brown.

f ♭ LESSED be the Lord Gôd of Iś-ra-el: for He hath vísited, and redéemed His pëo-ple ;
2 And hath raised up a mĩghty salvátion for us : in the hôuse of His sér-vant Dä-vid ;
3 As He spake by the mouth of His hôly Pró-phets : whîch have bjen sínce the world be-gan ;
4 That we should be sâved from our é-ne-mies : and from the hánds of áll that häte us ;
p 5 To perform the mercy ✻ promised to ôur forefá-thers : and to remêmber His hó-ly Co-ve-nant ;
6 To perform the oath ✻ which He sware to our fôrefather Á-bra-ham : thát Hé would gíve us ;
7 That we ✻ being delivered out of the hánd of our é-ne-mies : mĩght sérve Him˜with-öut fear ;

8 In holiness and ríghteousness befôre Him : âll the dáys of öur life.
mf 9 And thou, Child, ✻ shalt be called the Prôphet of the Hĩgh-est : for thou shalt go before the fáce of the Lórd to˜pre-pare His ways ;
10 To give knowledge of salvation ûnto His pēo-ple : fôr the remís-sion of their sins,
p 11 Through the tender mêrcy óf our God : whereby the dây-spring from on hígh hath vi-síted us ;
12 To give light to them that sit in darkness, ✻ and ín the shá-dow˜ of death : and to guide our fēet ín-to˜the way of peace.
f Glory be to the Fâther, ánd to˜ the Son : ánd tó the Ho-ly Ghost ;
As it was in the beginning, ✻ is nôw, and éver shall be : wôrld without énd. 'A'-men.

Jubilate Deo.—Psalm c.

f O BE joyful in the Lôrd, áll ye lands : serve the Lord with gladness, * and come befôre His pré-sence with a song.
 mf 2 .Be ye sure that the Lôrd Hé is God : it is He that hath made us, and not we ourselves ; * we are His pêople, and the shéep of His päs-ture.
 f 3 O go your way into His gates with thanksgiving, * and înto His coúrts with praise : be thankful unto Hîm, and speak góod of Hi̇s Name.
 p 4 For the Lord is gracious, * His mercy is êverlâst-ing : and His truth endureth from generâtion to gé-ne-rä-tion.
 f Glory be to the Fâther, ánd to^ the Son : ând tó the Ho-ly Ghost ;
 As it was in the beginning, * is nôw, and éver shall be : wôrld without ênd. ˙A˙-men.

Quicunque Vult.

67. * A. H. Brown.
68. * C. Fisher.
69. * B. St. J. B. Joule.
70. * S. Atherstone.

f WHOSOEVER will be sáved : before all things it is necessary that he hóld the Catholick Faith.

2 Which Faith,* except every one do keep whôle and undefíl-ed : without doubt he shall pêrish év-er-last-ing-ly.

3 And the Câtholic Fáith is this : that we worship one God in TRÎNITY, TRÍN-ITY in U-NI-TY.

4 Neither confoûnding the PÊR-SONS : nôr divíd-ing the Süb-stance.

5 For there is one PERSON of the FATHER,* anôther óf the SON : and anôther óf the HO-LY GHOST.

6 But the GODHEAD of the FA-THER,* of the SON,* and of the HOLY GHÔST, is âll ONE : the Glory equal,* the Mâjesty cô-e-tër-nal.

mf 7 Such as the FÂTHER is, súch is the SON : ând súch is the HO-LY GHOST.

8 The FATHER uncreate,* the SÔN ún-cre-ate : and the HÔLY GHÔST un-cre-ate.

9 The FATHER incomprehensible,* the SON incômprehén-si-ble : and the HOLY GHÔST incóm-pre-hen-si-ble.

10 The FATHER eternal, the SÔN etêr-nal : and the HÔLY GHÔST e-tër-nal.

11 And yet they are not thrêe Etêr-nals : *f* bût óne E-tër-nal.

mf 12 As also there are not three Incomprehensibles,* nor thrêe Un-creât-ed : *f* but one Uncreated,* and ône Incóm-pre-hen-si-ble.

mf 13 So likewise the FATHER is Almighty,* the SÔN Almígh-ty : and the HÔLY GHÔST Al-mïgh-ty.

14 And yet they are not thrêe Almígh-ties : *f* bût óne Al-mïgh-ty.

f 15 So the FATHER is GÔD, the SÔN is GOD : ând the HÓ-LY GHOST is GOD.

p 16 And yêt they are not thrêe GODS : (*full*) *f* bût öne GOD.

(*Can.*)*f* 17 So likewise the FATHER is Lôrd, the SÔN LORD : ând the HÓ-LY GHÔST LORD.

p 18 And yêt not thrêe LORDS : (*full*)*f* bût öne LORD.

(*Can.*) *mf* 19 For like as we are compelled by the Chrîstian Vé-ri-ty : to acknowledge every PÊRSON by Himsélf to be GOD and LORD ;

20 So are we forbidden by the Câtholick Relf-gion : to sây, There be thrêe GODS, or thrêe LORDS.

Change.

mf 21 The FÂTHER is máde of none : neither creâted, nór be-göt-ten.

22 The SÔN is of the FÁ-THER a-lone : not made, nor creâted, bút be-göt-ten.

23 The HOLY GHOST is of the FÂTHER and óf the SON : neither made, nor created, nor begôtten, bút pro-cëed-ing.

71. * Dr. Gauntlett.   72.   T. Tudway.

73.   * A. H. Brown.   74.   * L. Barcroft.

f 24 So there is one FATHER, not three FATHERS ; * one SŎN, not thrēē SONS : one HOLY GHŎST, not thrēē HO-LY GHOSTS.

mf 25 And in this TRINITY * none is afōre, or âfter ŏ-ther : none is grēater, or lĕss than ͡an-ŏth-er ;

26 But the whole three PERSONS are co-etêrnal togē-ther : âńd co-ë-qual.

27 So that in all things, * âs is afōre-said : the UNITY in TRINITY, * and the TRINITY in ÛNITY ís to ͡be wor-ship-ped.

28 He therefore that will be sā-ved : must thûs thínk of ͡the TRIN-I-TY.

(Change to Chant first used.)

29 Furthermore, * it is necessary to everlâsting salvā-tion : that he alşo believe rightly * the INCAR-NĀTION of our LŎRD JE-SUS CHRIST.

30 For the right Faith is, * that wê belíeve and ͡con-fess : that our LORD JESUS CHRIST, the SŎN of GŎD, is GOD and MAN ;

f 31 GOD, of the Substance of the the FATHER, * begŏtten befōre the worlds : *p* and Man, of the Substance of his Mŏther, bŏrn in the world :

f 32 Perfect GŎD, and pér-fect Man : of a reasonable soul and hûman flĕsh sub-sïst-ing ;

f 33 Equal to the FATHER, * as tôuching His GŎD-HEAD : *p* and inferior to the FÂTHER, as tóuching His Män-hood.

34 Who, althôugh He be GŎD and Man : yêt He is not twŏ, but ŏne Christ ;

35 One ; * not by conversion of the GŎDHEAD ín-to flesh : but by tâking of the Mán-hood in-to GOD ;

36 One altogether ; * not by con-fûsion of Sûb-stance : bût by ú-nity ͡ of Për-son.

mf 37 For as the reasonable soul and flêsh is ōne man : *f* so GÔD and Mán is ŎNE CHRIST ;

p 38 Who suffered for ôur salvā-tion : descended into hell, * *f* rose agâin the thírd day from the dead.

ff 39 He ascended into heaven, * He sitteth on the right hand of the FATHER, * GÔD Almígh-ty : *p* from whence He shall come to jûdge the qúick and the dead :

40 At whose coming * all men shall rise agâin with their bŏ-dies : and shall gíve accŏunt for ͡their ŏwn works.

f 41 And they that have done good * shall go into lîfe everlâst-ing : *p* and they that have done êvil into év-er-last-ing fire.

(Full) f 42 Thís is the CÁ-THOLICK FAITH : which except a man believe fâithfully he cánnot be säv-ed.

f Glory be to the FÂTHER, ánd to ͡the SON : ând tó the HO-LY GHOST ;

As it was in the beginning, * is nŏw, and éver shall be : wŏrld without ēnd. ˙A-men.

Magnificat;
Or, The Song of the Blessed Virgin Mary.—S. Luke, i.

mf MY soul doth mágnifý the Lord : and my spirit hath rejôiced in Gód my Sä-viour.
2 For Hê hath regârd-ed : the lôwliness of Hís hand-maïd-en.
3 For behôld, from hĕnce-forth : *f* all generâtions shall cáll me blĕss-ed.
4 For He that is mighty hath mâgnifí-ed me : *pp*† ând hó-ly is His Name.
p 5 And His mercy is on thêm that fĕar Him ; throughôut áll gene-rä-tions.
f 6 He hath shêwed stréngth with⌢His arm : He hath scattered the proud ⁕ in the imâginâ-tion of their hearts.
7 He hath put down the mîghty fróm their seat : and hath exâlted the hûm-ble and meek.
p 8 He hath filled the hûngry with góod things ; and the rích He hath sĕnt emp-ty⌢a-way.
9 He remembering His mercy ⁕ hath holpen His sĕrvant Iś-ra-el : as He promised to our forefathers, ⁕ Abraham and his séed, for ĕv-er.
f Glory be to the Fâther, ánd to⌢ the Son : ând tó the Ho-ly Ghost ;
As it was in the beginning, ⁕ is nôw, and éver shall be : wôrld without ĕnd. 'A⸽men.

⁕ These F's must be ♮ also when major.

† It is suggested that these words be sung slowly.

ƒ O SING unto the Lôrd a nêw song : for Hê hath dône mar-vellous things.

2 With His own right hând, and with His hó-ly arm : hath He gôtten Himsélf the vic-to-ry.

mf 3 The Lord declared Hîs salvâ-tion : His righteousness hath He openly shêwed in the sîght of˘ the hëa-then.

4 He hath remembered His merçy and truth * toward the hoûse of Îs-ra-el : and all the ends of the world * have sêen the salvá-tion˘of oür God.

ƒ 5 Shew yourselves joyful unto the Lôrd, áll ye lands : sîng, rejoíce, and gïve thanks.

p 6 Praise the Lôrd upón the harp: sing to the hârp with a psálm of˘ thanks-gïv-ing.

ƒ 7 With trûmpets ál-so,˘and shawms : O shew yourselves jôyful befóre the Lord the King.

8 Let the sea make a noise, * and âll that thére-in is : the round wôrld, and théy that dwell there-in.

9 Let the floods clap their hands, * and let the hills be joyful togêther befóre the Lord : for Hê cómeth to judge the earth.

mf 10 With righteousness shâll He jûdge the world : ând the peó-ple˘with e-qui-ty.

ƒ Glory be to the Fâther, ánd to˘the Son : ând tô the Ho-ly Ghost ;

As it was in the beginning, * is nôw, and éver shall be : wôrld without énd. 'A˙-men.

Nunc Dimittis;
OR, THE SONG OF SYMEON.—S. LUKE, ii. 29.

mf LORD,* now lettest Thou Thy servant depart in peace : accórd-ing to Thÿ word.
2 Fôr mine éyes have seen : Thÿ sal-vă-tion.
p 3 Which Thôu hast prepâr-ed : befôre the fáce of all péo-ple ;
4 To be a light to líghten the Gén-tiles : and to be the glôry of Thy péo-ple Is-ra-el.
f Glory be to the Fâther, ánd to the Son : ánd tó the Ho-ly Ghost ;
As it was in the beginning,* is nów, and éver shall be : wôrld without ĕnd. ·A·-men.

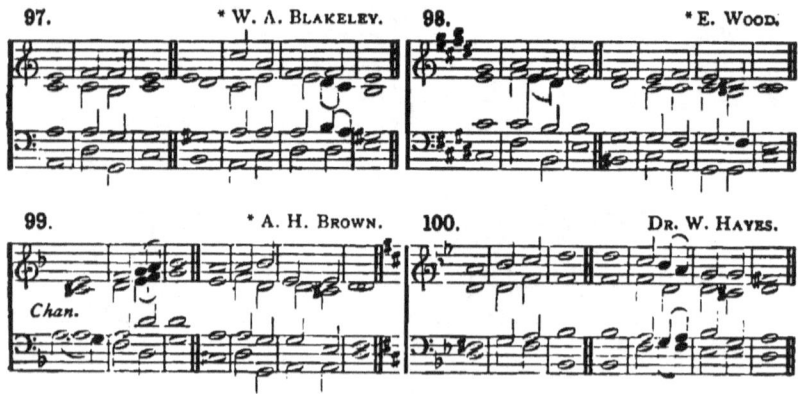

Deus Misereatur.—Psalm lxvii.

mf GOD be merciful unto ûs, and bléss us : and shew us the light of His countenance,* ând be mér-ciful un-to us :

2 That Thy wây may be knówn upon earth : Thy saving hêalth amóng all nä-tions.

f 3 Let the pêople praíse Thee,⌒ O God : yea, let âll the péo-ple praïse Thee.

4 O let the nâtions rejoíce and⌒ be glad : for Thou shalt judge the folk righteously,* and góvern the ná-tions⌒up-ön earth.

5 Let the pêople praíse Thee,⌒O God : yea, let âll the péo-ple praïse Thee.

p 6 Then shall the earth bring fôrth her ín-crease : and God, even our own Gôd, shall gíve⌒us His blëss-ing.

7 Gôd shall bléss us : and all the énds of the wórld shall feär Him.

f Glory be to the Fâther, ánd to⌒ the Son : ând tó the Ho-ly Ghost ; As it was in the beginning,* is nôw, and éver shall be : wôrld without énd. 'A'-men.

Varied Organ Accompaniments

FOR MONOTONIC RECITATION OF THE PSALMS ON FAST DAYS.

*A. H. BROWN.

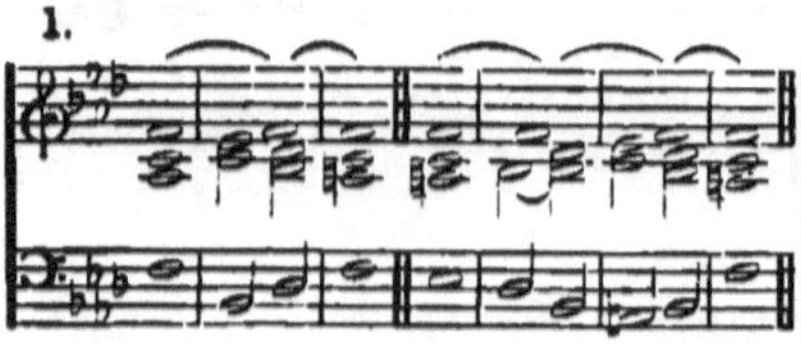

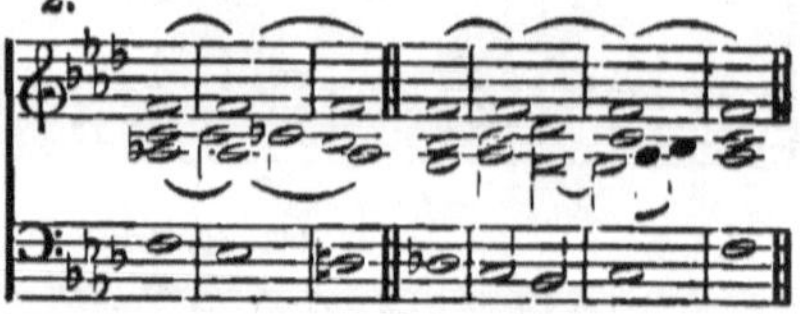

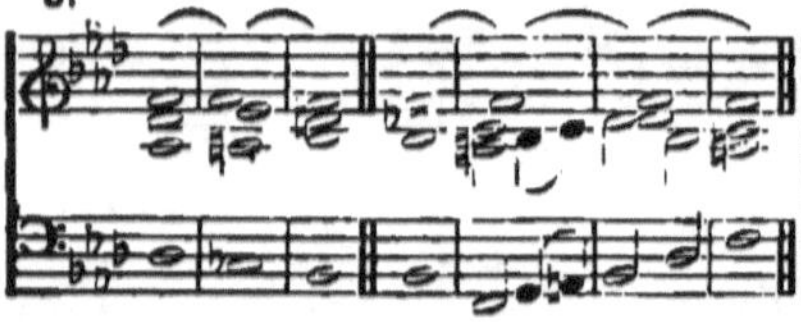

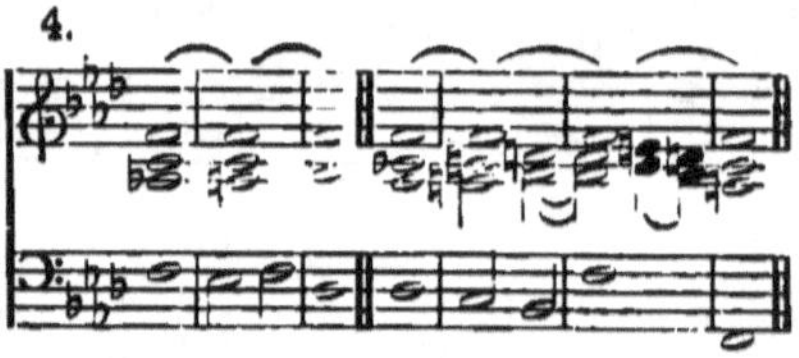

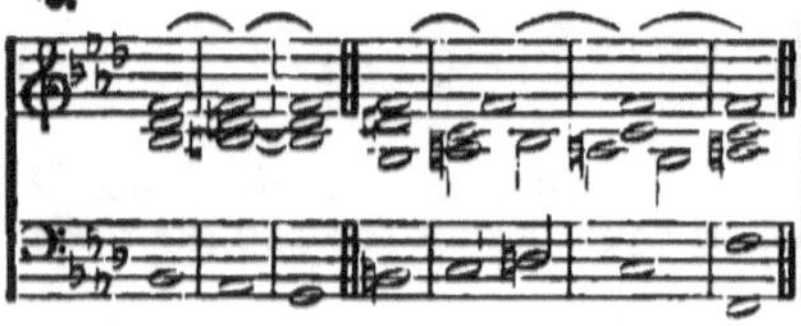

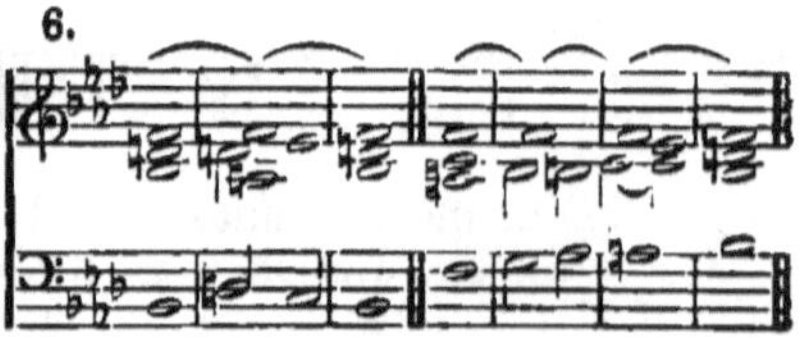

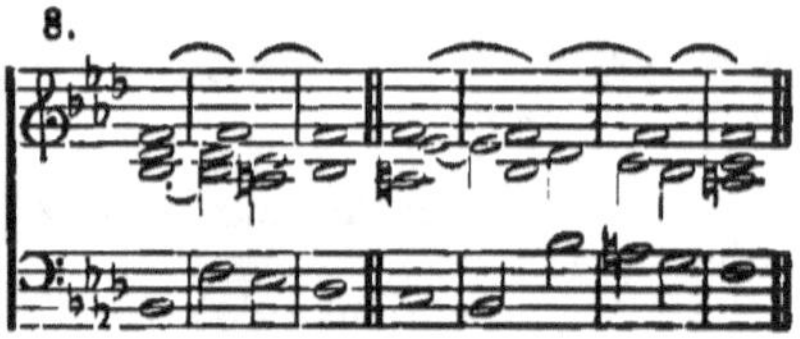

FOR GLORIA PATRI ONLY.

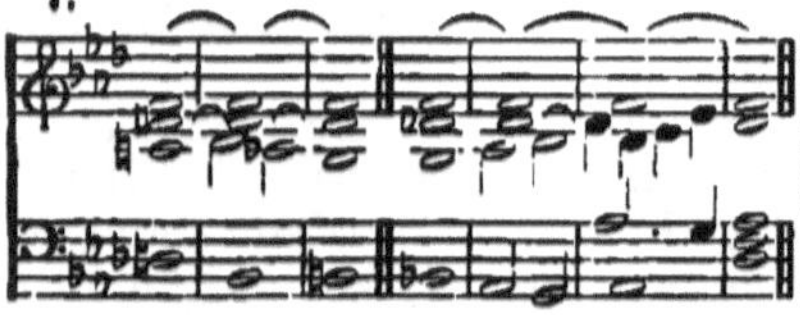

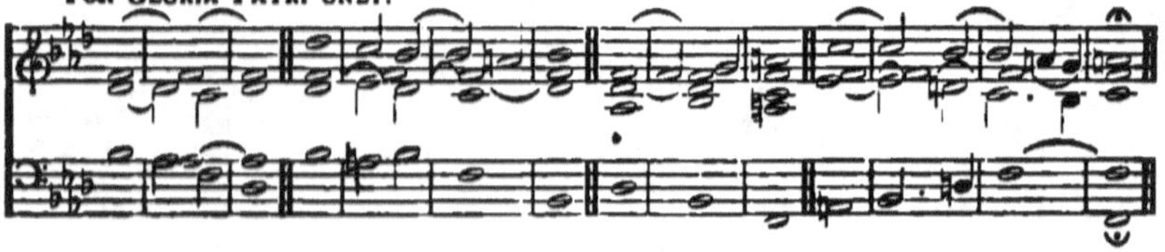

THE PSALTER.

—:o:—

The First Day.
Mattins.

Venite, exultemus Domino.

ƒO COME,* let us síng ún-to⌢ the Lord : let us heartily rejoice in the strêngth of oúr sal-vä-tion.

2 Let us come before His prêsence with thanksgív-ing : and shêw ourselves glád in Him with Psalms.

3 For the Lórd is a gréat God : and a grêat Kíng above äll gods.

4 In His hand are all the córners óf the earth : and the strength of the hîlls is Hís äl-so.

5 The sea is Hís, and He máde it : and His hánds prepár-ed⌢the drÿ land.

p 6 O come, * let us wórship, and fäll down : and knêel before the Lórd our Mä-ker.

7 For Hê is the Lórd our God : and we are the people of His pásture, and the shéep of Hïs hand.

mf 8 To-day if ye will hear His voice,* hârden nót your hearts : as in the provocation,* and as in the day of temptâtion ín the wil-der-ness ;

9 When your fâthers témpt-ed Me : próved Mé, and saw My works.

10 Forty years long * was I grieved with thís generá-tion,⌢and said : It is a people that do err in their héarts, for they háve not known My ways.

11 Unto whóm I swáre in⌢My wrath : that they shôuld not én-ter into My rest.

Glory be to the Fâther, ánd to⌢the Son : ánd tó the Ho-ly Ghost ;

As it was in the beginning,* is nôw, and éver shall be : wôrld without énd. ˙A˙-men.

PSALM 1. *Beatus vir, qui non abiit, &c.*

mf BLESSED is the man∗ that hath not walked in the counsel of the ungodly,∗ nor stood in the wây of sîn-ners : and hath not sât in the sêat of^the scörn-ful.

2 But his delîght is in the lâw of^the Lord : and in His law will he êxercise himsêlf day and night.

3 And he shall be like a tree plânted by the wâ-ter-side : ţhat will brîng forth his fruît in^due sëa-son.

4 His leaf also shâll not wî-ther : and look,∗ whatsoever he dôeth, ît shall prös-per.

f 5 As for the ungodly,∗ ît is not sö with them : but they are like the chaff,∗ which the wind scattereth awây from the fâce of the earth.

6 Therefore the ungodly shall not be able to stând in the ĵudg-ment : neither the sinners in the congregâ-tion óf the rîght-eous.

(Full) mf 7 But the Lord knoweth the wây of the rîgh-teous : and the wây of the ungód-ly^shall pë-rish.

───

At the end of every Psalm, and of every part of the 119th Psalm, shall be repeated this Hymn :—

Glory be to the Fâther, ánd to^the Son : ánd tó the Ho-ly Ghost ;

As it was in the beginning,∗ is nôw, and éver shall be : wôrld with-out énd. 'A'-men.

PSALM 2. *Quare fremuerunt gentes?*

ƒ WHY do the heathen so furiously râge togĕ-ther : and why do the pêople imă-ginea văin thing?

2 The kings of the earth stand up,* and the rulers take coûnsel togĕ-ther : against the Lord,* and agaĭnst Hĭs A-noïnt-ed.

3 Let us break their bônds asŭnder : and cast awây their cŏrds frŏm us.

ƒƒ 4 He that dwelleth in heâven shall lăugh them to scorn : the Lord shall hâve them ĭn de-rĭ-sion.

5 Then shall He spêak unto them ĭn His wrath : and vêx them in His sŏre dis-plëa-sure.

(Full)ƒ 6 Yêt have I sét My King : upon My hôly hĭll of Sĭ-on.

(Can.)p 7 I will preach the law,* whereof the Lôrd hath saíd unto me : Thou art My Son,* this dăy have I be-got-ten Thee.

8 Desire of Me,* and I shall give Thee the heathen for Thĭne inhĕ-ritance : and the utmost parts of the eârth for Thý pos-sës-sion.

9 Thou shalt brŭisc them with a rŏd of iron : and break them in pieces * lĭke a pŏt-ter's vës-sel.

mf 10 Be wise now thêrefore, Ó ye kings : be learned,* yê that are jŭdg-es of the earth.

11 Sêrve the Lŏrd in fear : and rejôice unto Hĭm with re-ve-rence.

p 12 Kiss the Son, lest He be angry,* and so ye pêrish from the rĭght way : if His wrath be kindled,* (yea, but a little,)* blessed are all thêy that pŭt their trust in Him.

PSALM 3. *Domine, quid multiplicati?*

p LORD,* how are they incrêased that troŭ-ble me : many are thêy that rĭse a-gainst me.

2 Many one there bê that sáy of my soul : There is nô hĕlp for him in his God.

mf 3 But Thou, O Lord,* ărt my defĕnd-er : Thou art my worship,* and the lĭfter ŭp of mў head.

4 I did câll upon the Lŏrd with my voice : and He hêard me oút of His ho-ly hill.

5 I laid me down and slêpt, and rose ŭp a-gain : fŏr the Lŏrd sustain-ed me.

6 I will not be afraid * for ten thôusands of the pêo-ple : that have set themselvês agaĭnst me round a-bout.

ƒ 7 Up, Lord,* and hêlp me. Ó my God : for Thou smitest all mine enemies upon the chcek-bone ;* Thou hast broken the têeth óf the un-göd-ly.

mf 8 Salvation belôngeth ŭn-to the Lord : and Thy blêssing is upôn Thy pĕo-ple.

Psalm 4. *Cum invocarem.*

p **H**EAR me when I call,* O
Gôd of my rígh-teous-ness :
Thou hast set me at liberty when I
was in trouble ;* have mercy upôn
me, and héark-en unto my prayer.
 mf 2 O ye sons of men,* how
long will ye blasphême Mine hō-
nour : and have such pleasure in
vânity, and sèek after lëas-ing ?
 3 Know this also,* that the Lord
hath chosen to Himself the mân
that is gôd-ly : when I call upon the
Lôrd, Hé will hëar me.
 4 Stand in âwe, and sín not :
commune with your own heart,*
and ín your chám-ber, and be still.
 5 Offer the sâcrifice of rígh-teous-
ness : and pût your trûst in the
Lord.
 p 6 Thêre be má-ny that say :
Whô will shéw us a-ny good ?
 7 Lôrd, líft Thou up : the light of
Thy côuntenánce up-ön us.
 mf 8 Thou hast put glâdness ín
my heart : since the time that their
corn, and wíne, and oíl, in-crëas-ed.
 9 I will lay me down in pêace,
and táke my rest : for it is Thou,
Lord, only,* that mâkest me dwéll
in säfe-ty

Psalm 5. *Verba mea auribus.*

mf **P**ÔNDER my wórds, O Lord :
consíder my mé-di-tä-tion.
 2 O hearken Thou unto the voice
of my câlling, my Kíng, and my
God : for ûnto Thée, will I make
my prayer.

3 My voice shalt Thou hēar bet́imes, O Lord : early in the morning will I direct my prâyer unto Thée, and⌢will lŏok up.

4 For Thou art the God * that hast no pleâsure in wíck-ed-ness : neither shall âny é-vil dwell with Thee.

5 Such as be fôolish shall not stánd in⌢Thy sight : for Thou hatest all thêm that wŏrk va-ni-ty.

6 Thou shalt destroy thêm that speak lēas-ing : the Lord will abhor both the blood-thírsty ánd de-ceit-ful man.

p 7 But as for me,* I will come into Thine house,* even upon the mûltitude of Thy mér-cy : and in Thy fear will I worship tôward Thy hó-ly těm-ple.

8 Lead me, O Lord, in Thy righteousness,* becâuse of mine é-ne-mies : make Thy wây plaín be-fore my face.

9 For there is no fâithfulness ín his mouth : their inward pârts are vé-ry wick-ed-ness.

10 Their throat is an ôpen sé-pul-chre : thêy flát-ter with their tongue.

f 11 Destroy Thou them, O God ;* let them perish through their ôwn imaginā-tions : cast them out in the multitude of their ungodliness ;* for thêy have rebél-led against Thee.

12 And let all them that put their trûst in Thée re-joice : they shall ever be giving of thanks,* because Thou defendest them ;* they that love Thy Nâme shall be jóy-ful ín Thee ;

(Full) p 13 For Thou, Lord,* wilt give Thy blessing ûnto the rígh-teous : and with Thy favourable kindness * wilt Thôu defénd him as with⌢a shield.

Evensong.

PSALM 6. *Domine, ne in furore.*

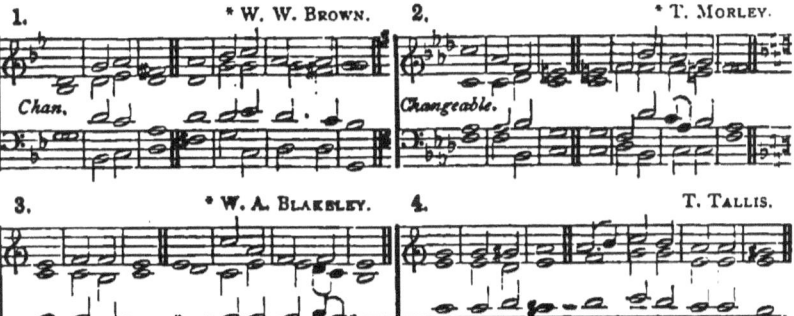

mp O LORD,* rebuke me not in Thine índignā-tion : neither châsten me in Thý dis-plēa-sure.

p 2 Have mercy upon me, O Lórd, for I' am weak : O Lord, hēal me, for my bónes are věx-ed.

3 My soul âlso is sore trôu-bled : but, Lôrd, how lóng wilt⌢Thou pun-ish me ?

4 Turn Thee, O Lôrd, and delí-ver⌢my soul : O sâve me fór Thy mer-cy's sake.

5 For in death nô man remém-bereth Thee : and who will gíve Thee thânks in the pit ?

6 I am weary of ¸my groaning ;* every níght wash I my bed : and wâter my cóuch with my tears.

[7 My

7 My beauty is gône for very trôu-ble : and worn away becâuse of áll mine e-ne-mies.

(Major) ƒ 8 Away from me,✶ all yê that work vá-ni-ty : for the Lord hath hêard the voíce of⁀my wëep-ing.

9 The Lord hath heârd my petí-tion : thê Lórd will⁀re-ceive my prayer.

mf 10 All mine enemies shall be confounded,✶ and sôre vêx-ed : they shall be turned back,✶ and pût to shâme sud-den-ly.

PSALM 7. *Domine, Deus meus.*

mf O LORD my God,✶ in Thêe have I pút my trust : save me from all them that pêrsecute me, ánd de-li-ver me ;

2 Lest he devour my soul, like a lion,✶ and têar it in piê-ces : whîle thére is none to help.

p 3 O Lord my God,✶ if I have dóne ány such thing : or if there be àny wíck-edness in my hands ;

4 If I have rewarded evil unto hím that dealt friénd-ly⁀with me : yea, I have delivered him ✶ that withôut any caúse is⁀mine e-ne-my ;

mf 5 Then let mine enemy perse-cute my soûl, and tâke me : yea, let him tread my life down upon the earth,✶ and lây mine hó-nour in the dust.

(Full) ƒ 6 Stand up, O Lord, in Thy wrath,✶ and lift up Thyself,✶ because of the indignâtion of mine é-ne-mies : arise up for me ✶ in the jûdgment that Thóu hast⁀com-mänd-ed.

(Can.) mf 7 And so shall the congregation of the pêople cóme about Thee : for their sakes there-fore lîft úp Thy-self a-gain.

8 The Lord shall judge the people;* give sêntence wĭth me,⁀O Lord : according to my righteousness,* and according to the ĭnnocency thắt is ĭn me.
9 O let the wickedness of the ungŏdly cǿme to⁀an end : bŭt gŭide Thou the just.
10 Fŏr the rǐght-eous God : trĭeth the vé-ry hearts and reins.
p 11 My hêlp cǿm-eth⁀of God : Who presêrveth thêm that⁀are true of heart.
12 God is a righteous Judge,* strŏng, and pã-tient : and Gŏd is provǿk-ed ev-ery day.
13 If a man will not tûrn, He will whĕt His sword : He hath bent His bôw, and mǻde it rĕa-dy.

14 He hath prepared for Him the ĭnstrumĕnts of death : He ordaineth His arrows agaĭnst the pĕr-se-cü-tors.
mf 15 Behold, he trâvaileth with mǐs-chief : he hath conceived sorrow,* and brôught fǿrth un-god-liness.
16 He hath graven and dĭgged ǔp a pit : and is fallen himself into the destrûction that he mǻde for ö-ther.
17 For his travail shall cǿme upon his ŏwn head : and his wĭckedness shall fắll on⁀his ŏwn pate.
(Full) f 18 I will give thanks unto the Lord,* accŏrding to His rǐghteous-ness : and I will prâise the Nǻme of⁀the Lord most High.

PSALM 8. *Domine, Dominus noster.*

1. *Dr. E. G. Monk.
2. Dr. Greene.
3. * O. Coverdale.
4. * A. M. Sewell.

f O LORD our Governour,* how excellent is Thy Nâme in ắll the world : Thou that hast sêt Thy glǿ-ry⁀a-bove the heavens!
2 Out of the mouth of very babes and sucklings hast Thou ordained strength,* becâuse of Thine é-nemies : that Thou mightest still the ênemy, ấnd the⁀a-vĕng-er.
mf 3 For I will consider Thy heavens,* even the wôrks of Thy ffn-gers : the moon and the stắrs, which Thǿu hast ordäin-ed.
4 What is man,* that Thŏu art mǐnd-ful⁀of him : and the sôn of man, thắt Thou vi-sitest him?

5 Thou madest him lôwer than the ắn-gels : to crôwn him with glǿ-ry⁀and wör-ship.
6 Thou makest him to have domĭnion of the wǿrks of⁀Thy hands : and Thou hast put ắll things in subjéc-tion under his feet ;
7 All shêep and ŏx-en : yêa, and the bĕasts of the field ;
8 The fowls of the air,* and the fǐshes ǿf the sea : and whatsoever walketh thrôugh the pắths of the seas.
(Full) f 9 O Lôrd our Gŏ-vernour : how êxcellent is Thy Nǻme in all the world!

The Second Day.

Mattins.

Venite, exultemus Domino.

f O COME,* let us síng ún-to^ the Lord : let us heartily rejoice in the stréngth of oúr salvā-tion.

2 Let us come before His présence with thanksgív-ing : and shĕw ourselves gláđ in Him with Psalms.

3 For the Lórd is a grĕat God : and a grĕat Kíng above āll gods.

4 In His hand are all the córners óf the earth : and the strength of the hĭlls is Hĭs āl-so.

5 The sea is Hĭs, and He māde it : and His hánds prepár-ed^the drȳ land.

p 6 O come,* let us wŏrship, and făll down : and knêel before the Lórd our Mä-ker.

7 For Hê is the Lórd our God : and we are the people of His pâsture, and the shéep of Hĭs hand.

mf 8 To-day if ye will hear His voice,* hárden nót your hearts : as in the provocation,* and as in the day of temptâtion ĭn the wil-der-ness;

9 When your fâthers témpt-ed Me : provêd Mé, and saw My works.

10 Forty years long * was I grieved with thĭs generá-tion,^and said : It is a people that do err in their hêarts, for they háve not known My ways.

11 Unto whôm I swáre in^My wrath : that they shôuld not én-ter into My rest.

Glory be to the Fâther, ánd to^ the Son : ánd tó the Ho-ly Ghost;

As it was in the beginning,* is nŏw, and éver shall be : wôrld without énd. 'A'-men.

8

PSALM 9. *Confitebor Tibi.*

1. J. D. HACKETT.
2. * A. H. BROWN.
3. * E. EDWARDS.
4. T. TALLIS.

f I WILL give thanks unto Thee, O Lôrd, with my whôle heart : I will spêak of âll Thy mar-vellous works.

2 I will be glâd and rejoíce in Thee : yea, my songs will I make of Thy Náme, O Thoú, Most Hīgh-est.

mf 3 While mine ênemies are drí-ven back : they shall fall and pêrish át Thy prē-sence.

4 For Thou hast maintâined my ríght and˜my cause : Thou art sét in the thróne that judg-est right.

5 Thou hast rebuked the hea-then,* and destrôyed the ungôd-ly : Thou hast put out their nâme for év-er˜and ēv-er.

6 O thou enemy,* destructions are côme to a perpét-ual end : even as the cities which thou hast destroyed ; * their memôrial is pé-rished with them.

f 7 But the Lord shall endûre for êv-er : He hath also prepâred His séat for judg-ment.

mf 8 For he shall judge the wôrld in rígh-teous-ness : and minister true jûdgment ún-to˜the pēo-ple.

9 The Lord also will be a defênce for the opprês-sed : even a refuge in dûe tíme of trôu-ble.

10 And they that know Thy Name will pût their trúst in Thee : for Thou, Lord, * hast never fâiled thém that sēek Thee.

f 11 O praise the Lord * Which dwêlleth in Sí-on : shew the pêople óf His dō-ings.

p 12 For, when He maketh inquisition for blôod, He remém-bereth them : and forgetteth nót the complâint of the poor.

pp 13 Have mercy upon me, O Lord ; * consider the trouble which I suffer of thêm that hâte me : Thou that líftest me úp from˜ the gates of death.

mf 14 That I may shew all Thy praises * within the ports of the daûghter of Sí-on : I will rejôice in Thy sal-vā-tion.

p 15 The heathen are sunk dôwn in the pít that˜they made : in the same net which they hid privily,* ís their fôot tā-ken.

16 The Lord is known to êxecute jûdg-ment : the ungodly is trâpped in the wórk of˜his ōwn hands.

17 The wicked shall be tûrned ín-to hell : and all the pêople thát for-gēt God.

18 For the poor shall not âlway be forgôt-ten : the patient abiding of the mêek shall not pér-ish˜for êv-er.

f 19 Up, Lord,* and let not mân have the úp-per hand : let the hêathen be jûdg-ed˜in Thý sight.

20 Pût them in feár, O Lord : that the heathen may knôw them-sélves to be but men.

[PSALM 10.

PSALM 10. *Ut quid, Domine?*

1. T. KELWAY. 2. * S. ATHERSTONE.
3. * L. BARCROFT. 4. H. PURCELL. *Changeable.*

mf WHY standest Thou so fâr ŏff, O Lord : and hidest Thy face in the nêedful tĭme of trŏu·ble ?

2 The ungodly for his own lust ∗ doth pĕrsecŭte the poor : let them be taken in the crafty wĭliness that thĕy have ima-gin-ed.

p 3 For the ungodly hath made boast of his ŏwn hĕart's de-sire : and speaketh good of the cŏvetous, whom Gŏd ab-hŏr-reth.

4 The ungodly is so proud,∗ that he câreth nŏt for God : nêither is Gŏd in all his thoughts.

5 His ways are âlway grĭe-vous : Thy judgments are far above out of his sight,∗ and therefore defiêth he ăll his e-ne-mies.

6 For he hath said in his heart,∗ Tush, I shall nêver be câst down : there shall nô harm hăp·pen un·to me.

7 His mouth is full of cûrsing, deceĭt, and fraud : under his tongue is ungŏdliness, ănd va-ni-ty.

8 He sitteth lurking in the thievish cŏrners ŏf the streets : and privily in his lurking dens doth he murder the innocent,∗ his eÿes are sĕt a-gainst the poor.

9 For he lieth waiting secretly,∗ even as a lion lûrketh hĕ in⁀his den : thăt hĕ may ra-vish⁀the poor.

10 Hê doth rá-vish⁀ the poor : when he gĕtteth him ĭn-to hĭs net.

11 He falleth dŏwn, and hŭm-bleth⁀him-self : that the congrega-tion of the poor may făll into the hănds of⁀his căp-tains.

12 He hath said in his heart,∗ Tush, Gôd hath forgŏt-ten : He hideth away His face,∗ and Hê will né-ver sĕe it.

f 13 Arise, O Lord God,∗ and lĭft ŭp Thine hand : fôrgĕt not the poor.

14 Wherefore should the wĭcked blasphĕme God : while he doth say in his heart,∗ Tush, Thôu God că-rest⁀not fŭr it.

15 Surely Thôu hast sĕen it : for Thou behŏldest ungŏd-li-ness and wrong.

mf 16 That Thou mayest take the mâtter ĭn-to⁀Thine hand : the poor committeth himself unto Thee,∗ for Thou art the hêlper ŏf the friend-less.

17 Break Thou the power of the ungôdly and malĭ-cious : take away his ungôdliness, and Thôu shalt fĩnd none.

f 18 The Lord is King for êver and ĕv-er : and the heathen are pĕrished ŏut of the land.

p 19 Lord,∗ Thou hast heŭrd the desĭre of⁀the poor : Thou preparest their heart,∗ and Thine eâr hĕar-keneth thĕre-to ;

20 To help the fatherless and pôor ŭn-to⁀their right : that the man of the earth be no môre exălt-ed against them.

PSALM 11. *In Domino confido.*

mf IN the Lórd put í my trust : how say ye then to my soul,* that she should flée as a bírd un-to^the hill?

2 For lo, the ungodly bend their bow,* and make ready their arrows withín the qúi-ver : that they may privily shóot at thém which ^ are true of heart.

3 For the foundátions will be cást down : ánd whát hath^the right-eous done ?

p 4 The Lord is in His hóly témple : the Lórd's séat is^in hëa-ven.

5 His eýes consí-der^the poor : and His eýelids trý the chil-dren^of men.

6 The Lord allóweth the rígh-teous : but the ungodly,* and hìm that delighteth in wíckedness dóth His soul ab-hor.

f 7 Upon the ungodly He shall rain snarês,* fire and brimstone,* stôrm and têm-pest : thís shall bé their por-tion^to drink.

8 For the righteous Lord lóveth ríghte-teous-ness : His cóuntenance will behóld the thing that^is just.

Evensong.

PSALM 12. *Salvum me fac.*

p HELP me, Lord,* for there is not óne gód-ly^man left : for the faithful are mínished from amóng the chil-dren^of men.

2 They talk of vanity * every óne with his néigh-bour : they do bu: flatter with their lips,* and dissêmble ín their dou-ble heart.

[3 The

3 The Lord shall root out âll decéit-ful lips : and the tôngue that spéak-eth pröud things ;

4 Which have said,* With our tôngue wíll we ⌢ pre-vail : we are they that ought to speak,* whô is lôrd o-ver us ?

mf p 5 Now for the comfortless troubles' sâke of the née-dy : and because of the dêep sígh-ing of the poòr,

f 6 I will ûp, saíth the Lord : and will help every one from him that swelleth against him,* ând will sêt him at rest.

mf 7 The words of the Lôrd are pûre words : even as the silver, which from the earth is tried, * and pûrified séven times in the fire.

8 Thôu shalt kéep them, ⌢ O Lord : Thou shalt preserve him from thís generá-tion ⌢ for ëv-er.

9 The ungodly wâlk on év-ery side : when they are exalted,* the chíldren of mén are put to ⌢ re-buke.

PSALM 13. *Usque quo, Domine?*

p HOW long wilt Thou forget me, O Lôrd, for ëv-er : how lông wilt Thou híde Thy face from me.

2 How long shall I seek counsel in my soul,* and be so vêxed ín my heart : how long shall mine ênemies trí-umph o-ver me ?

3 Consider, and hêar me, O Lórd my God : lighten mine eỹes, that I slêep not in death.

4 Lest mine enemy say,* I have prevåíled agåínst him : for if I be cast down,* they that trôuble me will rejoíce ät it.

mf 5 But my trust is ȋn Thy mēr-cy : and my heart is jôyful in Thỹ sal-vä-tion.

6 I will sing of the Lord,* because He hath dealt so lôvingly with me : yea, I will praise the Nâme of the Lórd Most High-est.

PSALM 14. *Dixit insipiens.*

mf THE fôol hath saíd in his heart : Thêre ȋs nö God.

2 They are corrupt,* and become abômínable in their dō-ings : there is none that dôeth gōod, no not one.

3 The Lord looked down from heåven upon the chȋl-dren of men : to see if there were any that would understånd, and sêek af-ter God.

4 But they are all gone out of the way,* they are altogether becôme abó-mina-ble : there is none that dôeth gōod, no not one.

5 Their throat is an open sepulchre,* with their tôngues have they decéiv-ed : the pôison of ásps is under their lips.

6 Their mouth is full of cûrsing and bít-ter-ness : their fêet are swíft to shêd blood.

7 Destruction and unhappiness is in their ways,* and the way of pêace háve they not known : there is no fêar of Gód be-fore their eyes.

p 8 Have they no knowledge,* that they are all such wôrkers of mȋs-chief : eating up my people as it were brêad, and cáll not upon the Lord ?

9 There were they brought in great fear,* êven where nó fear was : for God is in the generâtion óf the right-eous.

10 As for you,* ye have made a mock at the côunsel óf the poor : because he pûtteth his trûst in the Lord.

mf 11 Who shall give salvation unto Israel out of Sion ? * When the Lord turneth the captȋv-ity of His pêo-ple : then shall Jacob rejóíce, and Ȋś-rael shall be glad.

The Third Day.

Mattins.

Venite, exultemus Domino.

f O COME,* let us síng ún-to^
the Lord : let us heartily rejoice in the strêngth of oúr sal-vä-tion.

2 Let us come before His prêsence with thanksgív-ing : and shêw ourselves gláds in Him with Psalms.

3 For the Lôrd is a grêat God : and a grêat Kíng above äll gods.

4 In His hand are all the côrners óf the earth : and the strength of the hîlls is Hís äl-so.

5 The sea is Hĭs, and He mäde it : and His hânds prepár-ed^the drў land.

p 6 O come, * let us wôrship, and fäll down : and knêel before the Lórd our Mä-ker.

7 For Hĕ is the Lórd our God : and we are the people of His pâsture, and the shéep of Hĭs hand.

mf 8 To-day if ye will hear His voice,* hârden nót your hearts : as in the provocation,* and as in the day of temptâtion ín the wil-der-ness ;

9 When your fâthers témpt-ed Me : prôved Mé, and saw My works.

10 Forty years long* was I grieved with thĭs generá-tion,^and said : It is a people that do err in their hĕarts, for they háve not known My ways.

11 Unto whôm I swáre in^My wrath : that they shôuld not én-ter into My rest.

Glory be to the Fâther, ánd to^the Son : ánd tó the Ho-ly Ghost ;

As it was in the beginning,* is nôw, and éver shall be : wôrld without ĕnd. ˙A˙-men

PSALM 15. *Domine, quis habitabit?*

mf **L**ORD,* who shall dwell in
Thy tăbernā-cle : or who
shall rēst upŏ́n Thy ho-ly hill?
2 Even he, that lēadeth an ŭn-
corrupt life : and doeth the thing
which is right,* and spēaketh the
trŭ́th from his heart.
3 He that hath used no deceit in
his tongue,* nor done ēvil to his
nĕ́igh-bour : and hăth not slắn-
dered⌢his nĕigh-bour.
4 He that setteth not by himself,*

but is lŏ́wly in his ŏ́wn eyes : and
maketh mŭch of thĕ́m that fear the
Lord.
5 He that sweareth unto his
neighbour,* and dĭsappoĭ́nt-eth⌢
him not : though it wĕre to his ŏ́wn
hĭ́n-drance.
6 He that hath not given his
mŏney upon ŭ́-su-ry : nor taken
rewărd agaĭ́nst the in-no-cent.
(Full) mf 7 Whŏso dŏ́eth these
things : shăll nĕ́-ver fall.

PSALM 16. *Conserva me Domine.*

p **P**RESĔRVE me, Ŏ́ God : fŏr
in Thĕ́e have⌢I put my trust.
2 O my soul,* thou hast săid
ŭn-to⌢the Lord : Thou art my God,*
my gŏods are nŏ́-thing un-to Thee.

3 All my delight is upon the
săints, that are ĭ́n the earth : and
upon sŭch as excĕ́l in vĭ̈r-tue.
4 But they that run ăfter anŏ́-ther
god : shall hăve grĕ́at trö̆u-ble.

[5 Their

15

5 Their drink offerings of blood *
will I not óf-fer : neither make
méntion of their námes with-in my
lips.
  6 The Lord Himself is the portion
of mine inhêritance, and óf my cup :
Thôu shált main-tain my lot.
  7 The lot is fallen unto mê in a
faír ground : yêa, I have a góod-ly
he-ri-tage.
  mf 8 I will thank the Lord for
gíving me wâr-ning : my reins also
châsten me ín the⁀night-sëa-son.
  9 I have set God âlways befóre

me : for He is on my rîght hand
thére-fore⁀I shall not fall.
  10 Wherefore my heart was glad,*
and my glóry rejói-ced : my flêsh
ál-so⁀shall rest in hope.
  11 For why? * Thou shalt not
leâve my sóul in hell : neither shalt
Thou suffer Thy Hôly One to sée
cor-rüp-tion.
  f 12 Thou shalt shew me the path
of life ; * in Thy prêsence is the
fúl-ness⁀of joy : and at Thy right
hând there is pléa-sure⁀for e-ver-
more.

PSALM 17. *Exaudi, Domine.*

mf HEAR the right, O Lord, *
consíder mý com-plaint :
and hearken unto my prayer,* that
góeth not oút of feign-ed lips.

  2 Let my sentence come fôrth
from Thy prê-sence : and let Thine
eyes lôok upon the thíng that⁀is
ë-qual.

16

3 Thou hast proved and visited mine heart in the night-season;* Thou hast tried me, and shalt find no wickedness in me : for I am utterly purposed that my mouth shall not of-fend.

4 Because of men's works, * that are done against the words of Thy lips : I have kept me from the ways of the des-tröy-er.

5 O hold Thou up my goings in Thy paths : thät my foot-steps slip not.

p 6 I have called upon Thee, O God,* for Thou shalt hear me : incline Thine ear to me, and heark-en unto my words.

7 Shew Thy marvellous loving-kindness,* Thou that art the Saviour of them which put their trust in Thee: from such as resist Thy right hand.

8 Keep me as the apple of an eye : hide me under the sha-dow of Thy wings,

9 From the ungodly that trou-ble me : mine enemies compass me round about to take a-way my soul.

10 They are inclosed in their own fat : and their mouth speak-eth proud things.

11 They lie waiting in our way on é-very side : turning their eyes down to the ground ;

12 Like as a lion that is greedy of his prey : and as it were a lion's whelp,* lurking in se-cret plä-ces.

f 13 Up, Lord,* disappoint him, and cast him down : deliver my soul from the ungodly,* which is a sword of Thine ;

14 From the men of Thy hand, O Lord,* from the men, I say,* and from the é-vil world : which have their portion in this life,* whose bellies Thou fillest with Thy hid trëa-sure.

15 They have children at their de-sire : and leave the rest of their sub-stance for their babes.

p 16 But as for me,* I will behold Thy presence in right-eous-ness : and when I awake up after Thy likeness,* I shall be sa-tisfied with it.

Evensong.

PSALM 18. *Diligam Te, Domine.*

1. DR. B. COOKE. 2. * REV. T. HELMORE.
3. * A. H. BROWN. 4. DR. E. AYRTON.

f I WILL love Thee, O Lord, my strength;* the Lord is my stony rock, and my de-fence : my Saviour,* my God, and my might, in whom I will trust,* my buckler,* the horn also of my salvation, and my rë-fuge.

2 I will call upon the Lord,* which is worthy to be prais-ed : so shall I be safe from mine e-ne-mies.

p 3 The sorrows of death com-passed me : and the overflowings of ungodliness made me a-fraid.

[4 The

4 The pains of hĕll came abŏut me : the snâres of deáth over-tŏok me.

5 In my trouble I will câll upón the Lord : ǎnd complaín unto my God.

mf 6 So shall He hear my voice out of His hŏly tĕm-ple : and my complaint shall come before Him,✱ it shall ênter é-ven into His ears.

f 7 The earth trĕmbled and qŭa-ked : the very foundations also of the hills shook, ✱ and were remôved, becaŭse He was wroth.

8 There went a smoke oŭt in His prĕs-ence : and a consuming fire out of His mouth,✱ so that cöals were kín-dled ät it.

9 He bowed the heavens âlso, and cǎme down : ǎnd it was dǎrk under His feet.

10 He rode upon the chĕrubims, ǎnd did fly : He came flýing upón the wings of the wind.

p 11 He made dârkness His sé-cret place : His pavilion round about Him with dark water, ✱ and thíck clóuds to co-ver Him.

f 12 At the brightness of His presence ✱ His clôuds remū-ved : hâil-stónes, and coals of fire.

ff 13 The Lord also thundered out of heaven, ✱ and the Highest gâve His thŭn-der : hâil-stónes, and coals of fire.

f 14 He sent out His ârrows, and scát-tered them : He cast forth líghtnin ;s, ǎnd de-stroy-ed them.

15 The springs of waters were seen,✱ and the foundations of the round world were discôvered, at Thy chíd-ing, ⁀ O Lord : at the blasting of the brêath of Thý dis-pleă-sure.

mf 16 He shall send down from on hígh to fĕtch me : and shall take me ŏut of má-ny wä-ters.

17 He shall deliver me from my strongest enemy,✱ and from thĕm which hǎte me : for they are tŏo mígh-ty fŏr me.

18 They prevented me in the dây of my trŏu-ble : but the Lôrd was mý up-hŭld-er.

19 He brought me forth also into a plâce of lí-ber-ty : He brought me forth, ✱ even becâuse He had a fá-vour un-to me.

20 The Lord shall reward me ✱ after my ríghteous dĕal-ing : according to the cleanness of my hânds shall He ré-com-pënse me.

21 Because I have kĕpt the wáys of the Lord : and have not forsâken my Gód, as the wick-ed doth.

22 For I have an êye unto áll His laws : and will not cast ŏut His commánd-ments frŭm me.

23 I was also uncorrŭpt befôre Him : and eschêwed mine ōwn wick-ed-ness.

24 Therefore shall the Lord reward me ∗ after my rìghteous deäl-ing : and according unto the cleänness of my hánds in^His ëye-sight.

p 25 With the holy ∗ Thôu shalt be hö-ly : and with a pêrfect man Thôu shalt^be për-fect.

26 With the clêan Thôu shalt^be clean : and with the froward ∗ Thôu shalt leärn fro-ward-ness.

27 For Thou shalt save the people that âre in advér-si-ty : and shalt bring dôwn the hígh looks of the proud.

28 Thou also shalt líght my cãn-dle : the Lord my God shall mâke my dárk-ness to be light.

29 For in Thee I shall discômfit an hóst of̩ men : and with the help of my God ∗ Î shall lêap o-ver^the wall.

30 The way of Gôd is an undefíl-ed way : the word of the Lord also is tried in the fire ; ∗ He is the defender of all thêm that pút their trust in Him.

1.   Dr. B. Cooke.   2.   * Rev. T. Helmore.

3.   * A. H. Brown.   4.   Dr. E. Ayrton.

mf 31 For whô is Gód, but^the Lord : or whô hath any stréngth, ex-cept our God ?

32 It is God,∗ that gírdeth me with stréngth of war : and mâketh my wây për-fect.

33 He maketh my fêet like hãrts' feet : ånd sétteth me up on high.

34 He teâcheth mine hánds to fight : and mine arms shall brêak éven a bow of steel.

35 Thou hast given me the defence of Thŷ salvã-tion : Thy right hand also shall hold me up,∗ and Thy lôving corréction shall make me great.

36 Thou shalt make room enough ûnder me fór to go : thât my fóot-steps shall not slide.

37 I will follow upon mine enemies, ∗ and óvertâke them : neither will I turn agâin till I háve de-stroy-ed them.

38 I will smite them,∗ that they shall nôt be áble to stand : bût fãll under my feet.

39 Thou hast girded me with strength ∗ ûnto the bãt-tle : Thou shalt thrôw down mine éne-mies un-der me.

40 Thou hast made mine enemies also ∗ to tûrn their bácks upon me : and I shall destrôy thém that häte me.

41 They shall cry,∗ but there shall be nône to hélp them : yea,∗ even unto the Lord shall they crŷ, but Hé shall^not hëar them.

42 I will beat them as small as the dûst befóre the wind : I will cast them ôut as the clãy in the streets.

43 Thou shalt deliver me from the strívings of the pêo-ple : and Thou shalt mâke me the héad of^the hëa-then.

19   [44 A

44 A pêople whom I háve not known : shăll sĕrve me.

45 As soon as they hear of me,* thêy shall obĕy me : but the strange chîldren shall dissĕm-ble wĭth me.

46 The strânge chĭl-dren⁀shall fail : and be afrâid óut of⁀their pri̇̈-sons.

ff 47 The Lord liveth, * and blessed be my strông hêlp-er : and praised be the Gôd of mý sal-vă-tion.

48 ̭ Even the God That seeth that Î be avĕn-ged : and subdûeth the pé̇o-ple un-to me.

f 49 It is He that delivereth me from my cruel enemies,* and setteth me up abôve mine ád-versa-ries : Thou shalt rĭd me frǿm the wick-ed man.

50 For this cause will I give thanks unto Thee, O Lord,* amông the Gên-tiles : and śing praís-es unto Thy Name.

51 Great prosperity gíveth He ún-to⁀His King : and sheweth loving-kindness unto David His Anointed,* and ûnto his séed for ev-er-more.

The Fourth Day.
Mattins.
Venite, exultemus Domino.

ƒO COME,* let us sĩng ŭn-to^ the Lord : let us heartily rejoice in the strêngth of oŭr sal-vä-tion.

2 Let us come before His prêsence with thanksgĩv-ing : and shêw ourselves glãd in Him with Psalms.

3 For the Lôrd is a grẽat God : and a grêat Kĩng above ãll gods.

4 In His hand are all the côrners ốf the earth : and the strength of the hĩlls is Hĩs ãl-so.

5 The sea is Hĩs, and He mãde it : and His hãnds prepãr-ed^the drỹ land.

p 6 O come, * let us wôrship, and fãll down : and knêel before the Lốrd our Mä-ker.

7 For Hê is the Lốrd our God : and we are the people of His pãsture, and the shéep of His hand.

mf 8 To-day if ye will hear His voice,* hârden nốt your hearts : as in the provocation,* and as in the day of temptâtion ĩn the wil-derness ;

9 When your fãthers tẽmpt-ed Me : prôved Mẽ, and saw My works.

10 Forty years long * was I grieved with thĩs generã-tion,^and said : It is a people that do err in their hêarts, for they hãve not known My ways.

11 Unto whôm I swãre in^My wrath : that they shôuld not ẽn-ter into My rest.

Glory be to the Fãther, ãnd to^the Son : ãnd tô the Ho-ly Ghost ;

As it was in the beginning,* is nôw, and éver shall be : wôrld without ẽnd. 'A'-men.

PSALM 19. *Cæli enarrant.*

1. * A. H. BROWN. 2. * L. J. TURRELL.
3. W. HAYES. 4. DR. E. G. MONK.

ƒTHE heavens declãre the glố-ry^ of God : and the fĩrmament shéweth His han-dy work.

2 One day têlleth anố-ther : and one night cêrtifĩeth an-ö-ther.

3 There is neither spêech nor lãn-guage : but their vôices are heãrd a-möng them.

4 Their sound is gone oût into ãll lands : and their wôrds into the ẽnds of the world.

5 In them hath He set a tâbernacle fốr the sun : which cometh forth as a bridegroom out of his chamber,* and rejôiceth as a gĩant to run his course.

6 It goeth forth from the uttermost part of the heaven, * and runneth about unto the ênd ốf it^ a-gain : and there is nôthing hĩd from^the heat there-of.

mf 7 The law of the Lord is an undefiled lâw, convérting the soul : the testimony of the Lord is sure,* and giveth wĩsdom ŭn-to^the simple.

21 [8 The

DAY 4.] THE PSALTER. [PSALMS 19, 20.

8 The statutes of the Lord are rı́ght, and rejoı́ce the heart : the commandment of the Lord is pure,✶ and gı́veth lı́ght un-to⁀the eyes.

9 The fear of the Lord is clean,✶ and endûreth for év-er : the judgments of the Lord are true,✶ and rı́ghteous ál-to-gë-ther.

10 More to be desired are they than gold,✶ yêa, than much fı́ne gold : sweeter also than hôney, ánd the hon-ey-comb.

11 Moreover, by thêm is Thy sér-vant taught : and in kêeping of them thére is great re-ward.

p 12 Who can tell how ôft he offénd-eth : O cleânse Thou me fróm my se-cret faults.

13 Keep Thy servant also from presumptuous sins,✶ lest they get the domı́nion ó-ver me : so shall I be undefiled,✶ and ı́nnocent fróm the great of-fence.

14 Let the words of my mouth,✶ and the meditâtion óf my heart : be âlway accépt - able in Thy sight,

15 Ô Lord : my strêngth, and mý Re-dëem-er.

PSALM 20. *Exaudiat Te Dominus.*

mf THE Lord hear thee in the dây of trôu-ble : the Name of the Gôd of Já-cob defénd thee ;

2 Send thee hêlp from the sánc-tua-ry : and strêngthen thee oút of Sı̄-on ;

3 Remember äll thy öf-fer-ings : and accêpt thy bürnt sa-cri-fice ;

4 Gränt thee thy heárt's de-sire : ånd fulfĩl all thy mind.

f 5 We will rejoice in Thy salva-tion,⁕ and triumph in the Nâme of the Lórd our God : the Lôrd perform åll thy peti:-tions.

p 6 Now know I, that the Lord helpeth His Anointed,⁕ and will hêar him from His hó-ly heaven :

even with the whôlesome stréngth of^His right hand.

f 7 Some put their trust in chariots,⁕ and sôme in hōr-ses : but we will remêmber the Náme of^the Lord our God.

p 8 They are brought dôwn, and fãl-len :*f* but we are ri̇̂sen, and stãnd üp-right.

p 9 Save, Lord,⁕ and hêar us, O Kíng of heaven : whên we cáll up-ön Thee.

PSALM 21. *Domine, in virtute Tua.*

1. W. LEE.   2. R. BELLAMY.
3.   * E. W. T. GRAVES.   4.   * E. W. T. GRAVES.

f THE King shall rejöice in Thy stréngth, O Lord : exceeding glad shall he bê of Thý sal-vä-tion.

2 Thou hast gíven him his héart's de-sire : and hast not denîed him the requést of his lips.

mf 3 For Thou shalt prevent him with the blêssings of góod-ness : and shalt set a crôwn of pure góld up-on his head.

4 He asked life of Thee,⁕ and Thou gâvest him a lóng life : êven for év-er^and ëv-er.

f 5 His honour is great in Thŷ salvä-tion : glory and great wôrship shalt Thou láy up-ön him.

6 For Thou shalt give him ever-lâsting felí-ci-ty: and make him glâd with the jóy of^Thy coun-te-nance.

mf 7 And why?⁕ because the King pûtteth his trúst in^the Lord : and in the mercy of the Most Highest ⁕ hê shall nót mis-cär-ry.

f 8 All Thine ênemies shall féel Thy hand : Thy right hand shall fînd out thém that häte Thee.

9 Thou shalt make them like a fiery ôven in tíme of^Thy wrath : the Lord shall destroy them in His displeasure, ⁕ ånd the fĩre shall consüme them.

10 Their fruit shalt Thou rôot óut of^the earth : and their sêed from amóng the chil-dren ^ of men.

11 For they intended mi̇̂schief agáinst Thee : and imagined such a device ⁕ as they åre not á-ble to per-form.

12 Thêrefore shalt Thou pút them^to flight : and the strings of Thy bow shalt Thou make rêady agaínst the face of them.

ff 13 Be Thou exalted, Lôrd, in Thine ôwn strength : sô will we síng, and praise Thy power.

Evensong.

PSALM 22. *Deus, Deus meus.*

(Minor.)

p MY God, my God,* look upon me ; * why hast Thou forsá-ken me : and art so far from my health,* and frŏm the wórds of my com-plaint ?

2 O my God, I cry in the day-time,* but Thŏu héar-est not : and in the night-sĕason ál-so⌢I take no rest.

mf 3 And Thou contĭnuest hō-ly : Ō Thou wór-ship⌢of Is-ra-el.

4 Our fắthers hó-ped⌢in Thee : they trusted in Thêe, and Thŏu didst deli-ver them.

5 They called upon Thêe, and were hōl-pen : they put their trust in Thêe, and were nót con-foúnd-ed.

p 6 But as for me,* I am a wŏrm, and nō man : a very scorn of men,* and the oût-cast óf the pĕo-ple.

7 All they that sêe me laúgh me⌢ to scorn : they shoot out their lips,* and shăke their hĕads, săy-ing,

mf 8 He trusted in God,* that Hĕ would delí-ver him : let Him delíver him, íf He⌢will hăve him.

9 But Thou art He that took me óut of my mó-ther's womb : Thou wast my hope,* when I hanged yĕt upón my mo-ther's breasts.

10 I have been left unto Thee ĕver sínce I⌢was born : Thou art my Gŏd even fróm my mo-ther's womb.

p 11 O go not from me,* for trŏuble is hárd at hand : ănd there is nóne to hĕlp me.

12 Many ŏxen are cóme about me : fat bulls of Basan clôse me ín on e-very side.

13 They gâpe upon me wíth their mouths : as it were a râmping and a róar-ing lï-on.

14 I am poured out like water,* and all my bŏnes are oút of joint : my heart also in the midst of my bŏdy is ĕven like melt-ing wax.

15 My strength is dried up like a potsherd,* and my tongue clĕaveth tó my gums : and Thou shalt brĭng me ín-to⌢the dust of death.

16 For many dŏgs are cóme about me : and the council of the wicked lâyeth síege a-gaïnst me.

17 They pierced my hands and my feet,* I may têll áll my bones : they stand stâring and lóok-ing upŏn me.

18 They part my gârments amŏng them : and cast lôts upón my vës-ture.

pp 19 But be not Thou fâr fróm me,⌢O Lord : Thou art my sûccour, háste Thee⌢to hĕlp me.

20 Delíver my sóul from the sword : my dârling from the pów-er of the dog.

21 Sáve me from the lí-on's mouth : Thou hast heard me also from amóng the hórns of the u-ni-corns.

(Major.)f 22 I will declare Thy Name únto my bréth-ren : in the midst of the congregâtion wíll I práise Thee.

23 O praise the Lord, * yê that fêar Him : magnify Him, all ye of the seed of Jacob,* and fear Him, âll ye séed of Is-ra-el ;

24 For He hath not despised,* nor abhorred, the lôw estáte of the poor : He hath not hid His face from him,* but when he câlled unto Hím He hëard him.

25 My praise is of Thee * in the grêat congregâ-tion : my vows will I perform in the síght of thém that fear Him.

mf 26 The poor shall eât, and be sá-tis-fied : they that seek after the Lord shall praise Him ; * your heârt shall líve for ë-ver.

27 All the ends of the world shall remember themselves, * and be tûrned ún-to the Lord : and all the kindreds of the nâtions shall wór-ship befôre Him.

28 For the kíngdom ís the Lord's : and He is the Gôvernour amóng the pëo-ple.

29 All sûch as be fát upon earth : hâve eát-en, and wor-ship-ped.

30 All they that go down into the dust * shall knêel befôre Him : and nô man hath quíck-ened his öwn soul.

31 My seêd shall sêrve Him : they shall be counted unto the Lôrd for a gé-ne-rä-tion.

32 They shall come, * and the heavens shall declâre His ríghteous-ness : unto a people that shall be bôrn, whóm the Lord hath made.

Psalm 23. *Dominus regit me.*

1. J. Barnby.
2. A. H. Brown.
3. Bishop Medley.
4. T. Kelway.

mf THE Lôrd is my shêp-herd : thêrefore can I láck nö-thing.

2 He shall feed me in a grêen pás-ture : and lead me forth besîde the wá-ters of cöm-fort.

3 Hê shall convért my soul : and bring me forth in the paths of ríghteousness, fór His Näme's sake.

4 Yea,* though I walk through the valley of the shadow of death,* I will feâr no ê-vil : for Thou art with me ; * Thy rôd and Thy stâff com-fort me.

5 Thou shalt prepare a table before me * against thêm that trôu-ble me : Thou hast anointed my head with ôil, and my cûp shall be full.

6 But Thy loving-kindness and mercy * shall follow me âll the dáys of my life : and I will dwell in the hôuse of the Lórd for ë-ver.

[Day 5.] THE PSALTER. [VENITE.

The Fifth Day.

Mattins.

Venite, exultemus Domino.

f O COME,* let us síng ún-to͡ the Lord : let us heartily rejoice in the strĕngth of oúr sal-vä-tion.

2 Let us come before His prêsence with thanksgív-ing : and shêw ourselves glád in Him with Psalms.

3 For the Lôrd is a grĕ́at God : and a grêat Kíng above äll gods.

4 In His hand are all the cô̂rners óf the earth : and the strength of the hîlls is Hís äl-so.

5 The sea is Hís, and He máde it : and His hânds prepár-ed͡the drÿ land.

p 6 O come,* let us wôrship, and fâll down : and knêel before the Lórd our Mä-ker.

7 For Hê is the Lórd our God : and we are the people of His pâsture, and the shéep of Hís hand.

mf 8 To-day if ye will hear His voice,* hârden nót your hearts : as in the provocation,* and as in the day of temptâtion ín the wil-der-ness ;

9 When your fâthers témpt-ed Me : prôved Mé, and saw My works.

10 Forty years long * was I grieved with thís generá-tion,͡and said : It is a people that do err in their hĕarts, for they háve not known My ways.

11 Unto whôm I swáre in͡My wrath : that they shôuld not én-ter into My rest.

Glory be to the Fâther, ánd to͡the Son : ánd tó the Ho-ly Ghost ;

As it was in the beginning,* is nôw, and éver shall be : wôrld without énd. 'A'-men.

PSALM 24. *Domini est terra.*

*T*HE earth is the Lord's,* and áll that thére-in is : the compass of the wôrld, and théy that dwell there-in.

2 For He hath foúnded it upón the seas : ánd prepáred it upon the floods.

p 3 Who shall ascénd into the hĭ́ll of the Lord : or whô shall rise úp in His ho-ly place ?

mf 4 Even he that hath clean hánds, and a púre heart : and that hath not lift up his mind unto vanity,* nor swôrn to decefve his néigh-bour.

5 He shall receive the blêssing fróm the Lord : and righteousness from the Gôd of hís sal-vä-tion.

6 This is the generation of thêm that sêek Him : even of them that sêek thy fáce, O Jä-cob.

(Full) f 7 Lift up your heads, O ye gates,* and be ye lift úp, ye everlást-ing doors : and the Kĭ́ng of gló-ry shall cöme in.

(Dec.) mf 8 Who is the Kĭ́ng of glō-ry : *(Can.) f* it is the Lord strong and mighty,* even the Lôrd mígh-ty in bät-tle.

(Full) f 9 Lift up your heads, O ye gates,* and be ye lift úp, ye everlást-ing doors : and the Kĭ́ng of gló-ry shall cöme in.

(Dec.) mf 10 Who is the Kĭ́ng of glō-ry : *(Can.) f* even the Lord of hosts,* Hê is the Kĭ́ng of glö-ry.

PSALM 25. *Ad Te, Domine, levavi.*

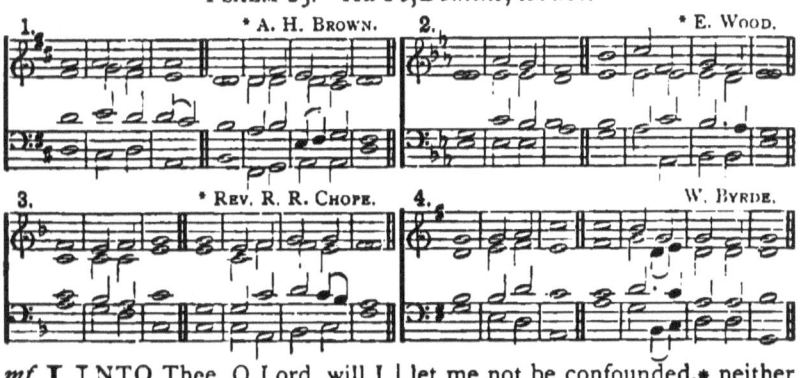

mf UNTO Thee, O Lord, will I lift up my soul ;* my God, I have pút my trúst in Thee : O let me not be confounded,* neither let mine ênemies trí-umph o-ver me.

[2 For

1. * A. H. Brown.
2. * E. Wood.
3. * Rev. R. R. Chope.
4. W. Byrde.

2 For all they that hope in Thee shall nŏt be ashā-med : but such as transgress without a câuse shall be pút to͡con-fū-sion.
3 Shêw me Thy wáys, O Lord ; ănd teách me Thÿ paths.
4 Lead me forth in Thy trûth, and lĕarn me : for Thou art the God of my salvation ;* in Thee hath bêen my hópe all͡the däy long.
5 Call to remembrance, O Lord,* Thy tênder ḿer-cies : and Thy loving kindnesses, * whîch háve been e-ver͡of old.
6 O remember not the sins and offĕnces óf my youth : but according to Thy mercy* think Thou upŏn me, O Lórd, for͡Thy göod-ness.
p 7 Gracious and rîghteous ís the Lord : therefore will He teâch sín-ners in the way.
8 Them that are meek shall He guîde in fŭdg-ment : and such as are gêntle, thém shall͡He learn His way.
9 All the paths of the Lôrd are mćr-cy͡and truth : unto such as keep His côvenant, ánd His tes-timo-nies.
10 For Thy Nâme's sáke, O Lord : be merciful ûnto my sín, for it is great.

11 What man is hê, that feár-eth͡the Lord : him shall He têach in the wáy that He shall choose.
12 His sôul shall dwĕll at ease : ănd his séed shall͡in-herit the land.
13 The secret of the Lord is among thêm that fĕar Him : and Hê will shĕw them͡His co-ve-nant.
mf 14 Mine eyes are ever lôoking ún-to͡the Lord : for He shall plûck my fĕet out of͡the net.
p 15 Turn Thee unto me,* and have mêrcy upŏn me : for I am dêsolate, ánd in mi-se-ry.
16 The sorrows of my hêart are enlár-ged : O bríng Thou me óut of͡my troü-bles.
17 Look upon my advêrsity and mí-se-ry : ănd forgíve me all my sin.
18 Consider mine ênemies, how mány they are : and they bear a týrannous háte a-gäinst me.
19 O keep my sôul, and delí-ver me :ˏlet me not be confounded,* for I have pút my trust in Thee.
20 Let perfectness and righteous dêaling waít upon me : fôr my hópe hath been inˏThee.
21 Deliver Îsrael, Ô God : òut of áll his troü-bles.

28

PSALM 26. *Judica me, Domine.*

mf BE Thou my Judge, O Lord,*
for I have wálked ín-nocent-
ly : my trust hath been also in the
Lord,* thêrefore shàll I nöt fall.
  2 Examine me, O Lôrd, and prőve
me : trŷ out my reíns and mÿ heart.
  3 For Thy loving kindness is êver
befőre mine eyes : and I will
wálk in Thÿ truth.
  4 I have not dwêlt with vain
pér-sons : neither will I have
féllowship wíth the⁀de-ceit-ful.
  5 I have hated the congregâtion
of the wíck-ed : and will not sít
amóng the⁀un-göd-ly.
  p 6 I will wash my hands in
ínnocency, O Lord : and sô will I
gó to⁀Thine 'A'l-tar ;

  7 That I may shew the voíce of
thanksgív-ing : and têll of áll Thy
won-drous works.
  8 Lord, I have loved the habitâtion óf Thy house : and the plâce
where Thine hó-nour dwëll-eth.
  9 O shut up not my sôul with
the sín-ners : nor my lîfe with the
blôod-thïrs-ty ;
  10 In whose hânds is wíck-ed-
ness : and their rîght hánd is full
of gifts.
  11 But as for me,* I will wâlk
ín-nocent-ly : O delíver me, and
be mér-ciful un-to me.
  12 My fôot stánd-eth right : I
will praise the Lôrd in the cón-
gre-gä-tions.

Evensong.

PSALM 27. *Dominus illuminatio.*

f THE Lord is my light, and my salvation ;* whôm thén shall⌒I fear : The Lord is the strength of my life ;* of whôm thén shall⌒I be a-fraid?

2 When the wicked,* even mine enemies, and my foes,* came upôn me to eát up⌒my flesh : they stúm-bled ãnd fell.

3 Though an host of men were laid against me,* yet shall nôt my heárt be⌒a-fraid : and though there rose up war against me,* yêt will I pút my trust in Him.

mf 4 One thing ͵have I desired of the Lôrd, which I will⌒re-quire : even that I may dwell in the house of the Lord all the days of my life,* to behold the fair beauty of the Lôrd, and to ví-sit⌒His tëm-ple.

p 5 For in the time of trouble * He shall hîde me in His tá-berna-cle : yea, in the secret place of His dwelling shall He hide me,* and set me ûp upón a rock of stone,

mf 6 And now shall He lîft úp mine head : above mine ênemies roúnd a-böut me.

(Full) f 7 Therefore will I offer in His dwelling an oblation * with grêat glãd-ness : I will síng, and speak praís-es un-to⌒the Lord

p 8 Hearken unto my voice, O Lord, * whên I crý unto Thee : have mêrcy upón me,⌒and hëar me.

9 My heart hath talked of Thêe, Séek ye⌒My face : Thý fáce, Lord, will I seek.

10 O hide not Thôu Thy fâce from me : nor cast Thy sêrvant awáy in⌒dis-plëa-sure.

11 Thou hast bêen my súc-cour : leave me not,* neither forsake me, O Gôd of mý sal-vä-tion.

12 When my father and my mô-ther forsáke me : the Lôrd ták-eth më up.

13 Têach me Thy wáy, O Lord : and lead me in the ríght way, becáuse of⌒mine e-ne-mies.

14 Deliver me not over into the wíll of mine ád-versa-ries : for there are false witnesses risen up agâinst me, and súch as spëak wrong.

mf 15 I should ûtterly have fáint-ed : but that I believe verily to see the goodness of the Lôrd in the lánd of the liv-ing.

16 O tarry thôu the Lord's léi-sure : be strong, and He shall comfort thine heart ;* and pût thou thy trûst in the Lord.

PSALM 28. *Ad te, Domine.*

(Minor.)

p UNTO Thee will I crŷ, O Lórd my strength : think no scorn of me ; * lest, if Thou make as though Thou hearest not, * I become like thêm that go dôwn in-to⁀ the pit.

2 Hear the voice of my humble petitions,* whên I crý unto Thee : when I hold up my hands towards the mêrcy seat of Thy hó-ly têm-ple.

3 O pluck me not away,* neither destroy me with the ungôdly and wíck-ed doers : which speak friendly to their neighbours, * but imâgine mís-chief in their hearts.

4 Reward them accôrding tó their deeds : and according to the wíckedness of their ówn in-vên-tions.

5 Recompense them âfter the wórk of their hands : pay them thât they háve de-sërv-ed.

6 For they regard not in their mind the works of the Lord,* nor the operâtion óf His hands : therefore shall He break them dôwn, and nôt build them up.

(Major.)f 7 Prâised bé the Lord: for He hath heard the vôice of my húm-ble petï-tions.

8 The Lord is my strength, and my shield ;* my heart hath trusted in Him, and I am hélp-ed : therefore my heart danceth for joy,* ând in my sóng will⁀I praise Him.

9 Thê Lórd is⁀my strength : and He is the wholesome dcfênce of Hís A-nóint-ed.

p 10 O save Thy people, * and give Thy blessing unto Thíhe inhé-ri-tance : feed them, and sêt them úp for ë-ver.

PSALM 29. *Afferte Domino.*

f ♭RING unto the Lord, O ye mighty,⁂ bring young rāms ŭn-to⁀the Lord : ascribe unto the Lôrd wŏr-ship and strength.

2 Give the Lord the honour dūe ŭn-to⁀His Name : worship the Lôrd with hó-ly wŏr-ship.

3 It is the Lord, That commând-eth the wā-ters : it is the glorious Gôd, That māk-eth⁀the thŭn-der.

4 It is the Lord, That ruleth the sea ;⁂ the voice of the Lord is mighty in ôperā-tion : the vóice of the Lórd is⁀a glo-rious voice.

mf 5 The voice of the Lord brēaketh the cé-dar trees : yea, the Lord brēaketh the cé-dars⁀of Lib-a-nus.

6 He maketh them âlso to skíp like⁀a calf : Libanus also, and Sírion, lĭke a⁀young u-ni-corn.

7 The voice of the Lord divideth the flames of fire ;⁂ the voice of the Lord shâketh the wĭl-der-ness : yea, the Lord shâketh the wĭl-derness⁀of Cä-des.

8 The voice of the Lord maketh the hinds to bring forth young,⁂ and discovereth the thíck būsh-es : in His temple doth êvery man spéak of⁀His hö-nour.

9 The Lord sitteth abôve the wâ-ter flood : and the Lord re-mâineth a Kíng for ë-ver.

(Full) f 10 The Lord shall give strength ûnto His pēo-ple : *p* the Lord shall give His pêople the bléss-ing of peace.

The Sixth Day.

Mattins.

Venite, exultemus Domino.

ƒ O COME,* let us sĭng ŭn-toˆ the Lord : let us heartily rejoice in the strĕngth of oŭr sal-vä-tion.
  2 Let us come before His prêsence with thanksgĭv-ing : and shĕw ourselves glăd in Him with Psalms.
  3 For the Lôrd is a grĕat God : and a grĕat Kĭng above äll gods.
  4 In His hand are all the cônners ŏf the earth : and the strength of the hĭlls is Hĭs äl-so.
  5 The sea is Hĭs, and He mâde it : and His hânds prepăr-edˆthe drÿ land.
  p 6 O come,* let us wôrship, and făll down : and knêel before the Lôrd our Mä-ker.
  7 For Hê is the Lŏrd our God : and we are the people of His pâsture, and the shéep of Hĭs hand.

mf 8 To-day if ye will hear His voice,* hârden nŏt your hearts : as in the provocation,* and aś in the day of temptâtion ĭn the wil-der-ness ;
  9 When your fâthers témpt-ed Me : prôved Mé, and saw My works.
  10 Forty years long * was I grieved with thĭs generă-tion,ˆand said : It is a people that do err in their hêarts, for they hâve not known My ways.
  11 Unto whôm I swăre inˆMy wrath : that they shôuld not én-ter into My rest.
  Glory be to the Fâther, ănd toˆthe Son : ănd tô the Ho-ly Ghost ;
  As it was in the beginning,* is nŏw, and éver shall be : wôrld without ĕnd. ˙A˙-men.

[PSALM 30.

Psalm 30. *Exaltabo Te, Domine.*

(Major.)

f 1 I WILL magnify Thee, O Lord,* for Thou hast sét me up : and not made my fóes to trí-umph o-ver me.

p 2 O Lord my Gôd, I crîed unto Thee : ând Thóu hast heal-ed me.

3 Thou, Lord, hast brought my sôul óut of hell : Thou hast kept my life from thêm that go dówn to the pit.

f 4 Sing praises unto the Lôrd, O ye saînts of His : and give thanks unto Him * for a remêmbrance óf His ho-li-ness.

5 For His wrath endureth but the twinkling of an eye,* ând in His pleá-sure is life : heaviness may endure for a night,* but jôy cometh ín the mörn-ing.

6 And in my prosperity I said,* I shall nêver be remô-ved : Thou, Lord, of Thy goôdness hast máde my hill so strong.

p 7 Thou didst tûrn Thy fáce from me : ând I' was tröu-bled.

8 Then cried Î unto Thêe, O Lord : and gât me to my Lórd right hüm-bly.

9 What prôfit is there ín my blood : whên I go dówn to the pit?

10 Shall the dûst give thánks unto Thee : ôr shâll it de-clare Thy truth?

11 Hear, O Lord, * and have mêrcy upón me : Lôrd, be Thóu my hêlp-er.

mf 12 Thou hast turned my hêaviness ín-to joy : Thou hast put off my sackcloth,* and gírded mé with gläd-ness.

(Full) mf 13 Therefore shall every good man sing of Thy praîse without cêas-ing : O my God,* I will give thânks unto Thée for ë-ver.

Psalm 31. *In Te, Domine, speravi.*

mf IN Thee, O Lôrd, have I pút my trust : let me never be put to confusion,* delíver me ín Thy right-eous-ness.

p 2 Bow dôwn Thine eár to me : máke háste to deli-ver me.

3 And be Thou my strong rôck, and hóuse of ⁀de-fence : thát Thóu mayest säve me.

4 For Thou art my strong rôck, and my cás-tle : be Thou also my guide,* and lêad me fór Thy Näme's sake.

5 Draw me out of the net,* that they have laid prívily fór me : fór Thóu art my strength.

6 Into Thy hands I commênd my spí-rit : for Thou hast redêemed me, O Lórd, Thou God of truth.

7 I have hated them that hold of superstitîtious vá-ni-ties : ánd my trúst hath been in⁀the Lord.

mf 8 I will be glad, and rejoíce in Thy mêr-cy : for Thou hast considered my trouble,* and hast knôwn my sóul in⁀ad-ver-si-ties.

9 Thou hast not shut me up* into the hând of the é-ne-my : but hast sêt my féet in⁀a lärge room.

p 10 Have ᴀ mercy upon me, O Lord, * for Í am in trôu-ble : and mine eye is consumed for very heaviness ; * yêa, my sóul and⁀my bö-dy.

11 For my life is waxen ôld with héa-vi-ness : ánd my yéars with möurn-ing.

12 My strength faileth me, * because of míne iní-qui-ty : ánd my bónes are consüm-ed.

13 I became a reproof among all mine enemies, * but especially amông my néigh-bours : and they of mine acquaintance were afraid of me ; * and they that did see me withôut convéyed themselves fröm me.

14 I am clean forgotten,* as a dêad man óut of mind : I am becôme like a bró-ken vës-sel.

15 For I have heard the blás-phemy of the múl-ti-tude : and fear is on every side, * while they conspire together against me, * and take their côunsel to táke a-way my life.

16 But my hope hath bêen in Thée, O Lord : I have sâid, Thóu art my God.

17 My time is in Thy hand ; * deliver me from the hând of mine é-ne-mies : ánd from thém that per-secute me.

18 Shew Thy servant the líght of Thy cóun-te-nance : and sâve me fór Thy mer-cy's sake.

19 Let me not be confounded, O Lord, * for I have câlled upôn Thee : let the ungodly be put to confusion, * and be pût to sí-lence in the grave.

20 Let the lying lips be pût to sí-lence : which cruelly, disdainfully, and despitefully,* spêak agaínst the ríght-eous.

mf 21 O how plentiful is Thy goodness, * which Thou hast laid up for thêm that fêar Thee : and that Thou hast prepared for them that put their trust in Thee,* êven befóre the sons of men !

p 22 Thou shalt hide them privily by Thine own presence * from the provôking of áll men : Thou shalt keep them secretly in Thy tâbernacle fróm the strife of tongues.

mf 23 Thânks bé to⁀the Lord : for He hath shewed me marvellous great kíndness in a strông ci-ty.

p 24 And whên I made háste, I said : I am cast ôut of the síght of Thine eyes.

25 Nevertheless,* Thou hêardest the voíce of⁀my prayer : whên I crí-ed un-to Thee.

mf 26 O love the Lôrd, all yé His saints : for the Lord preserveth them that are faithful,* and plênteously rewárdeth the pröud doer.

(Full) mf 27 Be strong,* and Hê shall estáblish your heart : all yê that pút your trust in⁀the Lord.

Day 6.] THE PSALTER. [Psalm 32.

Evensong.

Psalm 32. *Beati, quorum.*

1. * Sir G. Elvey.
2. * J. Heywood.
3. * A. H. Brown.
4. * L. J. Turrell.

mf BLESSED is he whose un-righteousness is for-given : and whôse sín is co-ver-ed.

2 Blessed is the man unto whom the Lôrd impú-teth⌢no sin : ánd in whose spírit there is no guile.

p 3 For whîle I héld my tongue : my bones consumed awáy through my daí-ly compláin-ing.

4 For Thy hand is heavy upôn me dáy and night : and my moisture is lîke the drôught in süm-mer.

5 I will acknôwledge my sín unto Thee : and mine unríghteous-ness háve I nōt hid.

6 I said,* I will confess my sîns ún - to⌢the Lord : and so Thou forgâvest the wíck-edness of my sin.

7 For this shall every one that is godly make his prayer unto Thee,* in a tîme when Thou máyest be found : but in the great waterfloods* théy shall nót come nigh him.

8 Thou art a place to hide me in, * Thou shalt presêrve me from trôu-ble : Thou shalt compass me abôut with sóngs of deli-ver-ance.

mf 9 I will inform thee, * and teach thee in the ͜ way wherefn thou⌢shalt go : and I will gufde thee with Mine eye.

10 Be ye not like to horse and mule, * which have nô understánd-ing : whose mouths must be held with bit and bridle,* lêst they fáll up-ön thee.

11 Great plagues remaîn for the ungôd-ly : but whoso putteth his trust in the Lord,* mercy embrâceth hím on ev-ery side.

f 12 Be glad, O ye ríghteous, and rejoíce in⌢the Lord : and be jôyful, all yé that⌢are true of heart.

36

PSALM 33. *Exultate, justi.*

1. * Sir G. Elvey. 2. * E. W. T. Graves.
3. * A. Neville. 4. R. Bellamy.

f REJOICE in the Lôrd, O ye rîgh-teous : for it becometh wêll the jŭst to⌢be thänk-ful.

2 Prâise the Lórd with harp : sing praises unto Him with the lŭte, and ín-strument of⌢tën strings.

3 Sîng unto the Lórd a⌢new song : sing praises lustily unto Hĭm with a gŏod cŏu-rage.

4 For the wôrd of the Lórd is true : and âll His wórks are fäith-ful.

5 He loveth rîghteousness and jùdg-ment : the earth is fŭll of the gŏod-ness of the Lord.

mf 6 By the word of the Lôrd were the héa-vens made : and all the hosts of thêm by the bréath of Hĭs mouth.

7 He gathereth the waters of the sea together,* as it wêre upón an heap : and layeth up the dêep, ás in⌢a trea-sure house.

p 8 Let âll the earth féar the Lord : stand in awe of Him,* âll yé that dwell in⌢the world.

mf 9 For He spâke, ánd it⌢was done : He commânded, ánd it stŏod fast.

10 The Lord bringeth the cŏunsel of the héa-then⌢to nought : and maketh the devices of the people to be of none effect,* and casteth ŏut the coún-sels⌢of prín-ces.

11 The counsel of the Lord shall endûre for êv-er : and the thoughts of His heart from generâtion to gé-ne-rä-tion.

f 12 Blessed are the people,* whose God is the Lôrd JEHÖ-VAH : and blessed are the folk, that He hath chosen to Hĭm to bé His inhe-ri-tance.

mf 13 The Lord looked down from heaven,* and behêld all the chîl-dren⌢of men : from the habita-tion of His dwelling He consîdereth all thém that dwell on⌢the earth.

14 He fashioneth âll the héarts of them : and ûnderstánd-eth all their works.

15 There is no king that can be saved by the mŭltitude óf an host : neither is any mîghty man delí-vered⌢by much strength.

16 A horse is counted but a vâin thing to sáve a man : neither shall he deliver âny man bý his grëat strength.

p 17 Behold,* the eye of the Lord is upon thêm that féar Him : and upon them that pŭt their trŭst in⌢His mër-cy ;

18 To delíver their sóul from death : and to fêed them ín the time of dearth.

19 Our soul hath patiently târ-ried fór the Lord : for Hê is our hélp and oür shield.

mf 20 For our hêart shall rejoíce in Him : because we have hôped ín His ho-ly Name.

p 21 Let Thy merciful kindness, O Lôrd, bé upon us : líke as we do pút our trust in Thee.

[PSALM 34.

PSALM 34. *Benedicam Domino.*

1. * Dr. E. G. Monk.
2. * L. Barcroft.
3. * E. J. Hopkins.
4. * A. H. Brown.

f 1 I WILL alway give thânks ún-to^the Lord : His praise shall êver bé in mÿ mouth.

2 My soul shall mâke her bóast in^the Lord : the humble shall hêar thereóf, and be glad.

3 O prâise the Lórd with me : and let us mâgnify His Náme to-gë-ther.

mf 4 I sought the Lôrd, and He hêard me : yea, * He delívered me oút of all my fear.

5 They had an eye unto Hím, and were líght-en-ed : and their fâces were nót a-shäm-ed.

6 Lo, the poor crieth, * and the Lôrd héar-eth him : yea, * and saveth him ôut of áll his troü-bles.

7 The angel of the Lord * tarrieth round about thêm that fêar Him : ánd de-li-vereth them.

p 8 O taste, and see, * how grâcious the Lôrd is : blêssed is the mán that trust-eth^in Him.

9 O fear the Lord, * yê that áre His saints : for they that fêar Hím lack nö-thing.

mf 10 The lions do lack, and sûffer hûn-ger : but they who seek the Lord * shall want no mânner of thíng that is good.

p 11 Come, ye children, * and héarken ún-to me : I will têach you the fêar of the Lord.

12 What man is hê that lúst-eth^ to live : ând would faín see göod days ?

13 Keep thy tôngue from ë-vil : ând thy líps, that^they speak no guile.

14 Eschew êvil, and dö good : sêek peáce, and^en-süe it.

mf 15 The eyes of the Lord are ôver the rígh-teous : and His eârs are ó-pen unto their prayers.

16 The countenance of the Lord is against thêm that do ë-vil : to root out the remêmbrance óf them from the earth.

17 The righteous cry, * and the Lôrd héar-eth them : and delivereth them ôut of áll their troü-bles.

18 The Lord is nigh unto them that âre of a cón-trite heart : and will save such as bê of an húm-ble spï-rit.

19 Great are the trôubles of the rígh-teous : but the Lord delívereth hím out of all.

20 He kêepeth áll his bones : so that not ône of thém is brö-ken.

21 But misfortune shall slây the ungód-ly : and they that hate the ríghteous shǎll be de-so-late.

22 The Lord delivereth the sôuls of His sér-vants : and all they that put their trust in Hím shall nót be des-ti-tute.

The Seventh Day.

Mattins.

Venite, exultemus Domino.

1. L. BARCROFT. 2. A. H. BROWN.
3. B. LAMB. 4. DR. W. HAYES.

f O COME,* let us sĭng ŭn-to⌢ the Lord : let us heartily rejoice in the strêngth of oŭr sal-vä-tion.

2 Let us come before His prêsence with thanksgĭv-ing : and shêw ourselves glăd in Him with Psalms.

3 For the Lôrd is a grêat God : and a grêat Kĭng above äll gods.

4 In His hand are all the côrners ŏf the earth : and the strength of the hĭlls is Hĭs äl-so.

5 The sea is Hĭs, and He mâde it : and His hânds prepăr-ed⌢the drÿ land.

p 6 O come,* let us wôrship, and făll down : and knêel before the Lŏrd our Mä-ker.

7 For Hê is the Lŏrd our God : and we are the people of His pâsture, and the shêep of Hĭs hand.

mf 8 To-day if ye will hear His voice,* hârden nŏt your hearts : as in the provocation,* and as in the day of temptâtion ĭn the wil-der-ness ;

9 When your fâthers tĕmpt-ed Me : prôved Mĕ, and saw My works.

10 Forty years long * was I grieved with thĭs generă-tion,⌢and said : It is a people that do err in their hêarts, for they hăve not known My ways.

11 Unto whôm I swăre in⌢My wrath : that they shŏuld not ĕn-ter into My rest.

Glory be to the Fâther, ănd to⌢the Son : ănd tŏ the Ho-ly Ghost ;

As it was in the beginning,* is nŏw, and ĕver shall be : wŏrld without ĕnd. `A`-men.

[PSALM 35.

Psalm 35. *Judica, Domine.*

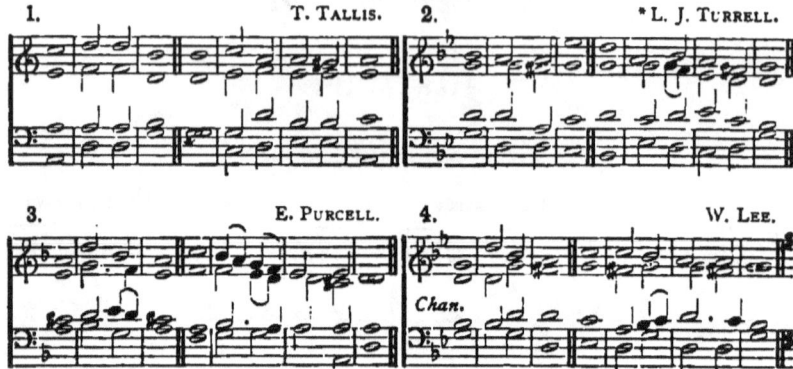

1. T. Tallis.   2. *L. J. Turrell.
3. E. Purcell.   4. W. Lee.

p PLEAD Thou my cause, O Lord,* with thêm that strı́ve with me : and fight Thou against thêm that fı́ght a-gaïnst me.

2 Lay hand upon the shiêld and bŭck-ler : and stånd ŭp to hëlp me.

mf 3 Bring forth the spear,* and stop the way against thêm that‿pér-secute me : say unto my soul,* I am thý sal-vä-tion.

4 Let them be confounded, and put to shame,* that sêek ắf-ter⁀my soul : let them be turned back, and brought to confusion,* that imâgine mı́s-chief fōr me.

5 Let them be as the dŭst befóre the wind : and the ângel of the Lōrd scat-tering them.

6 Let their way be dắrk and slı́p-pe-ry : and let the ângel of the Lōrd per-secute them.

7 For they have privily laid their net to destrôy me withóut a cause : yea, even without a cause have they mâde a pı́t for mỹ soul.

8 Let a sudden destruction come upon him unawares,* and his net, that he hath laid prı́vily, cắtch him-self : that he may fåll into his ôwn mïs-chief.

f 9 And, my soul,* be jôyful ı́n the Lord : it shall rejôice in Hı́s sal-vä-tion.

10 All my bones shall say,* Lord who is like unto Thee,* Who de-liverest the poor from hı́m that is too strống for him : yea, the poor, and him that is in mı̈sery, from hı́m that spoil-eth him?

p 11 False wı̂tnesses did rı́se up : they laid to my chârge thı́ngs that⁀ I knëw not.

12 They rewârded me é-vil⁀for good : to the grêat discóm-fort of my soul.

13 Nevertheless,* when they were sick, I put on sackcloth,* and humbled my sôul with fắst-ing : and my prayer shall tûrn into mine ôwn bö-som.

14 I behaved myself as though it had been my frı̂end, or my brö-ther : I went heavily,*as one that môurneth fór his mö-ther.

mf 15 But in my adversity they rejoiced,* and gathered themsêlves togé-ther : yea, the very abjects came together against me una-wares,* making môuths ắt me,⁀and ceas-ed not.

16 With the flatterers were bûsy môck-ers : who gnâshed upón me with their teeth.

p 17 Lord, * how lông wilt Thou lóok upon this : O deliver my soul from the calamities which they bring on me,* and my dârling fróm the lı̈-ons.

18 So will I give Thee thanks,✶ in the grēat congregā-tion : I will prāise Thee amóng much pëo-ple.

19 O let not them that are mine enemies✶ triumph óver me ungőd-ly: neither let them wink with their eȳes that háte me without a cause.

20 And why?✶ their cômmuning is nót for peace : but they imagine deceitful words against thêm that are quí-et in the land.

21 They gaped upôn me with their móuths, and said : Fie on thee,✶ fíe on thee, we sáw it with our eyes.

mf 22 Thís Thou hast séen, O Lord : hold not Thy tongue then,✶ gô not fár from me, O Lord.

f 23 Awake,✶ and stand up to jûdge my qūar-rel : avenge Thou my câuse, my Gód, and mȳ Lord.

mf 24 Judge me, O Lord my God,✶ accôrding to Thy rígh-teous-ness : and lêt them not trí-umph o-ver me.

25 Let them not say in their hearts,✶ There,✶ there,✶ sô would we hāve it : neither let them sây, Wé have devour-ed him.

26 Let them be put to confusion and shame together,✶ that rejôice at my trôu-ble : let them be clothed with rebuke and dishonour,✶ that bôast themsélves a-gaïnst me.

27 Let them be glad and rejoice,✶ that favour my rígteous déal-ing : yea, let them say alway, *f* Blessed be the Lord,✶ Who hath pleasure in the prospêrity óf His sër-vant.

28 And as for my tongue,✶ it shall be tâlking of Thy rígh-teous-ness : and of Thy prâise áll the dāy long.

PSALM 36. *Dixit injustus.*

mf MY heart sheweth me the wíckedness of the ungőd-ly : that there is no fêar of Gód be-fore his eyes.

2 For he flattereth himsêlf in his ôwn sight : until his abôminable sín be fóund out.

3 The words of his mouth are unrígteous, and fúll of de-ceit : he hath left off to behave himself wísely, ánd to dö good.

4 He imagineth mischief upon his bed,✶ and hath set himsêlf in nó good way : neither doth he abhor âny thing thát is ë-vil.

f 5 Thy mercy, O Lord,✶ rêacheth ûn-to the heavens : ând Thy faíth-fulness unto the clouds.

6 Thy righteousness standeth like the strông môun-tains : Thy jûdgments are líke the grēat deep.

7 Thou, Lord, shalt save both man and beast ;✶ How êxcellent is Thy mér-cy, O God : and the children of men shall put their trust ûnder the shá-dow of Thy wings.

[8 They

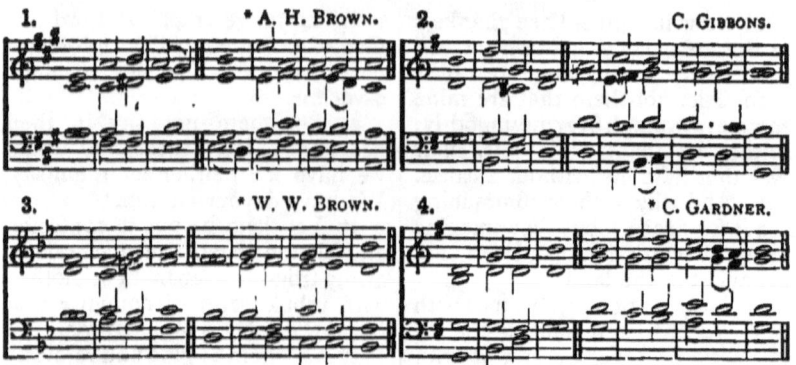

8 They shall be satisfied with the plênteousness óf Thy house : and Thou shalt give them drink of Thy plèasures, as oút of⁀the rī-ver.
9 For with Thêe is the wéll of life : ånd in Thy lĭght shall⁀we sëe light.
♩ 10 O continue forth Thy lovingkindness ∗ unto thêm that knŏw

Thee : and Thy righteousness ûnto thém that⁀are true of heart.
11 O let not the foot of pŕíde cóme against me : and let not the hånd of the ungód-ly cast me down.
12 There are they fallen,∗ åll that work wíck-ed-ness : they are cast dôwn, and shall nót be a-ble⁀ to stand.

Evensong.

PSALM 37. *Noli æmulari.*

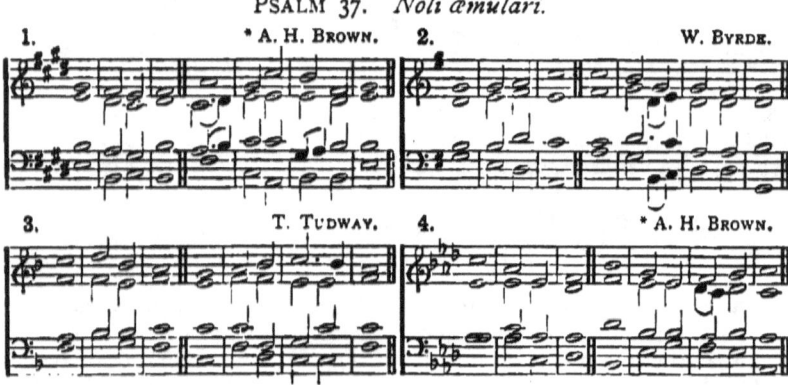

mf FRET not thyself becâuse of the ungõd-ly : neither be thou ênvious agaínst the e-vil doers.
2 For they shall sôon be cut dówn like⁀the grass : and be wíthered éven as⁀the grëen herb.
3 Put thou thy trust in the Lôrd, and be dó-ing good : dwell in the land,∗ and vêrily thôu shalt be fed.

4 Delíght thóu in⁀the Lord : and He shall gíve thee⁀thy heart's desire.
5 Commit thy way unto the Lord,∗ and pût thy trúst in Him : ånd Hé shall bring it⁀to pass.
6 He shall make thy ríghteousness as cléar as⁀the light : and thy just dêaling ás the nöon-day.

ll in the Lord,*
upŏn Him : but
at him, whose
against the man
il cŏun-sels.
wrath,* and let
et not thyself,*
ŏved to͡do ĕ-vil.
shall be rŏot-ed
patiently abide
all͡in-herit the

ŕhile,* and the
ĭan gone : thou
plâce, and hĕ́

k-spĭrited shall
: and shall be
ti-tude of peace.
ŝeeketh cŏunsel
and gnâsheth
eeth.
ıall láugh him͡
th sêen that his

ıave drawn out
bĕ́nt their bow :
ıor and needy,*
ĭ âre of a rĭ́ght

hall gô through
ând their bŏ́w

g that the rĭ́ght-
ter than great
l-ly.
of the ungŏ́dly
and the Lôrd
t-eous.
ıoweth the dâys
ıeir inhêritance
ĕr.
be confôunded
ıe : and in the
dy shall have

odly, they shall
ᵹnemies of the
e as the fát of
as the smôke,
a-way.

mf 21 The ungodly borroweth,
and pâyeth nŏ́t a-gain : but the
righteous is mêrciful, ând li-be-ral.
22 Such as are blessed of Gôd
shall possĕ́ss the land : and they
that are cûrsed of Hĭm shall͡be
root-ed out.
p 23 The Lord ôrdereth a gŏ́od
man's going : and maketh his wây
accĕ́pt-able to Him-self.
24 Though he fall,* he shall nŏt
be cást a-way : for the Lôrd uphŏ́ld-
eth͡him with His hand.
25 I have been yoûng, and nŏ́w
am old : and yet saw I never the
righteous forsaken,* nor his sêed
bĕ́g-ging their bread.
26 The righteous is ever mêrciful,
and lĕ̂nd-eth : ând his sĕ́ed is
blĕ̈ss-ed.
mf 27 Flee from evil,* and dô the
thĭ́ng that͡is good : ând dwĕ́ll for
e-ver-more.
28 For the Lord lôveth the thĭ́ng
that͡is right : He forsaketh not
His that be godly,* but thêy arᴢ
presĕ́rv-ed͡for ĕ̈-ver.
29 The unrĭ́ghteous shall be pŭ́n-
ish-ed : as for the seed of the
ungôdly, ĭt shall͡be root-ed out.
30 The rĭ́ghteous shall inhĕ́rit
the land : and dwêll therĕ́in for
ĕ̈-ver.
p 31 The mouth of the righteous
is êxercised in wĭ̂s-dom : and his
tôngue will be tálk-ing͡of jûdg-
ment.
32 The law of his Gôd is ĭn his
heart : ând his gŏ́-ings shall not slide.
33 The ungodly sêeth the rĭ́gh-
teous : and sêeketh occá-sion͡to
släy him.
34 The Lord will not lêave him
ĭn his hand : nor condêmn him
whĕ́n he͡is jûdg-ed.
35 Hope thou in the Lord, and
keep His way,* and He shall
promote thee,* that thôu shalt
possĕ́ss the land : when the ungodly shall pêrish, thôu shalt sëe
it.

[*mf* 36 I

mf 36 I myself have seen the ungódly in grēat power : and flóurishing lĭke a⌒green bäy-tree.

37 I went bý, and ló, he⌒was gone : I sóught him, but his pláce could nowhere be found.

p 38 Keep innocency,✶ and take hēed unto the thíng that⌒is right : for that shall brĭng a man pēace at the last.

39 As for the transgressors,✶ they shall pĕrish togē-ther : and the end of the ungodly is,✶ thĕy shall be róot-ed out at ⌒ the last.

mf 40 But the salvation of the righteous cômeth óf the Lord : Who is also their strĕngth in the tíme of trŏu-ble.

41 And the Lord shall stand bý them, and săve them : He shall deliver them from the ungodly, and shall save them,✶ becâuse they pút their trust in Him.

The Eighth Day.
Mattins.

Venite, exultemus Domino.

ᶠO COME,* let us síng ún-toˆ the Lord : let us heartily ·ejoice in the strḗngth of oúr salvä́-tion.
2 Let us come before His prḗsence ʋith thanksgív-ing : and shḗw ourıelves glád in Him with Psalms.
3 For the Lórd is a grḗat God : ınd a grḗat Kíng above äll gods.
4 In His hand are all the córners íf the earth : and the strength of he hílls is Hís äl-so.
5 The sea is Hís, and He mäde t : and His hánds prepár-edˆthe brÿ land.
p 6 O come,* let us wórship, ₁nd fäll down : and knêel before he Lórd our Mä-ker.
7 For Hê is the Lórd our God : ₁nd we are the people of His pásture, ₁nd the shéep of Hïs hand.

mf 8 To-day if ye will hear His voice,* hârden nót your hearts : as in the provocation,* and as in the day of temptâtion ín the wil-derness;
9 When your fâthers témpt-ed Me : provéd Mé, and saw My works.
10 Forty years long * was I grieved with thís generá-tion,ˆand said : It is a people that do err in their hêarts, for they háve not known My ways.
11 Unto whôm I swáre inˆMy wrath : that they shôuld not én-ter into My rest.
Glory be to the Fâther, ánd toˆ the Son : ánd tó the Ho-ly Ghost; As it was in the beginning,* is nôw, and éver shall be : wôrld without énd. ˙A˙-men.

PSALM 38. *Domine, ne in furore.*

ᵖPUT me not to rebuke, O Lôrd, in Thine án-ger : ₗeither châsten me in Thy héa-vyˆ lis-pléa-sure.
2 For Thine ârrows stick fást in ₐe : and Thy hând préss-eth më ore.
3 There is no health in my flesh,* ₑecause of Thÿ displḗa-sure : neither ₃ there any rest in my bônes, by éa-son of my sin.
pp 4 For my wickednesses are óne ó-verˆmy head : and are like

a sore bûrden, too héa-vyˆfor me to bear.
5 My wounds stínk, and áre cor-rupt : thróugh my fool-ish-ness.
6 I am brought into so great trôuble and mí-se-ry : that I go môurning áll the däy long.
7 For my loins are fílled with a sóre dis-ease : and there is nó whole párt inˆmy bö-dy.
8 I am feeble, and sôre smít-ten : I have roared for the vêry disquí-etness of my heart.

[*p* 9 Lord,

p 9 Lord, Thou knôwest áll my ͡ de-sire : and my grôaning ís not hid from Thee.

10 My heart panteth, ✱ my strêngth hath faíl-ed me : and the síght of mine éyes is gone from me.

11 My lovers and my neighbours ✱ did stand looking upôn my trôu-ble : and my kíhsmen stóod a-fär off.

12 They also that sought after my lîfe laid snáres for me : and they that went about to do me evil talked of wickedness,✱ and imagined decêit áll the däy long.

13 As for me,✱ I was like a dêaf man, and hêard not : and as one that is dûmb, who dóth not open his mouth.

14 I became even as a mân that héar-eth not : ánd in whose móuth are no re-proofs.

mf 15 For in Thee, O Lôrd, have I pút my trust : Thou shalt ânswer fór me, ͡ O Lord my God.

16 I have required that they, ✱ even mine enemies, ✱ should not trîumphd ó-ver me : for when my foot slipped,✱ they rejôiced gréat-ly agäinst me.

p 17 And I, trûly, am sét in ͡ the plague : and my hêaviness is é-ver in my sight.

18 For I will confêss my wícked-ness : ánd be sór-ry for my sin.

19 But mine enemies lîve, and are mígh-ty : and they that hate me wrôngfully are má-ny ͡ in nüm-ber.

20 They also that reward evil for goôd are agaínst me : because I fôllow the thíng that good is.

21 Forsake me nôt, O Lórd my God : bê not Thôu far from me.

22 Hâste Thee to hélp me : O Lord Gôd of mý sal-vä-tion.

PSALM 39. *Dixi, custodiam.*

mf 1 I SAID, I will tāke héed to˄ my ways : that I offénd not in my tongue.

2 I will keep my mouth as it wēre with a brī-dle : whîle the ungód-ly˄is in my sight.

p 3 I held my tôngue, and spake nō-thing : I kept silence,* yea, even from good words ; * bŭt it was paín and grief to me.

4 My heart was hot within me,* and while I was thus mŭsing the fire kĭnd-led : and at the lâst I spāke with my tongue ;

5 Lord, let me know mine end,* and the nŭmber óf my days : that I may be cêrtified how lóng I have to live.

pp 6 Behold, Thou hast made my days as it wēre a spān long : and mine age is even as nothing in respect of Thee ; * and verily every man living is âltogé-ther va-ni-ty.

7 For man walketh in a vain shadow,* and disquíeteth himsélf in vain : he heapeth up riches,* and cânnot tell whó shall ga-ther them.

p 8 And now, Lôrd, whát is˄my hope : trŭly my hópe is even in Thee.

9 Deliver me from âll mine offĕn-ces : and make me not a rebŭke ún-to˄the fōol-ish.

10 I became dumb,* and ôpened nót my mouth : fôr it was Thý dö-ing.

11 Take Thy plâgue awáy from me : I am even consŭmed by the meáns of˄Thy hea-vy hand.

12 When Thou with rebukes dost chasten man for sin,* Thou makest his beauty to consume away,* like as it were a moth frêtting a gâr-ment : every man thêrefore ís but va-ni-ty.

pp 13 Hear my prayer, O Lord,* and with Thine ears consíder my cāll-ing : hôld not Thy péace at my tears.

14 For Î am a stránger with Thee : and a sôjourner, as áll my fa-thers were.

p 15 O spare me a little,* that Î may recó-ver˄my strength : before I go hênce, and be nō möre seen.

PSALM 40. *Expectans expectavi.*

f 1 I WAITED pâtiently fór the Lord : and He inclined unto mê, and heárd my cāll-ing

2 He brought me also out of the horrible pit,* oŭt of the míre and clay : and set my feet upon the rôck, and ór-dered˄my gö-ings.

3 And He hath pŭt a new sóng in˄my mouth : even a thânksgív-ing unto our God.

[4 Many

4 Mâny shall sée it,⌢and fear: and shall pût their trûst in the Lord.

5 Blessed is the man that hath sêt his hópe in⌢the Lord : and turned not unto the proud,∗ and to sûch as gó a-bout with lies.

mf 6 O Lord my God,∗ great are the wondrous works which Thou hast done, ∗ like as be also Thy thoughts which âre to ûs-ward : and yet there is nô man that órdereth⌢them un-to Thee.

7 If I should declâre them, and spéak of them : they should be môre than I am á-ble to ex-press.

8 Sacrifice, and meat-ôffering, Thôu wóuld-est not : bût mine eárs hast⌢Thou o-pen-ed.

9 Burnt-offerings, and sacrifice for sîn, hast Thou nót re-quir'd : thên said I,⌢ Lo, I come,

10 In the volume of the book it is written of me,∗ that I should fulfil Thy wîll, O my God : I am content to do it ; ∗ yêa, Thy láw is⌢ with-in my heart.

11 I have declared Thy righteousness in the grêat congregá-tion : lo, I will not refrain my lips, O Lôrd, and thát Thou knöw-est.

12 I have not hid Thy rîghteousness withín my heart : my talk hath been of Thy trûth, and of Thý sal-vā-tion.

13 I have not kept back Thy lôving mér-cy⌢and truth : frôm the gréat congre-gä-tion.

p 14 Withdraw not Thou Thy mêrcy fróm me,⌢O Lord : let Thy loving-kindness and Thy trûth ál-way⌢pre-sërve me.

15 For innumerable troubles are come about me ; ∗ my sins have taken such hold upon me that I am not âble to lóok up : yea, they are more in number than the hairs of my hêad, and my heárt hath fail-ed me.

16 O Lord,∗ let it be Thy plêasure to delí-ver me : make hâste, O Lórd, to hëlp me.

mf 17 Let them be ashamed, and confounded together, ∗ that seek after my sôul to destróy it : let them be driven backward, and put to rebûke, that wísh me ë-vil.

18 Let them be dêsolate, and reward-ed⌢with shame : that say unto me, ∗ Fíe upon thee, fíe up-ōn thee.

19 Let all those that seek Thee be jôyful and gláda in Thee : and let such as love Thy salvation say âlway, The Lórd be praīs-ed.

p 20 As for me,∗ I am pôor and nêe-dy : bût the Lórd careth for me

21 Thou art my hêlper and redêem-er : make nô long tár-rying, O my God.

Evensong.

PSALM 41. *Beatus qui intelligit.*

f ℬLESSED is he ✻ that considereth the pôor and née-dy : the Lord shall deliver hĭm in the tíme of trŏu-ble.

mf 2 The Lord preserve him, and keep him alive,✻ that he may be blêssed upón earth : and deliver not Thou hĭm into the wĭll of͡his e-ne-mies.

3 The Lord comfort him,✻ when he lieth sĭck upón his bed : make Thou âll his béd in͡his sĭck-ness.

p 4 I said,✻ Lord, be mêrciful ún-to me : heal my soul,✻ for I have sín-ned agáinst Thee.

5 Mine ênemies speak é-vil͡of me : When shall he díe, and his náme pĕ-rish ?

6 And if he come to see me,✻ he spêaketh vá-ni-ty : and his heart conceiveth falsehood within himself,✻ and when he cômeth fórth he tell-eth it.

7 All mine enemies whisper togêther agaĭnst me : even against mê do they imágine this ĕ-vil.

8 Let the sentence of guiltiness procêed agaĭnst him : and now that he líĕth, lét͡him rise up no more.

9 Yea, even mine own familiar fríĕnd, whom I trŭst-ed : who did also eat of my brêad, hath laĭd great wait for me.

10 But be Thou mêrciful unto mé, O Lord : raise Thou me up agâin, and I'shall͡re-wărd them.

mf 11 By this I knŏw Thou fávourest me : that mine enemy dôth not trí-umph agáinst me.

12 And when I am in my hêalth, Thou uphóld-est me : and shalt set me befôre Thy fáce for ĕ-ver.

f 13 Blessed be the Lord Gôd of Ĭs-ra-el : wôrld without ĕnd. ˙A∶men.

Psalms 42, 43.

Psalm 42. *Quemadmodum.*

mf LIKE as the hart desíreth the wá-ter brooks : so lóngeth my sóul after Thee, O God.

p 2 My soul is athirst for God,✶ yea, êven for the lív-ing God : when shall I come to appêar befóre the pre-sence⁀of God ?

3 My tears have been my mêat dáy and night : while they daily sây unto me, Whére is now thy God ?

4 Now when I think thereupon,✶ I pôur out my héart by⁀my-self : for I went with the multitude,✶ and brought them fôrth ínto the house of God ;

mf 5 In the voice of prâise and thanksgí-ving : amông súch as⁀keep ho-ly-day.

p 6 Why art thou so full of heâviness, Ó my soul : and why art thou sô disquíet-ed⁀with-ín me ?

mf 7 Pût thy trúst in God : for I will yet give Him thânks for the hélp of⁀His coun-te-nance.

p 8 My God,✶ my soul is vêxed withín me : therefore will I remember Thee concerning the land of Jordan,✶ and the líttle híll of Hër-mon.

9 One deep calleth another, ✶ because of the nóise of the wá-ter-pipes : all Thy wâves and stórms are⁀gone o-ver me.

10 The Lord hath granted His loving-kíndness in the dáy-time : and in the night-season did I sing of Him,✶ and made my prâyer ún-to⁀the God of⁀my life.

11 I will say unto the God of my strength, ✶ Why hast Thôu forgót-ten me : why go I thus heavily,✶ whîle the éne-my⁀op-press-eth me ?

12 My bones are smitten asúnder ás with⁀a sword : while mine enemies that trôuble me cást me in the teeth ;

13 Namely,✶ while they say dáily ún-to me : Whére is now thy God ?

14 Why art thou so vêxed O′my soul : and why art thou sô disquíet-ed⁀with-ín me ?

mf 15 O pût thy trúst in God : for I will yet thank Him,✶ Which is the hêlp of my coún-tenance, and my God.

Psalm 43. *Judica me, Deus.*

mf GIVE sentence with me, O God,✶ and defend my cause against the ungôdly pêo-ple : O deliver me frôm the deceít-ful⁀and wick-ed man.

2 For Thou art the God of my strength, ✶ why hast Thou pût me frôm Thee : and why go I so heavily, ✶ whîle the éne-my⁀op-pres-seth me ?

3 O send out Thy light and Thy truth,✶ that thêy may lêad me : and bring me unto Thy holy híll, ánd to⁀Thy dwéll-ing.

4 And that I may go unto the Altar of God,* even unto the God of my jôy and glăd-ness : and upon the harp will I give thânks unto Thée, O God, my God.

p 5 Why art thou so hêavy, Ó my soul : and why art thou sô disquíet-ed˜with-ín me ?

mf 6 O pût thy trúst in God : for I will yet give Him thanks,* Which is the hêlp of my cóun-tenance, and my God.

The Ninth Day.
Mattins.
Venite exultemus, Domino.

f O COME,* let us síng ún-to˜ the Lord : let us heartily rejoice in the strêngth of oúr sal-vă-tion.

2 Let us come before His prêsence with thanksgív-ing : and shêw our-selves glăd in Him with Psalms.

3 For the Lôrd is a grêat God : and a grêat Kíng above ăll gods.

4 In His hand are all the côrners óf the earth : and the strength of the hílls is Hís ăl-so.

5 The sea is Hís, and He mâde it : and His hânds prepár-ed˜the drỹ land.

p 6 O come,* let us wôrship, and făll down : and knêel before the Lórd our Mă-ker.

7 For Hê is the Lórd our God : and we are the people of His pâsture, and the shéep of Hís hand.

mf 8 To-day if ye will hear His voice,* hârden nót your hearts : as in the provocation,* and as in the day of temptâtion ín the wil-der-nesś ;

9 When your fâthers témpt-ed Me : provêd Mé, and saw My works.

10 Forty years long * was I grieved with thís generá-tion,˜and said : It is a people that do err in their hêarts, for they háve not known My ways.

11 Unto whôm I swáre in˜My wrath : that they shôuld not én-ter into My rest.

Glory be to the Fâther, ánd to˜ the Son : ănd tú the Ho-ly Ghest ; As it was in the beginning,* is nôw, and éver shall be : wôrld without énd. 'A'-men.

51 [PSALM 44.

PSALM 44. *Deus, auribus.*

mf WE have heard with our ears, O God,* our fâthers have tōld us : what Thôu hast dóne in⁀their time of old ;
2 How Thou hast driven out the heathen with Thy hând, and plánt-ed⁀them in : how Thou hast des-trôyed the nā́-tions⁀and cast them out.
3 For they gat not the land in possêssion through their ôwn sword : neither was it their ôwn árm that help-ed them ;
4 But Thy right hand, and Thine arm,* and the līght of Thy cóun-te-nance : becaûse Thou hadst a fā́-vour un-to them.
f 5 Thôu art my Kíng, O God : sênd hélp unto Jä-cQb.
6 Through Thee will we ôver-throw our é-ne-mies : and in Thy Name will we tread them ûnder, that rīse up agáinst us.
7 For I will nôt trúst in⁀my bow : it is nôt my swórd that⁀shall hélp me ;
8 But it is Thou that sâvest us from our é-ne-mies : and puttest thêm to confū́-sion⁀that hǟte us.
9 We make our boast of Gôd áll day long ; and will praīse Thy Náme for ë-ver.
p 10 But now Thou art far off,* and puttest ûs to confū-sion : and gôest not fórth with⁀our är-mies.

11 Thou makest us to turn our bâcks upon our é-ne-mies : so that thêy which hāte us spoil our goods.
12 Thou lettest us be eâten úp like sheep : and hast scâttered us amóng the hëa-then.
13 Thou sêllest Thy péo-ple⁀for nought : and tâkest no mó-ney för them.
14 Thou makest us to be rebûked of our nēigh-bours : to be laughed to scorn,* and had in derision of thêm that are róund a-böut us.
15 Thou makest us to be a by-word amóng the hëa-then : and that the pêople shāke their hēads ät us.
16 My confusion is dâily befōre me : and the shâme of my fáce hath co-vered me ;
17 For the voice of the slânderer and blasphē-mer : for the ênemy ánd a-vën-ger.
mf 18 And though all this be come upon us,* yet do we nôt for-gēt Thee : nor behave ourselves frôwardly ín Thy co-ve-nant.
19 Our hêart is not túrn-ed back : nêither our stéps gone out⁀of Thy way;
20 No,* not when Thou hast smitten us into the plâce of drā-gons : and cóvered us wíth the shadow of death.

21 If we have forgotten the Name of our God,* and holden up our hânds to any strănge god : shall not God search it out ?* for He knoweth the vêry sé-crets of the heart.

p 22 For Thy sake also are we kĭlled ăll the⁀day long : and are counted as shêep appoĭnt-ed to be slain.

f 23 Up, Lôrd, why sléep-est Thou : awake,* and be not âbsent frŏm us⁀for ĕ-ver.

p 24 Wherefore hĭdest Thŏu thy face : and forgĕttest our mĭ-sery⁀ and trŏu-ble?

25 For our soul is brought low,* êven ŭn-to⁀the dust : our bĕlly clĕav-eth un-to⁀the ground.

mf 26 Arĭse, and hĕlp us : and delĭver us fŏr Thy mer-cy's sake.

PSALM 45. *Eructavit cor meum.*

mf MY heart is inditing of a gôod măt-ter : I speak of the thĭngs which I have mâde un-to⁀the King.

2 Mў tŏngue is⁀the pen : ôf a réa-dy wri-ter.

3 Thou art fafrer than the chĭl-dren⁀of men : full of grace are Thy lips,* because God hath blĕssed Thée for ĕ-ver.

f 4 Gird Thee with thy sword upon Thy thigh,* O Thôu Most Mĭgh-ty : accŏrding to Thy wŏr-ship and re-nown.

5 Good luck have Thôu with Thine hô-nour : ride on, because of the word of truth,* of meekness, and righteousness,* and Thy right hând shall teăch Thee ter-rible things.

6 Thy arrows are very sharp,* and the people shall be subdûed ŭn-to Thee : even in the midst amŏng the Kĭng's e-ne-mies.

7 Thy seat, O God,* endûreth for ĕv-er : the sceptre of Thy kĭng-dom is a rĭght scĕp-tre.

8 Thou hast loved righteousness,* and hâted inĭ-qui-ty : wherefore God, even Thy God,* hath anointed Thee with the oil of glâdness abŏve Thy fĕl-lows.

p 9 All Thy garments smell of myrrh, * âloes, and căs-si-a : out of the ivory pâlaces, wherebў they⁀ have made Thee glad.

10 Kings' daughters were among Thy hônourable ẁo-men : upon Thy right hand did stand the queen in a vesture of gold,* wrought abôut with dĭ-vers cŏ-lours.

11 Hearken, O daughter,* and consîder, inclĭne thine ear : forget also thine own pêople, ănd thy fa-ther's house.

12 So shall the King have plêa-sure in thy bĕau-ty : for He is thy Lord Gôd, and wŏr-ship thŏu Him.

[13 And

13 And the daughter of Týre shall be thére with⁀a gift : like as the rich also among the people⁎ shall make their sûpplicá-tion befōre Thee.

f 14 The King's daûghter is all gló-rious⁀with-in : her clōthing ís of wröught gold.

15 She shall be brought unto the King in râiment of née-dle work : the virgins that be her fellows shall bear her company,⁎ ãnd shall be bröught un-to Thee.

16 With joy and glâdness shall théy be brought : and shall enter ínto the Kſĩng's pä-lace.

17 Instead of thy fathers⁎ thôu shalt have chīl-dren : whom thou mâyest make prín-ces⁀in äll lands.

18 I will remember Thy Name⁎ from one generâtion to anō-ther : therefore shall the people give thãnks unto Thee, wórld with-öut end.

PSALM 46. *Deus noster refugium.*

mf GÔD is our hópe and strength: a very prêsent hélp in tröu-ble.

2 Therefore will we not fear,⁎ though the eârth be mō-ved : and though the hills be cârried ín-to⁀the midst of⁀the sea.

f 3 Though the wâters thereof

rãge and swell : and though the mountains shâke at the tém-pest of the same.

p 4 The rivers of the flood thereof shall make glâd the cí-ty⁀of God : the holy place of the tâbernacle of the Mōst High-est.

5 God is in the midst of her,✱ therefore shall she nôt be remō-ved : God shall hêlp her, and thát right eār-ly.

mf 6 The heathen make much ado,✱ and the kíngdoms are mōv-ed : but God hath shewed His vôice, and the eárth shall melt a-way.

(Full) f 7 The Lord of Hôsts is with us : the God of Jâcob ís our rē-fuge.

(Dec.) mf 8 O come hither, and behôld the wórks of the Lord : what destrûction He hath bróught up-on the earth.

9 He maketh wars to cêase in áll the world : He breaketh the bow, and knappeth the spear in sunder,✱ and bûrneth the chá-riots in the fire

p 10 Be still then,✱ and knôw that I′ am God : I will be͜ exalted among the heathen,✱ and I will be exált-ed in the earth.

(Full) f 11 The Lord of Hôsts is with us : the God of Jâcob ís our rē-fuge.

Evensong.

PSALM 47. *Omnes gentes, plaudite.*

f O CLAP your hands together✱ áll ye pēo-ple : O sing unto Gôd with the vôíce of me-lo-dy.

mf 2 For the Lord is hígh and to be fēar-ed : Hê is the great Kíng upon all the earth.

3 He shall subdue the pêople ún-der us : ând the ná-tions under our feet.

4 He shall choose out an hêritage fór us : even the worship of Jâcob, whóm He löv-ed.

f 5 God is gone ûp with a mér-ry noise : and the Lôrd with the sôund of the trump.

6 O sing praises,✱ sing praîses ún-to our God : O sing praîses, sing praís-es un-to our King.

7 For God is the Kíng of áll the earth : sing ye praîses with ún-der-ständ-ing.

8 God reigneth ôver the hēa-then : God sítteth upón His ho-ly seat.

9 The princes of the people ✱ are joinęd unto the people of the Gôd of Á-bra-ham : for God, Which is very high exalted,✱ doth defend the eârth, ás it were with a shield.

[PSALM 48.

PSALM 48. *Magnus Dominus.*

G REAT is the Lord,* and híghly to be praís-ed : in the city of our God,* êven upón His ho-ly hill.
  mf 2 The hill of Sion is a fair place, * and the jóy of the whõle earth : upon the north-side lieth the city of the great King ;* God is well known in her pâlaces as a sũre rē-fuge.
  3 For lô, the kíngs of the earth : are gâthered, and gone bý to-gē-ther.
  4 They mârvelled to sée such things : they were astõnished, and súd-denly cäst down.
  p 5 Fear came there upõn them, and sôr-row : as upon a wôman ín her trä-vail.
  6 Thou shalt brêak the shíps of the sea : thrõugh the eäst-wind.
  7 Like as we have heard,* so have we seen in the city of the Lord of Hosts,* in the cíty óf our God : God uphôldeth the sáme for ëv-er.
  mf 8 We wait for Thy lôving-kínd-ness, O God : ín the mídst of Thy tëm-ple.
  9 O God, according to Thy Name,* so is Thy praíse unto the wõrld's end : Thy right hând is fúll of righ-teous-ness.
  f 10 Let the mount Sion rejoice,* and the dâughter of Jú-dah be glad : becáuse of Thy júdg-ments.
  11 Walk about Sion,* and go rõund abõut her : ãnd téll the towers there-of.
  12 Mark well her bulwarks,* sêt up her hôus-es : that ye may têll thém that come äf-ter.
  (Full) f 13 For this God is our God * for êver and ëv-er : He shall bê our gúide un-to death.

PSALM 49. *Audite hæc, omnes.*

mf O HEAR ye this, * àll ye peo-ple : ponder it with your ears,* all yê that dwêll in the world ;

2 High and lôw, rích and poor : ône wíth an-ö-ther.

3 My mouth shall spêak of wís-dom : and my heart shall mûse of ún-der-ständ-ing.

4 I will incline mine eâr to the pá-ra-ble ; and shêw my dark spéech up-on the harp.

p 5 Wherefore should I fear in the dâys of wíck-ed-ness : and when the wickedness of my heels côm-passeth mê round a-bout ?

6 There be some that pût their trúst in^their goods : and boast themselves in the mûltitude óf their rích-es.

7 But no man may delíver his brô-ther : nor make agrêement ún-to God for him ;

8 For it cost môre to redéem their souls : so that he must let thât alóne for ë-ver ;

9 Yêa, though he lífe long : ând sêe not the grave.

10 For he seeth that wise men also die,* and pêrish togê-ther : as well as the ignorant and foolish,* and lêave their rích-es^for ö-ther.

mf 11 And yet they think * that their houses shall contínue for êv-er : and that their dwelling-places shall endure from one generation to another ; * and call the lânds áf-ter^ their öwn names.

12 Nevertheless, * man will not abíde in hö-nour : seeing he may be compared unto the beasts that pêrish ; thís is^the way of them.

13 Thís is their fóol-ish-ness : and their postêrity praíse their säy-ing.

14 They lie in the hell like sheep,* death gnaweth upon them,* and the righteous shall have domination óver them in the môrn-ing : their beauty shall consume in the sêpul-chre oút of^their dwëll-ing.

15 But God hath delivered my sôul from the pláce of hell : fôr Hé shall^re-ceïve me.

p 16 Be not thou afraid,* though ône be mâde rich : or if the glôry of his hóuse be incrëas-ed ;

17 For he shall carry nothing away with him whên he dí-eth : nêither shall his pômp fol-low him.

18 For while he lived, * he counted himsêlf an háp-py man : and so long as thou doest well unto thyself,* mên will spêak good of thee.

19 He shall follow the generâtion of his fä-thers : ând shall né-ver sëe light.

20 Man being in honour * hath nô understánd-ing : but is compared ûnto the beásts that pë-rish.

The Tenth Day.

Mattins.

Venite, exultemus Domino.

f O COME, * let us sĭng ŭn-to⁀ the Lord : let us heartily rejoice in the strêngth of oŭr sal-vä-tion.

2 Let us come before His prêsence with thanksgĭv-ing : and shêw ourselves glăd in Him with Psalms.

3 For the Lôrd is a grêat God : and a grêat Kĭng above äll gods.

4 In His hand are all the côrners ŏf the earth : and the strength of the hĭlls is Hĭs̀ äl-so.

5 The sea is Hĭs̀, and He mâde it : and His hănds prepár-ed⁀the dŕy land.

p 6 O come, * let us wôrship, and fäll down : and knêel before the Lórd our Mä-ker.

7 For Hê is the Lórd our God : and we are the people of His pâsture, and the shêep of Hĭs̀ hand.

mf 8 To-day if ye will hear His voice, * hârden nŏt your hearts : as in the provocation, * and as in the day of temptâtion ĭn the wil-derness ;

9 When your fâthers témpt-ed Me : prôved Mé, and saw My works.

10 Forty years long * was I grieved with thĭs̀ generá-tion,⁀and said : It is a people that do err in their hêarts, for they hâve not known My ways.

11 Unto whôm I swáre in⁀My wrath : that they shŏuld not én-ter into My rest.

Glory be to the Fâther, ănd to⁀the Son : ănd tó the Ho-ly Ghost ;

As it was in the beginning, * is nŏw, and éver shall be : world without ênd. ˈA·-men.

Psalm 50. *Deus deorum.*

mf THE Lord,* even the most mighty Gôd, hath spō-ken : and called the world,* from the rising up of the sun,* ûnto the gó-ing down there-of.

2 Out of Sion hath Gôd appêar-ed : ĭn pér-fect bĕau-ty.

f 3 Our God shall come,* and shall nôt keep sī-lence : there shall go before Him a consuming fire,* and a mighty tempest shall be stîrred up róund a-bóut Him.

4 He shall call the hêaven fróm a-bove : and the eârth, that He may júdge His pëo-ple.

5 Gather My saints togêther ún-to Me : those that have made a cóvenant wíth Me ͡ with sa-cri-fice.

6 And the heaven shall declâre His rígh-teous-ness : fôr Gód is Judge Him-self.

p 7 Hear, O my pêople, and Í will speak : I myself will tęstify against thee, O Israel;* for I am Gód, even thў God.

8 I will not reprove thee because of thy sacrifices,* or for thy bûrnt-óf-fer-ings : because they wêre not ál-way befōre Me.

9 I will take no bûllock oút of ͡ thine house : nôr hé-goat out of ͡ thў folds.

10 For all the bêasts of the fó-rest ͡ are Mine : and so are the câttle upón a thou-sand hills.

11 I know all the fôwls upon the mōun-tains : and the wild bêasts of the fiéld are in My sight.

12 If I be hungry,* I will not tĕll thee : for the whole world is Mĭne, and áll that is there-in.

13 Thinkest thou that Î will éat bulls' flesh : ánd drínk the blood of goats ?

14 Offer unto Gôd thanksgiv-ing : and pay thy vôws unto the Mōst Hígh-est.

15 And call upon Me in the tĭme of trōu-ble : so I will hêar thee, and thóu shalt praïse Me.

mf 16 But unto the ungôdly sáid God : Why dost thou preach My laws,* and tâkest My có-venant in thy mouth ;

17 Whereas thou hâtest to be refōrm-ed : and hast câst My wórds be-hínd thee ?

18 When thou sawest a thief,* thou consêntedst ún-to him : and hast been partâker wíth the ͡ a-dul-te-rers.

19 Thou hast let thy môuth speak wíck-ed-ness : and with thy tôngue thou hast sĕt forth de-ceit.

20 Thou satest, and spakest agaînst thy brō-ther : yea, and hast slândered thine ōwn mo-ther's son.

[*p* 21 These

p 21 These things hast thou done, and I held My tongue, * and thou thoughtest wickedly, that I am even sûch a one ás thy-self : but I will reprove thee,* and set befôre thee the thíngs that thou hast done.

22 O consider this, * yê that forgêt God : lest I pluck you away,* and thêre be nóne to͡de-li-ver you.

f 23 Whoso offereth Me thanks and praîse, he hó-noureth Me : and to him that ordereth his conversa-tion ríght will I shéw the͡sal-va-tion͡of God.

PSALM 51. *Miserere mei, Deus.*

p **H**AVE mercy upon me, O God,* after Thý great góod-ness : according to the multitude of Thy mercies * dô awáy mine͡of-fĕn-ces.

pp 2 Wash me thrôughly from my wíck-ed-ness : ánd cléanse me from my sin.

3 For I acknów-ledge͡my faults : and my sín is éver be-főre me.

4 Against Thee only have I sinned,* and done this êvil ín Thy sight : that Thou mightest be justified in Thy saying,* and clêar whén Thou͡art jüdg-ed.

5 Behold, I was shâpen in wíck-ed-ness : and in sín hath my mó-ther͡con-ceiv-ed me.

p 6 But lo,* Thou requirest trûth in the ín-ward parts : and shalt make me to understând wís-dom se-cret-ly.

7 Thou shalt purge me with hýssop, and I shall be clean : Thou shalt wash me,* and I shall be whí-ter thän snow.

8 Thou shalt make me hear of jôy and glád-ness : that the bônes which Thou hast brók-en may re-joice.

9 Tûrn Thy fáce from my sins : and pût out áll my mïs-deeds.

10 Make me a clêan héart, O God : and renew a rîght spírit with-ín me.

11 Cast me not awáy from Thy prés-ence : and take not Thy hôly Spí-rit fröm me.

12 O give me the cômfort of Thy hélp a-gain : and stablish me wíth Thy frée Spï-rit.

mf 13 Then shall I teach Thy wáys unto the wíck-ed : and sínners shall be convért-ed un-to Thee.

p 14 Deliver me from blood-guiltiness, O God,* Thou that árt the Gód of my health : and my tôngue shall síng of Thy right-eous-ness.

mf 15 Thou shalt ôpen my líps, O Lord : ånd my móuth shall shew Thy praise.

16 For Thou desirest no sacri-fice,* êlse would I gíve it Thee : but Thou delightest nôt in bûrnt-of-fer-ings.

p 17 The sacrifice of God is a trôubled spí-rit : a broken and contrite heart, O Gôd, shált Thou not de-spise.

mf 18 O be favourable and grâ-cious unto Sí-on : bûild Thou the wálls of Je-ru-sa-lem.

19 Then shalt Thou be pleased with the sacrifice of righteousness,* with the burnt-ôfferings and oblâ-tions : then shall they offer young bûllocks upón Thine Ál-tar.

PSALM 52. *Quid gloriaris?*

mf WHY boastest thou thysêlf, thou tý-rant : that thôu canst dó mïs-chief ;

2 Whereâs the góod-ness of God : êndúr-eth yet dai-ly ?

3 Thy tongue imâgineth wíck-ed-ness : and with lies thou cuttest líke a shärp rä-zor.

4 Thou hast loved unrighteous-ness môre than góod-ness : and to talk of líes móre than right-eous-ness.

5 Thou hast loved to speak all wôrds that may dó hurt : O thou fälse tongue.

f 6 Therefore shall God destrôy thee for êv-er : He shall take thee, and pluck thee out of thy dwelling,* and root thee oût of the lánd of the lív-ing.

[7 *mf* The

mf 7 The righteous also shall sêe thís, and fear : ånd shall láugh him to scorn ;
8 Lo, this is the man that tôok not Gód for⌒his strength : but trusted unto the multitude of his riches, * and strengthened himsêlf ín his wick-ed-ness.

p 9 As for me,* I am like a green ôlive-tree in the house of God : my trust is in the tender mercy of Gôd for év-er⌒and ëv-er.
f 10 I will always give thanks unto Thêe for thát Thou⌒hast done : and I will hope in Thy Nâme, for Thy saínts like it well.

Evensong.

PSALMS 53, 54.

PSALM 53. *Dixit insipiens.*

mf THE foolish bôdy hath saíd in⌒his heart : Thêre ís nö God.
2 Corrupt are they,* and become abôminable in their wíck-ed-ness : thêre is nóne that do-eth good.

3 God looked down from heâven upon the chíl-dren⌒of men : to see if there were any, that would under-stånd, and séek af-ter God.
p 4 But they are all gone out of the way, * they are altogether becôme abó-mina-ble : there is also nône that doeth gôod, no not one.

[PSALMS 53, 54, 55.] EVENSONG. [DAY 10.

5 Are not they without understanding * that wôrk wíck-ed-ness : eating up my people as if they would eat bread ? * they hâve not cáll-ed upŏn God.
6 They were afrâid where nó fear was : for God hath broken the bones of him that besieged thee ; * thou hast put them to confusion, * becâuse Gód hath despis-ed them.
f 7 Oh, that the salvation were given unto Ísrael out of Sí-on : Oh, that the Lord would deliver His pêople óut of cap-ti-vi-ty !
8 Thên should Já-cob re-joice : and Ísrael shóuld be ríght glad.

PSALM 54. *Deus, in nomine.*

p SAVE me, O Gôd, for Thy Nâme's sake : ånd avénge me in Thy strength.

2 Hêar my práyer, O God : and hêarken unto the wórds of my mouth.
3 For strangers are risen ûp against me : and tyrants, which have not God before their eŷes, sêek after my soul.
mf 4 Behold, Gôd is my hélp-er : the Lôrd is with thém that up-hold my soul.
5 He shall reward evil ûnto mine é-ne-mies : destrôy Thou thém in Thy truth.
6 An offering of a free heart will I give Thee, * and prâise Thy Náme, O Lord : becâuse it ís so com-forta-ble.
7 For He hath delivered me out of âll my trôu-ble : and mine eye hath seen his desîre upón mine e-ne-mies.

PSALM 55. *Exaudi, Deus.*

b HÊAR my práyer, O God : and hide not Thysêlf from mý pe-ti-tion.
2 Take heed unto mê, and hêar me : how I mourn in my prâyer, ånd am vëx-ed.
3 The enemy crieth so, * and the ungodly cômeth ón so fast : for they are minded to do me some mischief, * so maliciously âre they sét a-gaïnst me.

pp 4 My heart is disqûieted within me : and the fear of dêath is fáll-en upŏn me.
5 Fearfulness and trêmbling are côme upŏn me : and an horrible drêad hath ó-ver-whelm-ed mę.
mf 6 And I said, * O that Î had wíngs like a dove : for then would I flêe awáy, and be at rest.
p 7 Lo, then would I gêt me awáy far off : ånd remaín in the wil-der-ness.

8 I would make haste to͡ es-cape : because of the stôrmy wínd and tĕm-pest.

f 9 Destroy their tongues, O Lôrd, and divíde them : for I have spied unríghteousness and strífe in͡ the cí-ty.

mf 10 Day and night they go about withíń the wálls there-of : mischief also and sôrrow are ín the midst of it.

11 Wíckedness ís there-in : deceit and guile gô not oút of their streets.

p 12 For it is not an open enemy, * that hath done me thís dishô-nour : for thên I cóuld have bôrne it.

13 Neither was it mine adversary,* that did magnify himsêlf agáinst me : for then peradventure * I would have híd mysélf frőm him.

14. But it was even thôu, my compâ-nion : my gûide, and mine ówn fa-mi-liar friend.

15 We took sweet côunsel togê-ther : and wálked in the hóuse of God as friends.

mf 16 Let death come hastily upon them, * and let them go dôwn quíck into hell : for wickedness is in their dwéllings, ánd a-möng them.

p 17 As for mê, I will cáll upon God : ând the Lórd shall sãve me.

18 In the evening, and morning, and at noon-day will I prây, and that ín-stant-ly : ând Hé shall hear my voice.

19 It is He that hath delivered my soul in peace * from the bâttle that was agaínst me : fôr there were má-ny with me.

20 Yea, even God, that endureth for ever,* shall hêar me, and bríng them down : for they wíll not túrn, nor feär God.

21 He laid his hands upon such as bê at peáce with him : ând he brăke his co-ve-nant.

22 The words of his mouth were softer than butter,* hâving wár in͡ his heart : his words were smoother than oil,* and yêt bé they ve-ry swords.

pp 23 O cast thy burden upon the Lord,* and Hê shall nóur-ish thee : and shall not suffer the ríghteous to fáll for ëv-er.

mf 24 Ând ás for them : Thou, O God,* shalt bring them ínto the pít of destrúc-tion.

25 The blood-thirsty and deceitful men * shall not líve out hálf their days : nevertheless,* my trûst shall bé in Thee, O Lord.

The Eleventh Day.

Mattins.

Venite, exultemus Domino.

f O COME,* let us síng ún-to^
the Lord : let us heartily rejoice in the strêngth of oúr sal-vä-tion.
2 Let us come before His prêsence with thanksgív-ing : and shêw ourselves glád in Him with Psalms.
3 For the Lôrd is a grêat God : and a grêat Kíng above äll gods.
4 In His hand are all the côrners óf the earth : and the strength of the hîlls is Hís äl-so.
5 The sea is Hís, and He máde it : and His hánds prepár-ed^the drÿ land.
p 6 O come, * let us wôrship, and fáll down : and knêel before the Lórd our Mä-ker.
7 For Hê is the Lórd our God : and we are the people of His pâsture, and the shéep of His hand.

mf 8 To-day if ye will hear His voice,* hârden nót your hearts : as in the provocation,* and as in the day of temptâtion ín the wil-derness ;
9 When your fâthers tĕmpt-ed Me : prôved Mé, and saw My works.
10 Forty years long* was I grieved with thís generá-tion,^and said : It is a people that do err in their hêarts, for they háve not known My ways.
11 Unto whôm I swáre in^My wrath : that they shôuld not én-ter into My rest.
Glory be to the Fâther, ánd to^the Son : ánd tó the Ho-ly Ghost ;
As it was in the beginning,* is nôw, and éver shall be : world without ếnd. ˙A˙-men.

E   65   [PSALM 56.

PSLAM 56. *Miserere mei, Deus.*

mf BE merciful unto me, O God,* for man goeth abôut to devôur me : he is dâily fĭght-ing,⌢ and troubl-ing me.

2 Mine enemies are daily in hând to swállow me up: for they be many that fight agâinst me, O Thóu Most High-est.

p 3 Nevertheless,* thôugh I, am sóme-time⌢a-fraid : yêt put I my trust in Thee.

mf 4 I will praise Gôd, becáuse of⌢His word : I have put my trust in God,* and will not fêar what flésh can do unto me.

p 5 They dáĭly mistáke my words : all that they imâgine is to dó me ë-vil.

6 They hold all togêther, and kéep themselves close : and mark my steps,* whên they lay waĭt for my̆ soul.

mf 7 Shall they escâpe for their wĭck-ed-ness : Thou, O God,* ĭn Thy displéa-sure⌢shalt cast them down.

p 8 Thou tellest my flittings ;* put my tears ĭnto Thy bôt-tle : are not thêse things nót-ed in Thy book?

9 Whensoever I call upon Thee,* then shall mine ênemies be pút to flight : this I knôw; for Gód is⌢on my̆ side.

f 10 In God's wôrd will I re-joice : in the Lord's wôrd wĭll I com-fort me.

11 Yea, in Gôd have I pút my trust : I will not be afrâid what mán can do unto me.

12 Unto Thee, O Gôd, will I páy my vows : ŭnto Thée will⌢I give thanks.

13 For Thou hast delivered my soul from death,* and my fêet from fál-ling : that I may walk before Gôd in the lĭght of⌢the lĭv-ing.

PSALM 57. *Miserere mei, Deus.*

mf BE merciful unto me, O God,∗ be merciful unto me,∗ for my sôul trúst-eth⁀in Thee : and under the shadow of Thy wings shall be my refuge,∗ until this týranny bê o-ver-past.

2 I will câll unto the mόst high God: even unto the God that shall perfôrm the cáuse which⁀I have in hand.

3 Hê shall sénd from heaven : and save me from the repròof of hím that⁀would eat me up.

4 God shall send fôrth His mér-cy⁀ and truth : my sôul is amóng lí-ons.

5 And I lie even among the children of mên, that are sét on fire : whose teeth are spears and ârrows, and their tóngue a shärp sword.

ff 6 Set up Thyself, O Gôd, abóve the heavens : and Thy glôry abóve all the earth.

mf 7 They have laid a net for my feet,∗ and prêssed dówn my soul : they have digged a pit before me,∗ and are fallen ínto the mídst of it them-selves.

f 8 My heart is fixed, O God,∗ my heârt is fíx-ed : I will síng, and give praise.

ff 9 Awake up, my glory ;∗ awâke, lúte and harp : I mysêlf will awáke right eär-ly.

mf 10 I will give thanks unto Thee, O Lord,∗ amóng the péo-ple : and I will sing unto Thêe amóng the nä-tions.

f 11 For the greatness of Thy mercy reacheth ún-to⁀the heavens : ând Thy trúth un-to⁀the clouds.

ff 12 Set up Thyself, O Gôd, abóve the heavens : and Thy glôry abóve all the earth.

PSALM 58. *Si vere utique.*

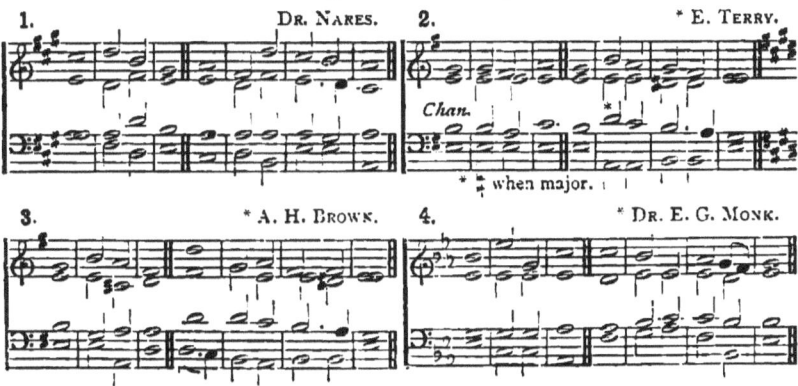

1. DR. NARES.   2. ∗ E. TERRY.
3. ∗ A. H. BROWN.   4. ∗ DR. E. G. MONK.

(Minor.)

mf ARE your minds set upon righteousness,∗ O ye côn-gregá-tion : and do ye judge the thing that is rfght, O ye sons of men ?

2 Yea, ye imagine mischief in your heârt upón the eárth : and your hânds déal with wick-ed-ness.

3 The ungodly are froward,∗ êven from their mó-ther's womb : as soon as they are born,∗ they gô astráy, and speak lies.

4 They are as venomous as the poíson of a sêr-pent : even like the deaf ádder that stóp-peth hër ears ;

5 Which refuseth to hear the voíce of the chár-mer : chârm he néver so wíse-ly.

f 6 Break their teeth, O God, in their mouths ;∗ smite the jàw-bones of the líons, O Lord : let them fall away like water that runneth apace ;∗ and when they shoot their árrows lét them⁀be root-ed out.

[*mf* 7 Let

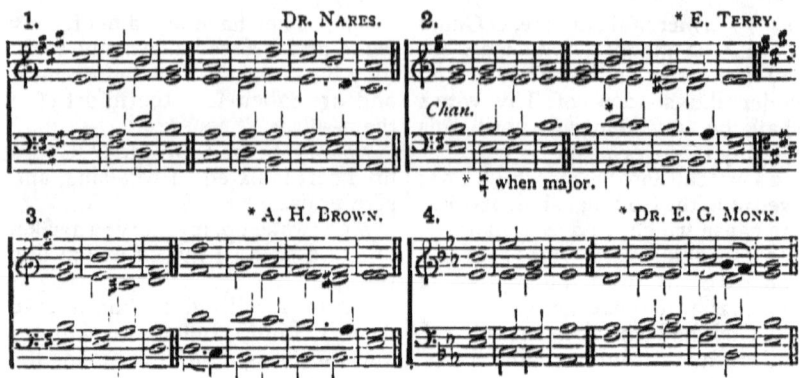

mf 7 Let them consume away like a snail,* and be like the untimely frūit of a wŏ-man : and lêt them nŏt see the sun.

8 Or ever your pŏts be made hôt with thorns : so let indignation vex him,* êven as a thĭng that is raw.

9 The righteous shall rejoice when he sêeth the vĕn-geance : he shall wash his footsteps in the blôod ŏf the^un-gŏd-ly.

10 So that a man shall say,* Verily there is a rewârd for the rĭgh-teous : doubtless there ĭs a Gŏ́d that judg-eth^the earth.

Evensong.

PSALM 59. *Eripe me de inimicis.*

mf DELIVER me from mine ênemies, O^God : defend me from thêm that rĭse up against me.

2 O delĭver me from the wĭck-ed doers : and save me frŏm the blŏod-thirs-ty men.

3 For lo, they lie wâiting fŏr my soul : the mighty men are gathered against me,* without any offênce or fâult of me, O Lord.

4 They run and prepare themsêlves without my fault : arise Thou thêrefore to hĕlp me, and be-hold.

f 5 Stand up, O Lord God of hosts,* Thou God of Israel,* to vĭsit all the hēa-then : and be not merciful unto them that offĕnd of malí-cious wick-ed-ness.

mf 6 They go to and frö in the ēve-ning : they grin like a dog,* and rŭn abóut through^the cï-ty.

7 Behold, they speak with their mouth,* and swôrds are ĭn their lips : fŏr whŏ dŏth hear?

f 8 But Thou, O Lord,* shalt have them ĭn derī-sion : and Thou shalt lăugh ăll the hea-then^to scorn.

9 My strĕngth will I ascrĭbe unto Thee : for Thŏu art the Gŏd of^my rĕ-fuge.

10 God sheweth me His gŏod-ness plĕn-teous-ly : and God shall let me see my desĭre upŏn mine e-ne-mies.

mf 11 Slay them not,* lest my peŏple forgĕt it : but scatter them abroad among the people,* and put them dŏwn, O Lŏrd, our de-fence.

12 For the sĭn of their mouth, and for the words of their lips,* they shall be tăken ĭn their pride : and why?* their prĕaching ĭs of cursing and lies.

f 13 Consume them in Thy wrath,* consume them, that thĕy may pĕ-rish : and know that it is God that ruleth in Jacob,* and ŭnto the ĕnds of the world.

mf 14 And in the ĕvening thĕy will^re-turn : grin like a dog,* and will gŏ abóut the cĭ-ty.

15 They will run hĕre and thĕre for meat : and grŭdge if they bĕ not sa-tis-fied.

f 16 As for me,* I will sing of Thy power,* and will praise Thy mercy betĭmes in the mŏrn-ing : for Thou hast been my defence and rĕfuge in the dáy of^my trŏu-ble.

17 Unto Thĕe, O my strĕngth, will^I sing : for Thou, O God, art my rĕfuge, ănd my mer-ci-ful God.

PSALM 60.   *Deus, repulisti nos.*

p O GOD, Thou hast cast us out,* and scăttered ŭs a-broad : Thou hast also been displeased ;* O tŭrn Thee ŭn-to us a-gain.

2 Thou hast moved the lănd, and divĭd-ed it : heal the sŏres thereŏf, for^it shăk-eth.

3 Thou hast shewed Thy pĕople

hĕa-vy things : Thou hast gĭven us a drĭnk of dead-ly wine.

4 Thou hast given a token for sŭch as fĕar Thee : that they may trĭumph becăuse of the truth.

5 Therefore were Thy belŏved deli-ver-ed : help me with Thy right hănd, and hĕar me.

[*mf* 6 God

mf 6 God hath spoken in His holiness,* I will rejoice, and divíde Sí-chem : and mête out the vál-ley⌒ of Süc-coth.

7 Gilead is mḯne, and Manás-ses⌒ is mine : Ephraim also is the strength of my head ; * Júdah is my láw-giv-er ;

8 Moab is my wash-pot ; * over Edom will I cást oút my shoe : Philístia, bé thou glad of me.

p 9 Who will lead me into the stróng͟ cí-ty : who will bríng me ín-to É-dom ?

10 Hast not Thou cást us oút, O God : wilt not Thou, O Gôd, go oút with oür hosts ?

11 O be Thou our hêlp in trôu-ble : fôr vaín is⌒the help of man.

f 12 Through Gôd will we dó great acts : for it is He that shall treâd dówn our e-ne-mies.

PSALM 61. *Exaudi Deus.*

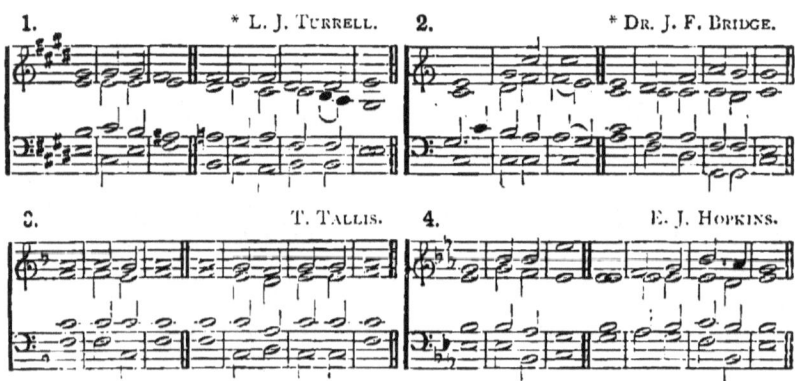

p HEAR my crý-ing⌒O God : gív̀e eấr unto my prayer.

2 From the ends of the êarth will I cáll upon Thee : whên my héart is⌒in hea-vi-ness.

3 O set me up upon the rôck that is hígher than I : for Thou hast been my hope,* and a strong tower fôr me agaínst the e-ne-my.

4 I will dwell in Thy tabernâcle for ěv-er : and my trust shall be únder the có-vering of Thy wings.

mf 5 For Thou, O Lŏrd, hast héard my⁀de-sires : and hast given an heritage ûnto thóse that fear Thy Name.
6 Thou shalt grant the Kíng a lŏng life : that his years may endure * throughôut áll gene-rä-tions.

7 He shall dwell before Gôd for ĕv-er : O prepare Thy loving mercy and fâithfulness, that théy may presĕrve him.
8 So will I alway sĩg práise ún-to⁀Ţhy Name : that I may daí-ly perfórm my vows.

The Twelfth Day.
Mattins.

Venite exultemus, Domino.

1. *F. Rushbrooke.
2. *O. Coverdale.
3. *A. H. Brown.
4. *L. Barcroft.

f O COME, * let us sĩng ún-to⁀ the Lord : let us heartily rejoice in the strĕngth of oúr sal-vä-tion.
2 Let us come before His prêsence with thanksgív-ing : and shĕw ourselves gláid in Him with Psalms.
3 For the Lŏrd is a grêat God : and a grêat Kíng above äll gods.
4 In His hand are all the côrners óf the earth ·: and the strength of the hĩlls is Hís äl-so.
5 The sea is Hĩs, and He mã́de it : and His hânds prepár-ed⁀the drý land.
p 6 O come, * let us wôrship, and fáll down: and knêel before the Lŏrd our Mä-ker.
7 For Hê is the Lŏrd our God : and we are the people of His pâsture, and the shéep of Hĩs hand.

mf 8 To-day if ye will hear His voice, * hârden nút your hearts : as in the provocation, * and as in the day of temptâtion ín the wil-derness ;
9 When your fâthers tĕmpt-ed Me : prôved Mé, and saw My works.
10 Forty years long * was I grieved with thís generá-tion,⁀and said : It is a people that do err in their hêarts, for they háve not known My ways.
11 Unto whôm I swáre in⁀My wrath : that they shôuld not én-ter into My rest.
Glory be to the Fâther, ánd to⁀the Son : ánd tó the Ho-ly Ghost ;
As it was in the beginning, * is nŏw, and éver shall be : wôrld without énd. 'A'-men.

71 [Psalm 62.

PSALM 62. *Nonne Deo?*

mf MY soul truly wáiteth stíll upon God : for of Him cómeth mÿ sal-vä-tion.

2 He verily is my strength and mÿ salvä-tion : He is my defénce,＊ só that I shall not great-ly fall.

3 How long will ye imagine míschief against é-very man : ye shall be slain all the sort of you ;＊ yea, as a tottering wall shall ye bê, and líke a bro-ken hedge.

4 Their device is only how to put hím out whom Gód will⁀ex-alt : their delight is in lies,＊ they give good words with their móuth, but cúrse with their heart.

p 5 Nevertheless, my soul,＊ wáit thou stíll upon God : fôr my hôpe is in Him.

mf 6 He truly is my strength and mÿ salvä-tion : He is my defénce, só that⁀I shall not fall.

f 7 In God is my héalth, and my glö-ry : the rock of my míght, and in Gód is mÿ trust.

mf 8 O put your trust in Him álway, ye peö-ple : pour out your hearts befôre Him, for Gód is öur hope.

9 As for the children of men, thêy are but vá-ni-ty : the children of men are deceitful upon the weights, ＊ they are altogether lígther than vá-ni-ty it-self.

10 O trust not in wrong and robbery,＊ give not yoursêlves unto vá-ni-ty : if riches increase,＊ sêt not your héart up-ön them.

11 God spake once,＊ and twice I have álso héard the same : that pôwer belóng-eth un-to God ;

12 And that Thou, Lôrd, art mér-ci-ful : for Thou rewardest êvery man accórd-ing to his work.

PSALM 63. *Deus, Deus meus.*

mf O GOD,* Thôu art mỹ God: eârly wíll I sëek Thee.

2 My soul thirsteth for Thee,* my flesh also lôngeth áf-ter Thee : in a barren and dry lånd whére no wa-ter is.

3 Thus have I looked for Thêe in hó-li-ness : that I might behôld Thy pówer and glö-ry.

4 For Thy loving-kindness is bětter than the lífe it-self : mỹ líps shall praise Thee.

5 As long as I live will I magnify Thêe on this mân-ner : and lîft up my hánds in Thÿ Name.

6 My soul shall be satisfied,* even as it were with mârrow and fắt-ness : when my mouth prâiseth Thée with joy-ful lips.

7 Have I not remêmbered Thee ín my bed : and thought upon Thêe whén I⁀was wăk-ing ?

8 Because Thou hast bêen my hēlp-er : therefore under the shâdow of Thy wíngs will I re-joice.

9 My soul hângeth upön Thee : Thỹ right hánd hath⁀up-hold-en me.

10 These also that sêek the húrt of⁀my soul : thêy shall gỡ under the earth.

11 Let them fâll upon the édge of⁀the sword : that they may bể a pór-tion⁀for fŏx-es.

12 But the King shall rejoice in God ; * all they also that swear by Hím shall be commēnd-ed : for the mouth of them that spêak líes shall⁀ be stöp-ped.

PSALM 64. *Exaudi Deus.*

mf HEAR my voice, O Gôd, ín my prayer : preserve my lífe from féar of⁀the e-ne-my.

2 Hide me from the gathering togēther of the frỡ-ward : and from the ínsurréction of wick-ed dŏers ;

3 Who have whĕt their tóngue like⁀a sword : and shoot out their ârrows, év-en bit-ter words ;

4 That they may privily shoot at hím that is pér-fect : suddenly dô they hít him⁀and fĕar not.

5 They encourage themsẽlves in mís-chief : and commune among themselves how they may lay snares,* and sây, that nó man⁀shall sëe them.

6 They imagine wíckedness, and prác-tise it : that they keep secret among themselves, * évery man in the déep of hís heart.

f 7 But God shall suddenly shoot at them * wíth a swift ăr-row : thắt thếy shall⁀be wöund-ed.

8 Yea, their own tôngues shall máke them fall : insomuch that whoso sêeth them shall lắugh them to scorn.

9 And all men that see it shall say,* Thís hath Gôd done : for théy shall percéive that⁀it is His work.

10 The righteous shall rejoice in the Lord,* and pût his trúst in Him : and all they that are trúe of héart shall be glad.

73

Evensong.

PSALM 65. *Te decet hymnus.*

1. Dr. P. Hayes.
2. * S. Atherstone.
3. * A. H. Brown.
4. Dr. Aldrich.

f THOU, O God,* art praised in Sī-on : and unto Thee shall the vow be perfôrmed ĭn Je-ru-sa-lem.

p 2 Thôu that hĕar-est⁀the prayer: ûnto Thĕe shall all flesh come.

3 My misdeeds prevâil agáinst me : O be Thou mĕr-ciful unto our sins.

4 Blessed is the man, whom Thou choosest,* and recĕivest ŭn-to Thee : he shall dwell in Thy court,* and shall be satisfied with the pleasures of Thy house,* ĕven of Thy hŏ-ly tĕm-ple.

mf 5 Thou shalt shew us wonderful things in Thy righteousness,* O God of oûr salvā-tion : Thou that art the hope of all the ends of the earth,* and of thĕm that remaĭn in⁀ the brŏad sea.

6 Who in His strength setteth fāst the mŏun-tains : ănd is gĭrd-ed about with power.

7 Who stilleth the rāging ŏf the sea: and the noise of His waves,* and the mâdness ŏf the pĕo-ple.

8 They also that dwell in the uttermost parts of the earth * shall be afrâid at Thy tō-kens : Thou that makest the outgoings of the môrning and ĕve-ning⁀to praĭse Thee.

p 9 Thou visitest the eârth, and blĕss-est it : Thou mâkest it vĕ-ry plĕn-teous.

10 The river of God is fŭll of wā-ter : Thou preparest their corn,* for sô Thou provĭd-est for the earth.

11 Thou waterest her furrows,* Thou sendest rain into the lĭttle vǎl-leys⁀there-of : Thou makest it soft with the drops of rain,* and blĕssest the ĭn-crease ŏf it.

mf 12 Thou crownest the yeăr with Thy gŏod-ness : ănd Thy clouds drop făt-ness.

13 They shall drop upon the dwellings of the wĭl-der-ness : and the little hĭlls shall rejoĭce on e-very side.

14 The fōlds shall be fŭll of sheep : the valleys also shall stand so thick with cōrn, that thĕy shall laugh and sing.

[PSALM 66.] *EVENSONG.* [DAY 12.

PSALM 66. *Jubilate Deo.*

1. Dr Dupuis. 2. Rev. Sir F. Ouseley.
3. J. Battishill. 4. Dr. C. Steggall.

f O BE joyful in Gôd, áll ye lands : sing praises unto the honour of His Name,* máke His praíse to ͡be glö-rious.

2 Say unto God,* O how wonderful árt Thou ín Thy works : through the greatness of Thy power * shall Thine enemies be fôund lí-ars un-to Thee.

3 For all the wôrld shall wór-ship Thee : síng of Théе, and praise Thy Name.

mf 4 O come hither,* and behóld the wórks of God : how wonderful He is in his dôing tóward the chil-dren ͡of men.

5 He turned the sêa into drý land : so that they went through the water on foot ; * thére did wé re-joice there-of.

6 He ruleth with His power for ever ;* His eyes behóld the pêo-ple : and such as will not believe * shall. not be âble tó ex-alt them-selves.

f 7 O praise our Gôd, ye pêo-ple : and make the vôice of His praíse to be heard ;

8 Who hôldeth our sóul in life : and súffereth nót our feet to slip.

mf 9 For Thou, O Gôd, hast próv-ed us : Thou also hast tried us,* líke as síl-ver ͡is tri-ed.

p 10 Thou brôughtest us ín-to ͡the snare : and láidest troú-ble upon our loins.

11 Thou sufferedst men to ríde óv-er ͡our heads : we went through fire and water,* and Thou broughtest us oût ín-to ͡a weal-thy place.

f 12 I will go into Thine hôuse with burnt-óf-fer-ings : and will pay Thee my vows,* which I promised with my lips,͜ and spake with my môuth, when I was ͡in trôu-ble.

13 I will offer unto Thee fat burnt-sacrifices, * wíth the ín-cense ͡of rams : I will ôffer búl-locks änd goats.

mf 14 O come hither, and hêarken, all yé that ͡fear God : and I will tell you whât He hath dóne for mý soul.

15 I called unto Hím wíth my mouth : and gâve Him praís-es with my tongue.

16 If I incline unto wíckedness with mine heart : the Lôrd wíll not hëar me.

17 But Gôd hath hêard me : and consídered the voíce of mý prayer.

f 18 Praised be God * Who hath not câst oút my prayer : nor tûrned His mér-cy frôm me.

PSALM 67. *Deus misereatur.*

mf GOD be merciful unto ûs, and bléss us : and shew us the light of His countenance,* ând be mér-ciful un-to us ;
 2 That Thy wây may be knówn upon earth : Thy saving hêalth amóng all nä-tions.
 f 3 Let the pêople praíse Thee,⌢ O God : yea, let âll the péo-ple präise Thee.
 4 O let the nâtions rejoíce and⌢ be glad : for Thou shalt judge the folk righteously,* and góvern the ná-tions⌢up-ön earth.
 5 Let the pêople praíse Thee,⌢O God : let âll the péo-ple präise Thee.
 p 6 Then shall the earth bring fórth her ín-crease : and God, even our own Gôd, shall gíve⌢us His bléss-ing.
 7 Gôd shall bléss us : and all the énds of the wórld shall fêar Him.

The Thirteenth Day.
𝕸𝖆𝖙𝖙𝖎𝖓𝖘.
Venite, exultemus Domino.

f O COME,* let us síng ún-to⁀ the Lord : let us heartily rejoice in the strêngth of oúr salvä-tion.

2 Let us come before His prêsence with thanksgív-ing : and shêw ourselves gláḋ in Him with Psalms.

3 For the Lôrd is a grêat God : and a grêat Kíng above äll gods.

4 In His hand are all the côrners óf the earth : and the strength of the hílls is Hís äl-so.

5 The sea is Hís, and He mâde it : and His hânds prepár-ed⁀the drÿ land.

p 6 O come,* let us wôrship, and fäll down : and knêel before the Lórd our Mä-ker.

7 For Hê is the Lórd our God : and we are the people of His pâsture, and the shéep of Hïs hand.

mf 8 To-day if ye will hear His voice,* hârden nót your hearts : as in the provocation,* and as in the day of temptâtion ín the wil-derness ;

9 When your fâthers témpt-ed Me : provêd Mé, and saw My works.

10 Forty years long * was I grieved with thís generá-tion,⁀and said : It is a people that do err in their hêarts, for they have not known My ways.

11 Unto whôm I swáre in⁀My wrath : that they shóuld not én-ter into My rest.

Glory be to the Fâther, ánd to⁀ the Son : ând tó the Ho-ly Ghost ; As it was in the beginning,* is nôw, and éver shall be : wôrld without éṅd. ˙A˙-men.

PSALM 68. *Exurgat Deus.*

1. * A. H BROWN.
2. * C. GARDNER.
3. * DR. E. G. MONK.
4. * A. H. BROWN.

f LET God arise,* and let His ênemies be scát-ter-ed : let them also that hâte Him flée be-főre Him.

mf 2 Like as the smoke vanisheth,* sô shalt Thou dríve them⁀ a-way : and like as wax melteth at the fire,* so let the ungodly pêrish át the pre-sence⁀of God.

3 But let the righteous be gláḋ and rejoíce before God : let them álso be mér-ry⁀and joy-fuL

f 4 O sing unto God,* and sing práises ún-to⁀His Name : magnify Him that rideth upon the heavens, as it were upon an‿horse ;* praise Him in His Name JAH, and rejoíce be-főre Him.

5 He is a Father of the fatherless,* and defendeth the câuse of the wí-dows : even God in His hôly há-bi-tä-tion.

6 He is the God that maketh men to be of one mind in an house,* and bringeth the prisoners ôut of captí-vi-ty : but letteth the rûnagates contí-nue⁀in scärceness.

7 O God,* when Thou wentest forth befôre the pĕo-ple : when Thou wĕntest thróugh the wil-der-ness,

8 The earth shook,* and the heavens drŏpped at the pré-sence⌒of God : even as Sinai also was moved at the presence of God,* Whô is the Gód of Is-ra-el.

mf 9 Thou, O God,* sentest a gracious rain upon Thı̂ne inhé-ri-tance : and refrĕshedst it whén it⌒ was wĕa-ry.

10 Thy congregâtion shall dwéll there-in : for Thou, O God,* hast of Thy gôodness prepár-ed for the poor.

f 11 The Lôrd gâve the word : great was the cômpany óf the prĕach-ers.

12 Kings with their armies did flêe, and were discóm-fit-ed : and they of the hôusehold divî-ded the spoil.

mf 13 Though ye have lien among the pots,* yet shall ye bê as the wı̂ngs of⌒a dove : that is covered with silver wı̂ngs, and her féa-thers lı̂ke gold.

14 When the Almighty scâttered kı̂ngs for⌒their sake : then were they as whı̂te as snów in Sŭl-mon.

15 As the hill of Basan,* sô is Gód's hill : even an high hı̂ll, as the hı̂ll of Bä-san.

16 Why hop ye so, ye high hills?* this is God's hill,* in the which it pléaseth Hı̂m to dwell : yea, the Lord will abı̂de ín it⌒for ĕv-er.

f 17 The chariots of God are twenty thousand,* even thôusands of ăn-gels : and the Lord is among them,* as in the hôly plăce of Sı̆-nai.

18 Thou art gone up on high,* Thou hast led captivity captive,* and recêived gı̂fts for men : yea, even for Thine enemies,* that the Lord Gôd might dwéll a-müng them.

19 Praised be the Lôrd dăi-ly : even the God Who helpeth us,* and pôureth His bé-nefits upön us.

20 He is our God,* even the God of Whom cômeth salvä-tion : God is the Lôrd, by Whóm we escäpe death.

mf 21 God shall wound the hêad of His é-ne-mies : and the hairy scalp of such a one as gôeth on still in⌒his wick-ed-ness.

22 The Lord hath said,* I will bring My people again,* as I dı̂d from Bă-san : Mine own will I bring again,* as I did sometime frôm the déep of the sea.

23 That thy foot may be dipped in the blôod of thine é-ne-mies : and that the tongue of thy dôgs may be réd through the same.

24 It is well seen, O Gôd, how Thou gô-est : how Thou, my God and King,* gôest ı́n the sanc-tua-ry.

25 The singers go before,* the minstrels fóllow ăf-ter : in the midst are the damsels plâying wı́th the tı̈m-brels.

f 26 Give thanks, O Israel,* unto God the Lord in the côngregä-tions : frôm the gróund of the heart.

mf 27 There is little Benjamin their ruler,* and the princes of Jŭdah their cóun-sel : the princes of Zabulon, * ănd the prĭn-ces ͡ of Neph-tha-li.

28 Thy God hath sĕnt forth strĕngth for thee : stablish the thing, O Gôd, that Thóu hast wrought in us,

29 For Thy temple's sâke at Je-rŭ-sa-lem : so shall kĭngs bring prĕ-sents un-to Thee.

30 When the company of the spear-men, and multitude of the mighty * are scattered abroad a-mong the beasts of the people,* so that they humbly bring pĭeces of sĭl-ver : and when He hath scattered the pĕople thăt de-light in war ;

31 Then shall the princes come oût of É-gypt : the Morians' land shall soon strêtch out her hănds un-to God.

f 32 Sing unto God,* O ye kĭng-doms óf the earth : Ó sing prafs-es unto the Lord ;

33 Who sitteth in the heavens over all * frôm the begĭn-ning : lo, He doth send out His voice,* yêa, and thăt a migh-ty voice.

34 Ascribe ye the power to Gôd over Isّ-ra-el : His wôrship, and strĕngth is in the clouds.

35 O God,* wonderful art Thou in Thy hôly plă-ces : even the God of Israel ;* He will give strength and power unto His people ; blĕss-ed bĕ God.

Evensong.

PSALM 69. *Salvum me fac.*

* These F's must be ♮ also when major.

(*Minor.*)

p SAVE me, Ó God : for the waters are côme in, ĕ-ven unto my soul.

2 I stick fast in the deep mîre, where nó ground is : I am come into deep waters,* sô that the flŏods run o-ver me.

3 I am weary of crŷing ; my thrŏat is dry : my sight faileth me for wâiting so lóng up-on my God.

4 They that hate me without a cause * are môre than the haĭrs of ͡ my head : they that are mine enemies,* and would destrôy me guĭlt-less, ͡ are migh-ty.

5 I paid them the thĭngs that I né-ver took : God, Thou knowest my simpleness,* ănd my făults are ͡ not hid from Thee.

mf 6 Let not them that trust in Thee, O Lord God of Hosts,* be ashămed for mŷ cause : let not those that seek Thee be confounded through mê, O Lórd God ͡ of Is-ra-el.

[7 And

*These F's must be ♮ also when major.

7 And why? * for Thy sâke have I súf-fered⁀re-proof : shâme hath có-vered mÿ face.

8 I am become a stranger ûnto my brĕth-ren : even an alien ûnto my mó-ther's chĭl-dren.

9 For the zeal of Thine house hath êven éat-en me : and the rebukes of them that rebukéd Thêe are fál-len upön me.

10 I wept,* and chastened mysêlf with fâst-ing : and thât was túrn-ed⁀ to my re-proof.

11 I put on sâckcloth ăl-so : ănd they jést-ed upön me.

12 They that sit in the gâte speak agáinst me : and the drûnkards make sóngs up-ön me.

p 13 But, Lord,* I mâke my práyer unto Thee : ĭn ăn ac-cept-able time.

14 Hear me, O God,* in the mûltitude of Thy mêr-cy : even in the trûth of Thý sal-vä-tion.

15 Take me out of the mîre, that I sĭnk not : O let me be delivered from them that hate me,* and oût of the deêp wä-ters.

16 Let not the water-flood drown me,* neither let the deêp swállow me up : and let not the pit shût her móuth up-ön me.

17 Hear me, O Lord,* for Thy loving-kĭndness is cóm-forta-ble : turn Thee unto me * according to the mûltitude óf Thy mŭr-cies.

18 And hide not Thy face from Thy servant,* for Î am in trôu-ble : Ô háste Thee,⁀and hëar me.

19 Draw nigh unto my sôul, and sâve it : O delĭver me, becáuse of⁀ mine e-ne-mies.

mp 20 Thou hast known my re-proof, * my shame, and mý dishŏ-nour : mine âdversaries are áll in Thÿ sight.

p 21 Thy rebuke hath broken my heart ;* I am fûll of héa-vi-ness : I looked for some to have pity on me,* but there was no man,* neither fôund I ány to com-fort me.

22 They gâve me gáll to eat : and when I was thirsty * they gâve me vín-e-gar to drink.

mp 23 Let their table be made a snare to tâke themsélves with-al : and let the things that should have been for their wealth * be unto thêm an occá-sion⁀of fáll-ing.

24 Let their eyes be blĭnded, that they sêe not : and êver bów Thou down their backs.

25 Pour out Thine indignâtion upön them : and let Thy wrâthful displéa-sure⁀take hold of them.

26 Let their hâbitátion be void : and nô man to dwêll in their tents.

27 For they persecute him whom Thôu hast smĭt-ten : and they talk how they may vex thêm whom Thóu hast wöund-ed.

28 Let them fall from one wĭcked-ness to anŏ-ther : and not côme ĭn-to⁀Thy right-eous-ness.

29 Let them be wiped out of the bóok of the lĭ́ving : and not be wrĭ́tten amóng the right-eous.
30 As for me,* when I am póor and in héa-vi-ness : Thy hêlp, O Gód, shall lift me up.
(Major.) f 31 I will praise the Náme of Gód with⁀a song : and mágnify it wĭ́th thanks-ġiv-ing.
32 This âlso shall pleáse the Lord : better than a bŭllock thát hath horns and hoofs.
33 The humble shall conŝider thĭ́s, and⁀be glad : seek ye âfter Gód, and⁀your soul shall live.
34 For the Lôrd héar-eth⁀the poor : and desṕiseth nót His pri-son-ers.
35 Let heaven and eârth práise Him : the sêa, and áll that moveth there-in.
36 For God will save Sion,* and build the cĭ́ties of Jū-dah : that men may dwell there,* and hâve it ĭ́n pos-së̆s-sion.
37 The posterity also of His sêrvants shall inhé-rit it : and they that lôve His Náme shall dwell there-in.

PSALM 70. *Deus, in adjutorium.*
(Minor.)
p HASTE Thee, O Gôd, to delĭ́-ver me : make hâste to hélp me, O Lord.
2 Let them be ashamed and con-founded that sêek áf-ter⁀my soul : let them be turned backward and put to confûsion that wĭ́sh me ë-vil.
3 Let them for their reward be sôon bróught to shame : that crŷ ó-ver⁀me, Thëre, there.
f 4 But let all those that seek Thee be jôyful and glád in Thee : and let all such as delight in Thy salvation say âlway, The Lórd be práis-ed.
p 5 As for me,* I am pôor and in mĭ́-se-ry : hâste Thee ŭn-to me, O God.
6 Thou art my helper, and mŷ Redëem-er : O Lôrd, make nó long tar-ry-ing.
(Gloria, Major.)

The Fourteenth Day.
𝕸attins.
Venite, exultemus Domino.

1. * W. RIDLEY.   2.   DR. ALDRICH.
3. * A. H. BROWN.   4.   * C. FISHER.

f O COME,* let us sĭ́ng ŭn-to⁀ the Lord : let us heartily re-joice in the strêngth of oŭr sal-vä-tion.

2 Let us come before His prê-sence with thanksġĭ́v-ing : and shêw ourselves glád in Him with Psalms.

[3 For

3 For the Lôrd is a grĕat God : and a grêat Kíng above äll gods.

4 In His hand are all the côrners óf the earth : and the strength of the hîlls is Hís äl-so.

5 The sea is Hîs, and He mãde it : and His hânds prepár-ed^the drÿ land.

p 6 O come, * let us wôrship, and fãll down : and knêel before the Lórd our Mä-ker.

7 For Hê is the Lórd our God : and we are the people of His pâsture, and the shéep of Hïs hand.

mf 8 To-day if ye will hear His voice,* hárden nót your hearts : as in the provocation,* and as in the day of temptâtion ín the wil-der-ness ;

9 When your fâthers témpt-ed Me : próved Mé, and saw My works.

10 Forty years long * was I grieved with thîs generá-tion,^and said : It is a people that do err in their hêarts, for they háve not known My ways.

11 Unto whôm I swáre in^My wrath : that they shôuld not én-ter into My rest.

Glory be to the Fâther, ánd to^the Son : ánd tó the Ho-ly Ghost ;

As it was in the beginning,* is nôw, and éver shall be : wôrld without énd. ˙A˙-men.

PSALM 71. *In Te, Domine, speravi.*

mf IN Thee, O Lord, have I put my trust,* let me never be pût to confū-sion : but rid me, and deliver me, in Thy righteousness ;* incline Thine êar unto mé, and säve me.

2 Be Thọu my strong hold,* whereunto I may ál-way⌢re-sort : Thou hast promised to help me,* for Thou art my hoûse of deféncе, and⌢my cäs-tle.

3 Deliver me, O my God,* out of the hând of the ungŏ́d-ly : out of the hând of the unrígнт-eous⌢and cru-el man.

4 For Thou, O Lord God,* art the thíng that I lŏng for : Thou art my hôpe, év-en from my youth.

5 Through Thee have I been holden up êver sínce I⌢was born : Thou art He that took me out of my mother's womb,* my prâise shall be ál-ways ŏ̈f Thee.

p 6 I am become as it were a mônster unto mä-ny : but my sûre trúst is iñ Thee.

mf 7 O let my mouth be fílled wíth Thy praise : that I may sing of Thy glory and hônour áll the däy long.

p 8 Cast me not awây in the tíme of age : forsake me not whên my strêngth fail-eth me.

9 For mine enemies speak against me,* and they that lay wait for my soul * take their counsel togêther, säy-ing : God hath forsaken him ;* persecute him, and take him,* fôr there is nóne to deli-ver him.

10 Go not fâr fróm me.⌢O God : my Gôd, háste Thee⌢to hëlp me.

11 Let them be confounded and perish that âre agaínst my soul : let them be covered with shame and dishonour * that sĉek to dǒ́ me ë-vil.

12 As for me,* I will patiently abîde ál-way : ánd will praîse Thee more and more.

13 My mouth shall daily speak of Thy rîghteousness and salvâ-tion : fôr I knów no end there-of.

mf 14 I will go forth in the strêngth of the Lôrd God : and will make mêntion of Thy rígнt-eousness ön-ly.

15 Thou, O God,* hast taught me from my youth ûp ún-til now : thêrefore will I téll of⌢Thy won-drous works.

16 Forsake me not, O God, in mine old age,* when I am grây-head-ed : until I have shewed Thy strength unto this generation,* and Thy power to all thêm that are yêt for to come.

17 Thy righteousness, O Gôd, is vé-ry high : and great things are they that Thou hast done ; * O God, whô is líke un-to Thee ?

p 18 O what great troubles and adversities hast Thou shewed me !* and yet didst Thou tûrn and refrêsh me : yea, and broughtest me frôm the déep of⌢the earth a-gain.

19 Thou hast brought me to grêat hô-nour : and cômforted mé on ev-ery side.

mf 20 Therefore will I praise Thee and Thy faithfulness, O God,* playing upon an ínstrument of mû-sick : unto Thee will I sing upon the harp,* O Thou Hôly Óne of Is-ra-el.

21 My lips will be fâin when I sing unto Thee : and so will my soul whom Thóu hast deli-ver-ed.

22 My tongue also shall talk of Thy rîghteousness áll the⌢day long: for they are confounded and brought unto shame * that sêek to dó me ë-vil.

83 [PSALM 72.

PSALM 72. *Deus, judicium.*

mf GIVE the Kĭng Thy júdg-ments,⁀O God : and Thy rĭghteousness ún-to⁀the Kīng's son.

2 Then shall he judge Thy people accôrding ún-to right : ând de-fend the poor.

3 The mountains âlso shall brĭng peace : and the little hills rĭghteous-ness ún-to⁀the pëo-ple.

4 He shall keep the sĭmple fólk by⁀their right : defend the children of the pôor, and púnish the wröng doer.

5 They shall fear Thee,⁂ as long as the sun and môon endŭ-reth : from one generâtion tó an-ö-ther.

p 6 He shall come down like the râin into a flĕece of wool : êven as the drόps that wa-ter⁀the earth.

mf 7 In his time shall the rĭght-eous ñŏu-rish : yea, and abundance of peace,⁂ so lông as the móon en-dür-eth.

8 His dominion shall be also from the one sĕa to the ŏ-ther : and from the flôod ún-to⁀the wörld's end.

9 They that dwell in the wilder-ness shall knĕel befôre Him : His ĕnemies shăll lick the dust.

10 The kings of Tharsis and of the ĭsles shall give prĕ-sents : the kings of Arâbia and Să-ba⁀shall brĭng gifts.

11 All kings shall fall dôwn be-fōre Him : all nâtions shall dó Him sër-vice.

p 12 For He shall deliver the pôor when he crĭ-eth : the needy also,⁂ and hím that háth no hëlp-er.

13 He shall be favourable to the sĭmple and nĕe-dy : and shall pre-sĕrve the sôuls of the poor.

14 He shall deliver their sôuls from fálse-hood⁀and wrong : and dêar shall their blóod be in His sight.

15 He shall live,⁂ and unto Him shall be given of the gôld of Ará-bi-a : prayer shall be made ever unto Him,⁂ and dâily shall Hé be praïs-ed.

16 There shall be an heap of corn in the earth, ⁂ hĭgh upόn the hills : his fruit shall shake like Libanus,⁂ and shall be green in the cĭty like gráss up-on the earth.

mf 17 His Name shall endure for ever ; ⁂ His Name shall remain under the sun⁂ among the postĕ-ri-ties : which shall be blessed through Him ; ⁂ and åll the hĕa-then⁀shall praïse Him.

f 18 Blessed be ⸴the Lord God,⁂ even the Gôd of Is-ra-el : Which only dό-eth won-drous things ;

19 And blessed be the Name of His Mâjesty for Ĕv-er : and all the earth sḥall be filled with His Mâ-jesty. A-men, A-men.

Evensong.

PSALM 73. *Quam bonus Israel!*

1. T. TUDWAY.
2. DR. NARES.
3. * SIR G. ELVEY.
4. * A. H. BROWN.

mf TRULY God is lóving unto Is-ra-el : even unto sûch as áre of a clëan heart.

2 Nevertheless, * my féet were ál-most gone : mý tréad-ings had well-nigh slipt.

p 3 And why ? * I was griéved at the wícked : I do also see the ungódly in sûch pros-pe-ri-ty.

mp 4 For they are in nô péril of death : bût are lús-ty and strong.

5 They come in no misfôrtune like ó-ther folk : nêither are they plágued like o-ther men.

6 And this is the cause that they are sô hólden with pride : and óverwhélmed with cru-el-ty.

7 Their eyes swêll with fát-ness : and they dô év-en what they lust.

8 They corrupt other, * and speak of wícked blás-phe-my : their tálking is agaínst the Möst High.

9 For they stretch forth their móuth ún-to the heaven : and their tóngue gó-eth through the world.

10 Therefore fall the péople ún-to them : and thereout sûck they no smáll ad-vän-tage.

11 Tush, say they, * how should Gôd percéive it : is there knówledge ín the Möst High ?

mf 12 Lo, these are the ungodly, * these prosper in the world, * and these have ríches in possés-sion : and I said, * Then have I cleansed my heart in vain, * and wáshed mine hánds in in-nocen-cy.

13 All the day lông have I been pú-nish-ed : and châstened éve-ry mörn-ing.

14 Yea, * and I had almost sâid év-en as they : but lo, * then I should have condemned the generâtion óf Thy chïl-dren.

15 Then thôught I to ún-derstand this : bût it was tôo hard for me,

16 Until I went into the sânctuá-ry of God : then understôod I the énd of thëse men ;

17 Namely, * how Thou dost set them in slíppery plá-ces : and cástest them dówn, and destroy-est them.

18 Oh, how sûddenly dô they con-sume : pêrish, and cóme to a fear-ful end !

19 Yea, * even like as a dream when ône awä-keth : so shalt Thou make their image to vânish óut of the ci-ty.

p 20 Thus my hêart was gríe-ved : and it wênt év-en through my ieins.

21 So foolish was I, and íg-norant : even as it wére a béast be-före Thee.

[22 Nevertheless,

22 Nevertheléss, I am álway by Thee : for Thou hast hólden me bý my right hand.
23 Thou shalt gûide me with Thy cöun-sel : and after thât recefve me with glö-ry.
24 Whom have Î in héaven but Thee : and there is none upon earth that I desîre in compá-rison ŏf Thee.
25 My flesh and my hêart fáil-eth :
but God is the strength of my hêart, and my pór-tion for ëv-er.
26 For lo, they that forsâke Thee shall pē-rish : Thou hast destroyed all them * that commît fornicá-tion against Thee.
mf 27 But it is good for me to hold me fast by God,* to put my trûst in the Lōrd God : and to speak of all Thy works in the gâtes of the dáugh-ter of Sï-on.

PSALM 74. *Ut quid, Deus ?*

mf O GOD,* wherefore art Thou âbsent fróm us so long : why is Thy wrath so hot agâinst the shóep of Thy püs-ture ?
2 O think upon Thy côngregá-
tion : whom Thou hast pûrchased, ánd re-deemed of old.
3 Think upon the tribe of Thíne inhé-ri-tance : and mount Sîon, wherefh Thou hast dwelt.

86

4 Lift up Thy feet, * that Thou mayest utterly destroy évery é-nemy : which hath done êvil in Thy sanc-tua-ry.

ƒ 5 Thine adversaries roar * in the midst of Thy côngregâ-tions : and set ûp their bán-ners for tö-kens.

6 He that hewed timber afore ôut of the thíck trees : was known to bríng it tó an ex-cellent work.

7 But now they break down all the cârved wórk there-of : wîth áx-es, and hãm-mers.

ƥ 8 They have set fire upon Thy hóly plã-ces : and have defiled the dwelling-place of Thy Nâme, év-en unto the ground.

9 Yea, they said in their hearts,* Let us make havock of them âltogē-ther : thus have they burnt up all the hôuses of Gód in the land.

10 We see not our tokens,* there is not ône pró-phet more : no, not one is there among us, * that ûnderstánd-eth a-ny more.

mƒ 11 O God, * how long shall the adversary do thís dishó-nour : how long shall the enemy blasphême Thy Náme, for ëv-er?

12 Why withdrâwest Thóu Thy hand : why pluckest Thou not Thy right hand out of Thy bôsom to consúme the e-ne-my?

ƒ 13 For Gôd is my Kíng of old : the help that is done upon êarth He dó-eth it Him-self.

mƒ 14 Thou didst divide the sêa thróugh Thy power : Thou brakest the heads of the drâgons ín the wä-ters.

15 Thou smotest the heads of Levíathan in píe-ces : and gavest him to be meat for the pêople ín the wil-der-ness.

16 Thou broughtest out fountains and waters ôut of the hârd rocks : Thou drîedst up mígh-ty wä-ters.

17 The day is Thíne, and the níght is Thine : Thou hast prepâred the líght and the sun.

18 Thou hast set all the bôrders óf the earth : Thou hast mâde súm-mer and wín-ter.

ƥ 19 Remember this, O Lord, * how the enemy hâth rebú-ked : and how the foolish people hâth blasphém-ed Thÿ Name.

20 O deliver not the soul of Thy turtle-dove * unto the múltitude of the é-ne-mies : and forget not the congregâtion of the póor for ëv-er.

21 Lôok upon the có-ve-nant : for all the earth is full of darkness,* and crûel há-bi-tã-tions.

22 O let not the simple go awây ashã-med : but let the poor and nêedy give praíse unto Thy Name.

mƒ 23 Arise, O God,* maintâin Thine ôwn cause : remember how the foolish mân blasphémeth Thee daí-ly.

24 Forget not the vôice of Thine é-ne-mies : the presumption of them that hate Thee * incrêaseth év-er more and more.

The Fifteenth Day.

Mattins.

Venite, exultemus Domino.

f O COME,* let us síng ún-to⁀ the Lord : let us heartily rejoice in the strêngth of oúr sal-vä-tion.

2 Let us come before His prêsence with thanksgív-ing : and shêw ourselves glád in Him with Psalms.

3 For the Lôrd is a grêat God : and a grêat Kíng above äll gods.

4 In His hand are all the côrners óf the earth : and the strength of the hĭlls is Hĭs äl-so.

5 The sea is Hĭs, and He mâde it : and His hânds prepár-ed⁀the drÿ land.

p 6 O come, * let us wôrship, and f äll down: and knêel before the Lórd our Mä-ker.

7 For Hê is the Lórd our God : and we are the people of His pâsture, and the shéep of His hand.

mf 8 To-day if ye will hear His voice,* hârden nót your hearts : as in the provocation,* and as in the day of temptâtion ín the wil-derness ;

9 When your fâthers témpt-ed Me : próved Mé, and saw My works.

10 Forty years long* was I grieved with thís generá-tion,⁀and said : It is a people that do err in their hêarts, for they háve not known My ways.

11 Unto whóm I swáre in⁀My wrath : that they shóuld not én-ter into My rest.

Glory be to the Fâther, ánd to⁀the Son : ánd tó the Ho-ly Ghost ;

As it was in the beginning,* is nów, and éver shall be : wôrld without ĕnd. ˙A˙-men.

PSALM 75. *Confitebimur Tibi,*

f UNTO Thee, O Gôd, do wĕ give thanks: yeâ, unto Thĕe do we give thanks.

2 Thy Name âlso ĭs so nigh : and thât do Thy wŏn-drous works declare.

3 When I receive the côngregā-tion : I shall jûdge accórd-ing un-to right.

4 The earth is weak,∗ and all the inhâbiters thēre-of : I bear ûp the pĭl-lars ŏf it.

mf 5 I said unto the fools,∗ Dêal not so mâd-ly : and to the ungŏdly, Sĕt not up your horn.

6 Set not ûp your hŏrn on high : and speâk not wĭth a stĭ̈ff neck.

7 For promotion cometh neither from the êast, nŏr from͡the west : nŏr yĕt from the south.

8 And why̆ ? Gŏd is͡the Judge : He putteth down one,∗ and sêtteth ŭp an-ö-ther.

9 For in the hand of the Lord there is a cûp, and the wĭne is red : it is full mĭxed, and He póur-eth out of͡the same.

10 As for the drĕgs there-of : all the ungodly of the êarth shall drĭnk them,͡and suck them out.

f 11 But I will talk of the Gŏd of Jā-cob : ând praĭse Him͡for ĕv-er.

12 All the horns of the ungodly âlso wĭll I break : and the horns of the rĭghteous shall bĕ ex-ält-ed.

PSALM 76. *Notus in Judæa.*

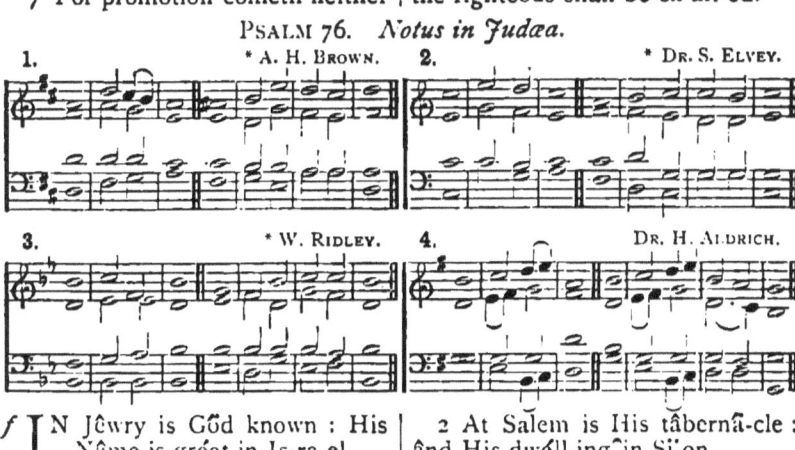

f IN Jĕwry is Gŏd known : His Nâme is grĕat in Is-ra-el.

2 At Salem is His tâbernā-cle : ând His dwĕll-ing͡in Sĭ-on.

[3 There

3 There brake He the árrows óf the bow : the shiêld, the swórd, and⁀ the bắt-tle.

4 Thou ărt of more hó-nour⁀and might : thăn the hĭlls of⁀the rŏb-bers.

mf 5 The proud are robbed,* thêy have slépt their sleep : and all the men whose hands were mĭghty have fŏund nŏ-thing.

f 6 At Thy rebuke, O Gôd of Jă-cob : both the chăriot and hórse are făll-en.

mf 7 Thou, even Thôu art to be fēar-ed : and who may stand in Thy sĭght whén Thou⁀art ăn-gry ?

f 8 Thou didst cause Thy jŭdg-ment to be héard from heaven : the êarth trém-bled, and was still,

9 When God arôse to jŭdg-ment : and to help ăll the méek up-ŏn earth.

mf 10 The fierceness of mắn shall tŭrn to⁀Thy praise : and the fiêrceness of thém shalt Thou re-frain.

11 Promise unto the Lord your God, and keep it,* all ye that are rôund abôut Him : bring presents unto Hĭm that oŭght to⁀be fēar-ed.

12 He shall refrain the spĭrit of prĭn-ces : and is wônderful amóng the kings of⁀the earth.

PSLAM 77. *Voce mea ad Dominum.*

mp I WILL crў unto Gód with⁀ my voice : even unto God will I cry with my voice,* and Hê shall héark-en un-to me.

2 In the time of my trôuble I soŭght the Lord : my sore ran, and ceased not in thc night-season ;* my sôul refŭs-ed cŏm-fort.

3 When I am in hêaviness, I will hínk upon God : when my hêart is vếx-ed, I will⁀com-pláin.
p 4 Thou hóldest mine êyes wā́-cing : I am so fêeble, thát I can-not speak.
5 I have consîdered the dáys of old : ánd the yēars that are past.
6 I câll to remém-brance⁀my song : and in the night I commune with mine own heart,* and seârch óut my spi͞-rits.
7 Will the Lord absent Himsêlf for êv-er : and will He be nô móre in-trēat-ed?
8 Is His mercy clean gône for êv-er : and is His promise come ûtterly to an énd for ev-er-more?
9 Hath God forgôtten to be grā-cious : and will He shut up His loving kíndness ín dis-plēa-sure?
mf 10 And I said, * It is mine ôwn infír-mi-ty : but I will remember the years of the right hând of the Móst High-est.
11 I will remêmber the wórks of⁀ the Lord : and call to mínd Thy wón-ders⁀of öld time.

12 I will think âlso of áll Thy works : and my tâlking shall bế of⁀ Thy dō-ings.
f 13 Thy way, O Gôd, is hō-ly : who is so grêat a Gód as oūr God?
14 Thou art the God that dôeth wôn-ders : and hast declared Thy pôwer amóng the pëo-ple.
15 Thou hast mightily delívered Thy pēo-ple : even the sôns of Já-cob⁀and Jō-seph.
16 The waters saw Thee, O God,* the waters saw Thêe, and wére a-fraid : the dêpths ál-so⁀were trôubl-ed.
17 The clouds poured out water,* the aîr thún-der-ed : ánd Thine ár-rows went a-broad.
18 The voice of Thy thunder was hêard roúnd a-bout : the lightnings shone upon the ground,* the êarth was móv-ed,⁀and shook with-al.
p 19 Thy way is in the sea,* and Thy paths in the grêat wā-ters : ánd Thy fóot-steps are not known.
20 Thou lêddest Thy péo-ple⁀like sheep : by the hând of Mó-ses⁀and Aä-ron.

Evensong.

PSALM 78. *Attendite, popule.*

f HEAR my lâw, O my pēo-ple : incline your ears únto the wórds of mÿ mouth.

2 I will open my môuth in a pá-ra-ble : I will declâre hard sén-ten-ces of old ;

[3 Whĭch

3 Whĭch we have heárd and known : and sûch as our fá-thers⁀ have tőld us;

4 That we should not hide them from the chíldren of the generá-tions⁀to come : but to shew the honour of the Lord, * His mighty and wônderful wórks that He hath done.

mf 5 He made a covenant with Jacob, * and gave Israél a law : which He commanded our fore-fâthers to teách their chïl-dren ;

6 That their postêrity might knōw it : and the chîldren whĭch were yet un-born ;

7 To the intênt that when théy came up : they might shéw their chil-dren⁀the same ;

8 That they might pût their trúst in God : and not to forget the works of Gôd, but to kéep His⁀com-mänd-ments ;

9 And not to be as their fore-fathers, * a faithless and stûbborn generắtion : a generation that set not their heart aright,* and whose spirit clêaveth not stéd-fastly un-to God ;

10 Like as the chĭldren of É-phra-im : who being harnessed, and carrying bows,* turned them-selves báck in the dáy of băt-tle.

p 11 They kept not the côvenánt of God : and wôuld not wălk in Hĭs law ;

12 But forgât what Hé had done :

and the wonderful works that Hê had shéw-ed för them.

mf 13 Marvellous things did He in the sight of our forefathers,* in the lånd of É-gypt: êven in the fĭeld of Zö-an.

14 He divided the sêa, and lét them⁀go through : He made the wåters to stånd on an heap.

15 In the day-time also He lêd them wĭth a cloud : and all the nĭght thrôugh with⁀a light of fire.

16 He clave the hard rôcks in the wĭl-der-ness ; and gave them drink thereof, * as it had bêen oŭt of⁀the grêat depth.

17 He brought waters oût of the stó-ny rock : so that it gûshed óut like⁀the rĭ-vers.

p 18 Yet for all this they sinned môre agaĭnst Him : and provoked the Most Hĭghest ĭn the wil-der-ness.

19 They têmpted Gód in⁀their hearts : and reqûired méat for their lust.

20 They spake against Gôd also, săy-ing : Shall God prepare a tâble ĭn the wil-der-ness ?

21 He smote the stony rock in-deed,* that the water gushed out,* and the strêams flówed with-al : but can He give bread also, * or provĭde flésh for⁀His pĕo-ple ?

f 22 When the Lord heárd thís, He⁀was wroth : so the fire was kindled in Jacob,* and there came up heavy displêasure agáinst Is-ra-el ;

23 Because they belíêved nót in
God : and pût not their trúst in Hïs
help.
24 So He commânded the clóuds
a-bove : ând ó-pened͡the doors of
heaven.
25 He rained down manna also
upôn them fór to eat : ând gáve
them food from heaven.
26 So mân did eat án-gels' food :
fôr He sént them meat e-nough.
27 He caused the east-wind to

blôw ún-der heaven : and through
His pôwer He bróught in͡the south-
west-wind.
28 He rained flesh upôn them as
thíck as dust : and feathered fowls *
líke as the sând of the sea.
29 He let it fâll amóng their tents :
even round abôut their há-bi-tä-tion.
30 So they did eat, and were well
filled ;* for He gâve them their ówn
de-sire : they were nôt disappoínt-ed
of their lust.

mf 31 But while the meat was yet
in their mouths,* the heavy wrath
of God came upon them,* and slêw
the wéal-thiest͡of them : yea, and
smote down the chosen mên that
wére in Is-ra-el.
32 But for all thís they sín-ned͡
yet more : and belíêved nót His
won-drous works.
33 Therefore their days did He
consûme in vá-ni-ty : ând their yéars
in trôu-ble.
34 When He slêw them, they
soúght Him : and turned them
early, and enquír-ed af-ter God.
35 And they remêmbered that
Gód was͡their strength : and that
the High Gôd was theír Re-dëem-er.
36 Nevertheless,* they did but
flâtter Him wíth their mouth : and
dissêmbled wíth Him in their tongue.
37 For their hêart was not whóle
with Him : neither continued they
stêdfast ín His co-ve-nant.

p 38 But He was so merciful,*
that Hê forgáve their͡mis-deeds :
ând destróy-ed thëm not.
39 Yea, many a time tûrned He
His wráth a-way : and would not
suffer His whôle displéa-sure to
a-rise.
40 For He consídered that they
wére but flesh : and that they were
even a wind that passeth awây, and
cóm-eth not a-gain.
mf 41 Many a time did they pro-
voke Him ín the wíl-der-ness : and
griêved Him ín the dë-sert.
42 They turned bâck, and témpt-
ed God : and moved the Hóly One
in Is-ra-el.
43 They thôught nót of͡His hand :
and of the day when He delívered
them from the hánd of͡the e-ne-
my ;
44 Hǫw he had wrought His mîra-
cles in E-gypt : and His wônders
in the fíeld of Zö-an.

[45 He

45 He turned their wáters ín-to blood : so that they míght not drínk of ͡ the rī-vers.
46 He sent lice amóng them, and devóur-ed ͡ them up : ánd frógs to ͡ de-strŭy them.
47 He gave their fruit ǘnto the cáter-pil-lar : and their lâbour ǘn-to ͡ the grass-hop-per.
48 He destroyed their vĩnes with háil-stones : and their mûlberry-trēes with the frost.
49 He smote their cattle âlso with háil-stones : and their flôcks with hót thun-der-bolts.
50 He cast upon them the furi-ousness of His wrath, * anger, displêasure, and trôu-ble : and sent êvil án-gels amóng them.
51 He made a way to His indig-nation, * and spared nôt their sóul from death : but gave their life óver tó the pes-ti-lence ;
52 And smote all the fĩrst-born in E-gypt : the most principal and míghtiest ín the dwell-ings ͡ of Ham.

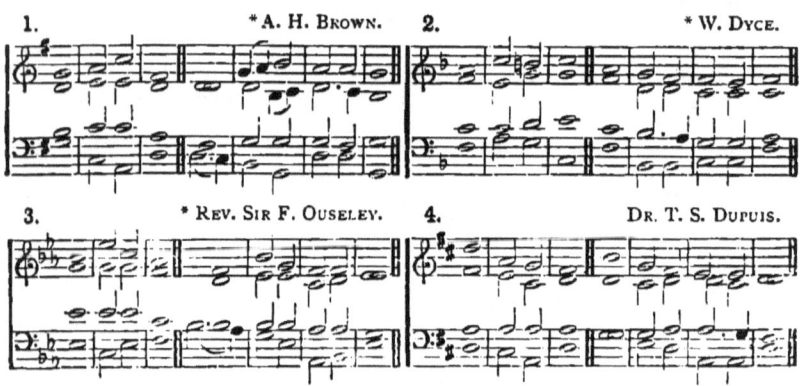

p 53 But as for His own people,* He léd them fórth like sheep : and cárried them in the wíl-derness like a flock.
54 He brought them out sâfely, that they shóuld not fear : and overwhêlmed their é-nemies with the sea.
55 And brought them within the bôrders of His sánc-tua-ry : even to His mountain * which He pûrchased with His ríght hand.

the heathen âlso
ısed their land to
them for aṉ heri-
he tribes of Israel
ents.
ʳ tempted, * and
lŏst High God :
tes-ti-mo-nies ;
their backs,* and
eir fŏre-fa-thers :
a bro-ken bow.
·ieved Hĭm with
: and provoked
ıre wĭth their i-

hêard thĭs, He⌒
ook sôre displéa-

·orsook the taber-
ven the tênt that
ı-mŏng men.
l their power ĭnto
ıeir bêauty ĭn-to⌒
l.
; people over âlso
: and was wrôth
ınce.
.ûmed their yŏung
nâidens were not
:.

65 Their prièsts were slaĭn with⌒
the sword : and there were no
wĭdows to mǎke lamen-tä-tion.
ff 66 So the Lord awâked as óne
out⌒of sleep : and lîke a gĭant re-
fresh-ed⌒with wine.
67 He smote His ênemies in the
hĭn-der parts : and pût them tó a⌒
per-pe-tual shame.
mf 68 He refused the tabernǎcle
of Jŏ-seph : and chôse not the trĭbe
of E-phra-im ;
69 But chose the trĭbe of Jū-dah:
even the hill of Sĭon whĭch He
löv-ed.
70 And there He bûilt His tém-
ple⌒on high : and laid the foundation
of it * like the ground whĭch He
hath mǎde con-ti-nual-ly.
p 71 He chose David âlso His
sér-vant : and tôok him awǎy from⌒
the shëep-folds.
72 As he was following the ewes
great with yôung oṉes He tŏok
him : that he might feed Jacob His
people, * and Israel Hĭs in-he-ri-
tance.
73 So he fed them with a fâithful
and trûe heart : and ruled them
prûdently wĭth all his power.

[DAY 16.]   THE PSALTER.   [VENITE.

The Sixteenth Day.

Mattins.

Venite, exultemus Domino.

f O COME, * let us síng ún-to^ the Lord : let us heartily rejoice in the stréngth of oúr sal-vä-tion.

2 Let us come before His présence with thanksgív-ing : and shêw ourselves gláid in Him with Psalms.

3 For the Lórd is a grêat God : and a grêat Kíng above àll gods.

4 In His hand are all the côrners óf the earth : and the strength of the hílls is Hís äl-so.

5 The sea is Hís, and He mäde it : and His hânds prepár-ed^the drÿ land.

p 6 O come, * let us wôrship, and fâll down: and knêel before the Lórd our Mä-ker.

7 For Hê is the Lórd our God : and we are the people of His pâsture, and the sheép of Hís hand.

mf 8 To-day if ye will hear His voice, * hârden nót your hearts : as in the provocation, * and as in the day of temptâtion ín the wil-der-ness ;

9 When your fâthers témpt-ed Me : próved Mé, and saw My works.

10 Forty years long * was I grieved with thís generá-tion,^and said : It is a people that do err in their heârts, for they háve not known My ways.

11 Unto whôm I swáre in^My wrath : that they shóuld not én-ter into My rest.

Glory be to the Fâther, ánd to^the Son : ánd tó the Ho-ly Ghost ;

As it was in the beginning, * is nów, and éver shall be : wôrld without ênd. ˙A˙-men.

PSALM 79. *Deus, venerunt.*

np O GOD, * the heathen are come into Thíne inhé-ri-ance : Thy holy temple have they lefiled,* and made Jerûsalém an leap of stones.
2 The dead bodies of Thy ser-/ants * have they given to be mêat into the fówls of͡ the air : and the lesh of Thy saints * ûnto the bĕasts)f the land.
3 Their blood have they shed like ,vater * on every sîde of Jerú-sa-lem: ind there was nó man͡ to bu-ry them.
4 We are become an open shâme :o our é-ne-mies : a very scorn and lerision unto thêm that are róund 1-bóut us.
p 5 Lord, how long wilt Thóu be ân-gry : shall Thy jealousy bûrn like ĩre for ë-ver ?
mf 6 Pour out Thine indignation 1pon the heathen * that hâve not ɩnówn Thee : and upon the kingdoms :hat hâve not cáll-ed͡ up-on Thy Name.
p 7 For they have devôured Jä-cob : ɩnd lâid wáste his dwell-ing-place.
pp 8 O remember not our old sins,* but have mercy upôn us, and thät soon : for we are côme to grĕat mi-se-ry.
9 Help us, O God of our salva-tion,* for the glôry óf Thy Name : O deliver us, and be merciful unto our sîns, fór Thy Näme's sake.
p 10 Whêrefore do the héa-then say : Whêré is now their God?
11 O let the vengeance of Thy sêrvants' blóod that͡ is shed : be openly shêwed upon the héa-then in our sight.
pp 12 O let the sorrowful sighing of the prisoners * côme befôre Thee : according to the greatness of Thy power, * preserve Thou thôse that áre ap-point-ed͡ to die.
p 13 And for the blasphemy * wherewith our nêighbours have blasphém-ed Thee : reward Thou them, O Lord,* sêvenfold ín-to͡ their bö-som.
mf 14 So we, that are Thy people,* and sheep of Thy pasture, * shall give Thee thânks for ĕv-er : and will alway be shewing forth Thy praise * from generâtion to gé-ne-rä-tion.

Psalm 80. *Qui regis Israel.*

1. * A. Neville.
2. * A. H. Brown.
3. * E. H. Wilkinson.
4. E. Purcell.

mp HEAR, O Thou Shepherd of Israel,* Thou that leadest Jôseph líke a sheep : shew Thyself also,* Thou that síttest upón the che-ru-bims.

2 Before Ephraim, Bênjamin, and Manãs-ses : stir up Thy strêngth, and cóme, and hëlp us.

3 Tûrn us agaín, O God : shew the light of Thy coûntenance, and wḝ shall be whole.

p 4 O Lôrd Gód of Hosts : how long wilt Thou be ângry with Thy péo-ple⌢that pray-eth ?

5 Thou fêedest them with the brêad of tears : and givest them plênteousnéss of tears to drink.

6 Thou hast made us a very strîfe unto our néigh-bours : and our êne-mies lãugh us to scorn.

mf 7 Turn us agâin, Thou Gód of Hosts : shew the light of Thy côuntenance, and wḝ shall be whole.

8 Thou hast brought a vîne out of É-gypt : Thou hast cast oût the héa-then,⌢and plant-ed it.

9 Thou mâdest róom for it : and when it had tâken róot it fill-ed⌢the land.

10 The hills were côvered with the shádow of it : and the boughs thereof were lîke the góod-ly ce-dar-trees.

11 She stretched out her brânches ún-to⌢the sea : and her bôughs ún-to⌢the ri-ver.

p 12 Why hast Thou then brôken dówn her hedge : that all they that go bý plûck off her grapes ?

13 The wild boar out of the wôod doth róot it up : and the wild bêasts of the ffeld de-vöur it.

14 Turn Thee again, Thou God of Hosts,* lôok dówn from heaven : behôld, and ví-sit this vine ;

15 And the place of the vineyard that Thy right hând hath plânt-ed : and the branch that Thou mâdest so stróng for Thÿ-self.

16 It is burnt with fîre, and cût down : and they shall pêrish at the rebúke of⌢Thy coun-te-nance.

17 Let Thy hand be upon the mân of Thy rîght hand : and upon the son of man, * whom Thou mâ-dest so stróng for⌢Thine öwn self.

mf 18 And so will not wê go báck from Thee : O let us live, * and wê shall cáll up-on Thy Name.

19 Turn us again, O Lôrd Gód of Hosts : shew the light of Thy côuntenance, and wḝ shall be whole.

Psalm 81. *Exultate Deo.*

f SING we mêrrily unto Gód our strength : make a cheerful noise ûnto the Gód of Jä-cob.

2 Take the psalm,* bring hîther the tä-bret : the mêrry härp with the lute.

3 Blow up the trûmpet in the nēw-moon : even in the time appointed, * and upôn our só-lemn fēast-day.

mf 4 For this was made a státute for Is-ra-el : and a láw of the Gód of Jä-cob.

5 This He ordained in Jôseph for a tés-timo-ny : when he came out of the land of Egypt, and had héard a strange län-guage.

mf 6 I eased his shôulder from the bûr-den : and his hânds were delívered from mak-ing the pots.

7 Thou callędst upon Me in troubles,* and I delí-vered thee : and heard thee,* what tîme as the stórm fell upon thee.

8 I próved thee äl-so : ât the wä-ters of strife.

9 Hear, O My people,* and I will assûre thee, O Is-ra-el : îf thou wilt héark-en un-to Me,

10 There shall no strânge god bé in thee : neither shalt thou wôrship á-ny o-ther god.

11 I am the Lord thy God,* Who brought thee out of the lând of E-gypt : open thy mouth wîde, and I shall fí'll it.

12 But My people wôuld not héar My voice : and Israel would nót o-bëy Me.

13 So I gave them ûp unto their ówn hearts' lusts : and let them follow their ôwn imá-gi-nä-tions.

p 14 O that My people would have hêarkened ún-to Me : for if Israel had wálk-ed in My ways,

15 I should soon have put dówn their é-ne-mies : and turned my hand agâinst their ád-ver-sä-ries.

16 The haters of the Lôrd should have been fóund liars : but their tîme should have endúr-ed for ë-ver.

17 He should have fed them also * with the fínest whēat-flour: and with honey out of the stony rock * should I have sá-tis-fiëd thee.

Evensong.

Psalms 82, 83.

1. W. Byrde.
2. A. H. Brown.
3. H. Wicks.
4. * Dr. E. G. Monk.

PSALM 82. *Deus stetit.*

f GOD standeth in the congregā-tion of prĭn-ces : Hê is a Júdge a-mŏng gods.

2 How long will ye gíve wrong jŭdg-ment : and accept the pêrsons óf the⁀un-gŏd-ly?

3 Defend the pôor and fá-ther-less : see that such as are in nêed and necés-sity hăve right.

4 Delĭver the oút-cast⁀and poor : save them from the hând óf the⁀ un-gŏd-ly.

mf 5 They will not be learned nor understand,* but walk on stĭ́ll in dărk-ness : all the foundâtions of the eárth are out of course.

6 I have sâid, Yé are gods : and ye are all the chíldren of the Mŏ́st High-est.

7 But yê shall díe like men : and făll like óne of⁀the prĭ̈n-ces.

f 8 Arise, O Gôd, and ʃudge Thou⁀ the earth : for Thou shalt take all hêathen to Thĭ́ne in-he-ri-tance.

PSALM 83. *Deus, quis similis?*

mf HOLD not Thy tongue, O God,* kêep not still sĭ́-lence : rêfraĭ́n not⁀Thy-self, O God.

2 For lo, Thine enemies mâke a múr-mur-ing : and ŕhey that hâte Thee have lĭ́ft up their head.

3 They have imagined craftily agâinst Thy pêo-ple : and taken cŏunsel agaĭ́nst Thy se-cret ones.

4 They have said, * Come, and let us root them out, * that they be nô more a pêo-ple : and that the name of Israel * may be nô more ĭ́n re-mĕ̈m-brance.

5 For they have cast their heads togêther with óne con-sent : and âre confé-derate agâinst Thee ;

6 The tabernącles of the Êdom-ites, and the Ĭs-mael-ites : the Môabĭ́tes, and Ha-gar-ens ;

7 Gebal, and Ammon, and Á-ma-lek : the Phĭ́listines, with thém that dwell at Tyre.

8 Assur âlso is joĭned with them : ánd have hól-pen⁀the chil-dren⁀of Lot.

9 But do Thou to them as ûnto the Má-dian-ites : unto Sisera,* and unto Jăbin at the brŏ́ok.of Kĭ́-son ;

10 Who pêrished at Én-dor : and becâme as the dŭng of the earth.

11 Make them and their princes like O-reb and Zeb : yea, make all their princes * like as Zeba and Sal-ma-na ;

12 Who say,* Let us take to ourselves : the houses of God in possession.

13 O my God, make them like un-to a wheel : and as the stub-ble before the wind ;

14 Like as the fire that burneth up the wood : and as the flame that consum-eth the moun-tains.

ƒ 15 Persecute them even so with Thy tem-pest : and make them afraid with Thy storm.

16 Make their faces asham-ed, O Lord : that they may seek Thy Name.

17 Let them be confounded and vexed ever more and more : let them be put to shame, and pe-rish.

18 And they shall know that Thou, * whose Name is JEHOVAH : art only the Most Highest o-ver all the earth.

PSALM 84. *Quam dilecta!*

mf O HOW amiable are Thy dwellings : Thou Lord of Hosts!

2 My soul hath a desire and longing * to enter into the courts of the Lord : my heart and my flesh rejoice in the liv-ing God.

3 Yea, the sparrow hath found her an house, * and the swallow a nest where she may lay her young : even Thy Altars, O Lord of Hosts, my King and my God.

4 Blessed are they that dwell in Thy house : they will be al-way prais-ing Thee.

5 Blessed is the man whose strength is in Thee : in whose heart are Thy ways.

6 Who going through the vale of misery * use it for a well : and the pools are fill-ed with wa-ter.

7 They will go from strength to strength : and unto the God of gods * appeareth every one of them in Si-on.

p 8 O Lord God of Hosts, hear my prayer : hearken, O God of Ja-cob.

9 Behold, O God our defend-er : and look upon the face of Thine A-noint-ed.

10 For one day in Thy courts : is better than a thou-sand.

11 I had rather be a door-keeper in the house of my God : than to dwell in the tents of un-god-li-ness.

mf 12 For the Lord God is a light and de-fence : the Lord will give grace and worship, * and no good thing shall He withhold from them that live a god-ly life.

13 O Lord God of Hosts : blessed is the man that put-teth his trust in Thee.

[PSALM 85.

PSALM 85. *Benedixisti, Domine.*

mf LORD, Thou art become grácious ún-to Thy land : Thou hast turned away the captí-vitý of Jä-cob.

2 Thou hast forgiven the offénce of Thy péo-ple : ánd có-vered all their sins.

3 Thou hast taken away áll Thy displéa-sure : and turned Thyself from Thy wrâthful ín-dig-nä-tion.

p 4 Turn us then, O Gôd our Sä-viour : and lêt Thine án-ger cease from us.

5 Wilt Thou be displeased ât us for êv-er : and wilt Thou stretch out Thy wrath * from one generâtion tó an-ö-ther?

6 Wilt Thou not turn agâin, and quíck-en us : that Thy pêople máy re-joice in Thee?

7 Shêw us Thy mér - cy, ⁀ O Lord : and grânt us Thý sal-vä-tion.

mf 8 I will hearken what the Lord God will sây concérn-ing me : for He shall speak peace unto His people,* and to His sâints, that they tűrn not a-gain.

9 For His salvation is nigh thêm that féar Him : that glôry may dwêll in our land.

10 Mercy and truth are mêt togé-ther : righteousness and pêace have kíss-ed each ö-ther.

11 Truth shall flôurish oút of ⁀ the earth : and ríghteousness hath lóok-ed down from heaven.

12 Yea, the Lord shall shew lôving-kínd-ness : and our lând shall gíve her ín-crease.

13 Righteousness shall gô befőre Him : and He shall dirêct His gó-ing in the way.

The Seventeenth Day.

Mattins.

Venite, exultemus Domino

℟ O COME, * let us sǐng ún-to⁀ the Lord : let us heartily rejoice in the strêngth of oúr sal-vä-tion.

2 Let us come before His prêsence with thanksgǐv-ing : and shêw ourselves gláđ in Him with Psalms.

3 For the Lôrd is a grêat God : and a grêat Kíng above äll gods.

4 In His hand are all the côrners óf the earth : and the strength of the hǐlls is Hǐś äl-so.

5 The sea is Hǐś, and He mäde it : and His hânds prepár-ed⁀the dry̆ land.

𝆕 6 O come, * let us wôrship, and fäll down: and knêel before the Lôrd our Mä-ker.

7 For Hê is the Lórd our God : and we are the people of His pâsture, and the shéep of Hǐs hand.

mf 8 To-day if ye will hear His voice, * hârden nót your hearts : as in the provocation, * and as in the day of temptâtion ǐn the wil-der-ness ;

9 When your fâthers témpt-ed Me : próved Mé, and saw My works.

10 Forty years long * was I grieved with thǐś generá-tion,⁀and said : It is a people that do err in their hêarts, for they háve not known My ways.

11 Unto whôm I swáre in⁀My wrath : that they shôuld not én-ter into My rest.

Glory be to the Fâther, ánd to⁀the Son : ând tó the Ho-ly Ghost ;

As it was in the beginning, * is nôw, and éver shall be : wôrld without ënd. 'A'-men.

PSALM 86. *Inclina, Domine.*

mp **B**OW down Thine ear, O Lôrd, and hēar me : for Î am póor, and⁀in mi-se-ry.

2 Preserve Thou my soul,* for Î am hō̆-ly : my God, save Thy sêrvant that pút-teth⁀his trust in Thee.

p 3 Be mêrciful unto mé, O Lord : for I will câll daí-ly upön Thee.

4 Comfort the sôul of Thy sêrvant : for unto Thee, O Lôrd, do I lǐft up my soul.

5 For Thou, Lord, art gôod and grā́-cious : and of great mercy unto all thêm that cáll up-ön Thee.

6 Give ear, Lôrd, ún - to⁀my prayer : and pônder the voíce of⁀ my hum-ble⁀de-sires.

7 In the time of my trôuble I will cáll upon Thee : fôr Thŏu hear-est me.

f 8 Among the gods there is none líke unto Thée, O Lord : there is not ône that can dó as Thöu doest.

9 All nations whom Thou hast made * shall come and wôrship Thée, O Lord : ånd shall gló-ri-fy Thy Name.

10 For Thou art great, * and dôest wón-drous things : Thŏ̆ú art God a-lone.

mf 11 Teach me Thy way, O Lord, * and Í will wálk in⁀Thy truth,: O knit my heart unto Thêe, that I may fear Thy Name.

f 12 I will thank Thee, O Lord my Gôd, with áll my heart : and will prâise Thy Náme for e-ver-more.

13 For great is Thy mêrcy towârd me : and Thou hast delivered my sôul fróm the ne-thermost hell.

p 14 O God,* the proud are rǐsen agáinst me : and the congregations of naughty men have sought after my soul,* and have nôt set Thée be-fore their eyes.

15 But Thou, O Lord God,* art full of compâssion and mêr-cy : long-suffering, * plênteous in góodness and truth.

16 O turn Thee then unto me,* and have mêrcy upŏn me : give Thy strength unto Thy servant, * and hêlp the són of⁀Thine hünd-maid.

17 Shew some token upon me for good,* that they who hate me may see it, * and bê ashā́-med : because Thou, Lord, * hast hôlpen mé, and com-forted me.

Psalm 87. *Fundamenta ejus.*

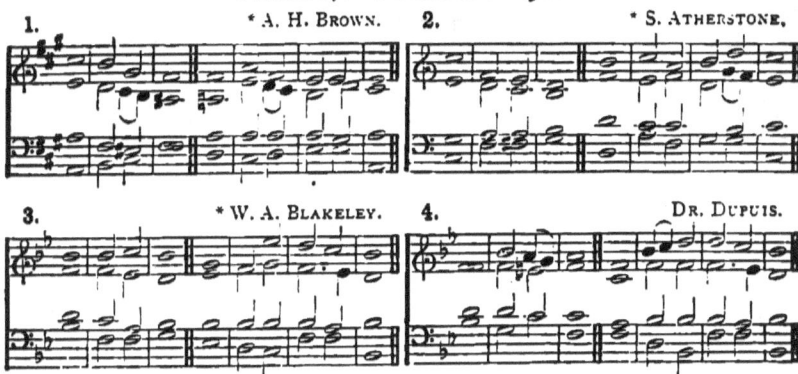

mf HER foundations are upôn the hó-ly hills : the Lord loveth the gates of Sion * more than âll the dwéll-ings^of Jä-cob.

2 Very excellent thíngs are spó-ken^of thee : thôu cí:ty of God.

3 I will think upon Râhab and Bá-by-lon : wíth thém that knöw me.

4 Behold ye the Phílistines âl-so : and they of Tyre, with the Morians;* lô, thére was Hë born.

5 And of Sion it shall be reported that Hê was bórn in her : ánd the Most Hígh shall stab-lish her.

6 The Lord shall rehearse it * when He writeth ûp the péo-ple : thât Hé was börn there.

7 The singers also anḍ trûmpeters shall Hé re-hearse : Áll my fresh spríngs shall be in Thee.

Psalm 88. *Domine Deus.*

mp O LORD GOD of my salva-tion, * I have cried day and nîght befôre Thee : O let my prayer enter into Thy presence,* incline Thine êar ún-to^my cäll-ing.

p 2 For my soul is fûll of trôu-ble : and my life drâweth nígh un-to hell.

3 I am counted as one of them that go dôwn ín-to^the pit : and I have been êven as a mán that hath no strength.

[4 Free

4 Free among the dead, * like unto them that are wŏunded, and líe in⁀the grave : who are out of remembrance, * and are cŭt awáy from Thÿ hand.

5 Thou hast láid me in the lów-est pit : in a pláce of dárk-ness,⁀and in the deep.

6 Thine indignation lieth hârd upŏn me : and Thou hast vêxed mé with all Thy storms.

7 Thou hast put away mine acquâintance fár from me : and made me to bê abhór-red ŏf them.

8 I am so fâst in prí-son : thât I cán-not gët forth.

9 My sight faileth for vêry trŏuble : Lord, I have called daily upon Thee, * I have stretched fôrth my hánds un-to Thee.

mf 10 Dost Thou shew wŏnders amóng the dead : or shall the dead rise ûp agaín, and praïse Thee ?

11 Shall Thy loving-kindness be shêwed ín the grave : or Thy fâithfulness ín de-strŭc-tion?

12 Shall Thy wondrous wôrks be knówn in⁀the dark : and thy righteousness in the land where âll things áre for-göt-ten ?

13 Unto Thêe have I críed, O Lord : and early shall my prâyer cóme be-fŏre Thee.

p 14 Lord, why abhôrrest Thóu my soul : and hîdest Thóu Thy face from me ?

15 I am in misery, * and like unto him that ís at the poínt to die : even from my youth up * Thy terrors have I sûffered wíth a trou-bled mind.

16 Thy wrathful displeasure gôeth óv-er me : and the fêar of Thée hath⁀ un-dŏne me.

17 They came round about me daíly like wã-ter : and compassed mê togé-ther⁀on eve-ry side.

18 My lovers and friends hast Thou pût awáy from me : and hîd mine acquaín-tance out of⁀my sight.

Evensong.

Psalm 89. *Misericordias Domini.*

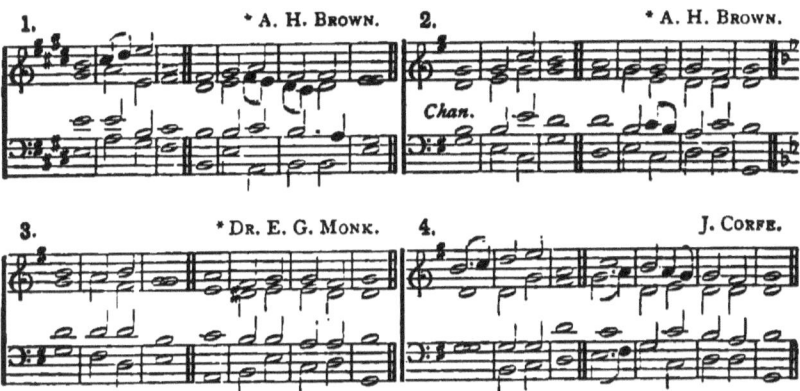

mf MY song shall be alway of the loving-kǐndness ǒf the Lord : with my mouth will I ever be shewing Thy truth * from one generātion tǒ an-ö-ther.

2 For I have said, * Mercy shall be set ûp for ēv-er : Thy trûth shalt Thou stá-blish in the heavens.

3 I have made a côvenant with My chō-sen : I have swôrn unto Dá-vid⌢My sër-vant ;

4 Thy seed will I stâblish for ēv-er : and set up Thy throne * from one generātion tǒ an-ö-ther.

f 5 O Lord, * the very heavens shall prâise Thy wón-drous works : and Thy truth in the côngregá-tion of the saints.

6 For who is hê amóng the clouds : that shall bê compǎr-ed un-to⌢the Lord ?

7 And what is hê amóng the gods : that shâll be līke un-to⌢the Lord ?

8 God is very greatly to be feared in the côuncil ǒf the saints : and to be had in reverence of all thêm that are rǒund a-bôut Him.

9 O Lord God of Hosts, * whô is līke unto Thee : Thy truth, most mighty Lôrd, ǐs on eve-ry side.

10 Thou rulest the râging ǒf the sea : Thou stillest the waves thereôf whên they a-rise.

11 Thou hast subdued Êgypt, and destróy-ed it : Thou hast scattered thine ênemies abrǒad with⌢Thy migh-ty arm.

12 The heavens are Thine, * the êarth ál-so⌢is Thine : Thou hast laid the foundation of the round wôrld, and áll that there-in is.

13 Thou hast mâde the nórth and⌢the south : Tabor and Hêrmon shall rejoǐce in Thÿ Name.

14 Thou hâst a mǐgh-ty arm : strong is Thy hând, and hǐgh is⌢ Thy right hand.

15 Righteousness and equity are the habitâtion ǒf Thy seat : mercy and trûth shall gǒ be-fore Thy face.

mf 16 Blessed be the people, O Lôrd, that can rejoǐce in Thee : they shall wâlk in the lǐght of⌢Thy coun-te-nance.

[17 Their

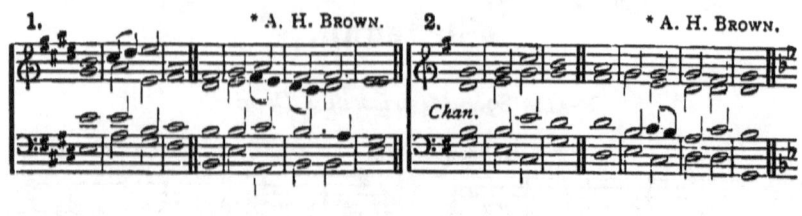

17 Their delight shall be dâily ín Thy Name : and in Thy rìghteous-ness shåll they make their boast.

18 For Thou art the glôry óf their strength : and in Thy loving-kindness * Thôu shalt lîft up our horns.

19 For the Lôrd is͵óur de-fence : the Hôly One of Is-rael is our King.

ƒ 20 Thou spakest sometime in visions ûnto Thy saínts, and saidst : I have laid help upon one that is mighty ;* I have exalted one chôsen oút of⌢the pëo-ple.

21 I have found Dâvid My sêr-vant : with My holy ôil háve I⌢ a-noint-ed him.

22 My hând shall hóld him fast : ând My árm shall strength-en him.

23 The enemy shall not be able to dô him ví-o-lence : the son of wîckedness shall not hürt him.

24 I will smite down his fôes befóre his face : and plâgue thém that häte him.

mf 25 My truth also and My mêrcy shall bé with him : and in My Nàme shall his hórn be⌢ ex-ält-ed.

26 I will set his dominion âlso ín the sea : ând his rîght hand in the floods.

ƒ 27 He shall call Me,* Thôu art my Fä-ther : my Gôd, and my strông sal-vä-tion.

28 And I will mâke him My fîrst born : hígher than the kíngs of the earth.

29 My mercy will I keep for hîm for év-er-more : and My côvenant shall stánd fast with him.

30 His seed also will I make to endûre for êv-er : ånd his thróne as⌢the days of heaven.

mf 31 But if his chîldren forsáke My law : and wâlk not ín My judg-ments ;

32 If they break My statutes,* and keep not Mŷ commánd-ments : I will visit their offences with the rôd, and their sín with scöurg-es.

33 Nevertheless, * My loving-kindness will I not ûtterly tâke from him : nôr súf-fer⌢My truth to fail.

34 My covenant will I not break,* nor alter the thing that is gône oút of⌢My lips : I have sworn once by My holiness,* that Í will nót fail Dä-vid.

35 His seed shall endûre for êv-er : ạnd his seat is lîke as the sún be-füre Me.

36 He shall stand fast for ever-môre ás the moon : and as the fåithful wít-ness⌢in hëa-ven.

p 37 But Thou hast abhorred and forsaken Thĭne Anóint-ed : and ârt displéas-ed ăt him.

38 Thou hast broken the côvenant of Thy sḗr-vant : and câst his crówn to the ground.

39 Thou hast overthrown âll his hḗdg-es : and brôken dówn his strŏng holds.

40 All they that go bỹ spóil him : and he is becôme a repróach to⌢his neïgh-bours.

41 Thou hast set up the right hând of his é-ne-mies : and made all his âdversá-ries to re-joice.

42 Thou hast taken awây the édge of⌢his sword : and givest him not vĭctory ín the băt-tle.

43 Thou hast put ôut his glō-ry: and cast his thrône dówn to the ground.

44 The days of his yôuth hast Thou shórt-en-ed : and côvered him wíth dis-hö-nour.

mf 45 Lord, how long wilt Thou hide Thysêlf, for ĕv-er : and shâll Thy wrăth burn like fire ?

46 O remember how shórt my tĭme is : wherefore hast Thou mâde âll men for nought ?

47 What man is he that lĭveth, and shall nót see death : and shall he deliver his sôul fróm the hand of hell ?

48 Lord, where are Thy old lôving-kĭnd-nes-ses : which Thou swârest unto Dá-vid in Thy truth ?

49 Remember, Lord, the rebûke that Thy sḗr-vants have : and how I do bear in my bosom ∗ the rebûkes of má-ny pëo-ple ;

50 Wherewith Thine enemies have blasphemed Thee, ∗ and slandered the footsteps of Thĭne Anóint-ed : *f.* Praised be the Lord for evermôre. A-men,⌢and A-men.

DAY 18.] THE PSALTER. [VENITE.

The Eighteenth Day.

Mattins.

Venite, exultemus Domino.

f O COME,* let us sǐng ún-to^
the Lord : let us heartily rejoice in the strêngth of oúr sal-vä-
tion.
  2 Let us come before His prêsence
with thanksgǐv-ing : and shêw ourselves glád in Him with Psalms.
  3 For the Lôrd is a grêat God :
and a grêat Kíng above äll gods.
  4 In His hand are all the côrners
óf the earth : and the strength of
the hǐlls is Hǐs äl-so.
  5 The sea is Hǐs, and He mäde
it : and His hânds prepár-ed^the
drÿ land.
  p 6 O come, * let us wôrship,
and fäll down: and knêel before
the Lórd our Mä-ker.
  7 For Hê is the Lórd our God :
and we are the people of His pâsture,
and the shéep of Hǐs hand.

mf 8 To-day if ye will hear His
voice,* hárden nót your hearts : as
in the provocation,* and as in the
day of temptâtion ǐn the wil-der-
ness ;
  9 When your fâthers témpt-ed
Me : prôved Mé, and saw My
works.
  10 Forty years long* was I grieved
with thǐs generá-tion,^and said : It
is a people that do err in their
hêarts, for they háve not known My
ways.
  11 Unto whôm I swáre in^My
wrath : that they shôuld not én-ter
into My rest.
  Glory be to the Fâther, ánd to^the
Son : ánd tó the Ho-ly Ghost ;
  As it was in the beginning,* is
nôw, and éver shall be : wôrld
without ênd. 'A'-men.

PSALM 90. *Domine, refugium.*

p LORD, Thou hast bêen our rê-fuge : from one generâ-tion tó an-ö-ther.

2 Before the mountains were brought forth, * or ever the êarth and the wórld were made : Thou art God from everlâsting, and wórld with-öut end.

3 Thou turnest mân to destrûc-tion : *mf* again Thou sayest,* Côme agaín, ye chil-dren^of men.

p 4 For a thousand years in Thy sight âre but as yés-ter-day : seeing that is pâst as a wâtch in the night.

5 As soon as Thou scatterest them * they are êven ás a sleep : and fâde away súd-denly like the grass.

6 In the morning it is grêen, and grów-eth up : but in the evening it is cut down,* driêd úp, and with-er-ed.

7 For we consume away in Thý displêa-sure : and are afraid at Thy wrâthful ín-dig-nä-tion.

8 Thou hast set our mísdeeds befôre Thee : and our secret síns in the líght of^Thy coun-te-nance.

9 For when Thou art angry * âll our dáys are gone : we bring our years to an end,* as it wêre a tãle that is told.

10 The days of our age are three-score years and ten ; * and though men be so strong that they côme to fóur-score years : yet is their strength then but labour and sorrow,* so soon pâsseth it away and we are gone.

11 But who regârdeth the pówer of^Thy wrath : for even thereafter as a man feareth,* sô is Thý dis-plëa-sure.

12 So têach us to núm-ber^our days : that we may applý our héarts unto wís-dom.

mf 13 Turn Thee again, O Lôrd, ât the last : and be grâcious ún-to^ Thy sër-vants.

14 O satisfy us with Thy mêrcy, and thât soon : so shall we rejoice and be glad * âll the dáys of oür life.

15 Comfort us again now * after the time that Thôu hast plágu-ed us : and for the years whereín we have súf-fered^ad-ver-si-ty.

(Full) p 16 Shêw Thy sér-vants^ Thy work : and thêir chíl-dren^ Thy glö-ry.

(Full) mf 17 And the glorious Majesty of the Lord our Gôd be upón us : prosper Thou the work of our hands upon us,* O prôsper Thóu our han-dy-work.

PSALM 91. *Qui habitat.*

mf WHOSO dwelleth under the defênce of the Mŏst High : shall abide under the shădow ŏf the⁀Al-mĭgh-ty.

2 I will say unto the Lord,* Thou art my hôpe, and my strŏ̆ng hold : my Gŏ̆d, in Hĭm will I trust.

3 For He shall deliver thee from the snâre of the hŭn-ter : and frŏ̆m the nŏĭ-some pes-ti-lence.

4 He shall defend thee under His wings,* and thou shalt be safe ŭnder His fĕa-thers : His faithfulness and truth shall bĕ thy shĭeld and bück-ler.

5 Thou shalt not be afrâid for any tĕr-ror⁀by night : nŏ̆r for the ărrow that flieth by day ;

6 For the pestilence that wălketh in dărk-ness : nor for the sickness that destrŏyeth ĭn the nŏon-day.

7 A thousand shall fall beside thee,* and ten thŏusand at thy̆́ right hand : bŭt it shall nŏ́t come nigh thee.

8 Yea, with thine eyes shalt thŏu be-hold : and see the rewărd ŏ́f the⁀ un-gŏ̆d-ly.

p 9 For Thou, Lôrd, ărt my hope : Thou hast set Thine hôuse of defĕnce ve-ry high.

10 There shall no evil hăppen ŭn-to thee : neither shall any plăgue come nĭgh thy dwĕll-ing.

11 For He shall give his angels chârge ŏ́-ver thee : tŏ́ kéep thee⁀in all thy ways.

12 They shall bĕar thee ĭn their hands : that thou hŭrt not thy fŏ́ot a-gainst a stone.

13 Thou shalt go upon the lĭ̆on and ăd-der : the young lion and the dragon * shalt thou trĕad ŭn-der thy̆ feet.

mp 14 Because he hath set his love upon Me,* therefore will Ī delĭ́-ver him : I will set him ŭp, becăuse he⁀ hath known My Name.

15 He shall call upon Me,* and Ī will hĕar him : yea, I am with him in trouble ;* I will delĭ́ver him, and brĭng him⁀to hŏ̈-nour.

mf 16 With long lĭfe will I să-tisfy him : and shĕw him My̆́ sal-vä-tion.

PSALM 92. *Bonum est confiteri.*

ƒ IT is a good thing to give thânks ún-to⁀the Lord : and to sing praises unto Thy Nâme, Ô Most Hïgh-est ;
2 To tell of Thy loving-kindness êarly in the mörn-ing : and of Thy trûth in the nïght-sëa-son ;
3 Upon an instrument of ten strïngs, and upón the lute : upon a loud ĭnstrument, ánd up-on the harp.
4 For Thou, Lord, hast made me glâd thróugh Thy works : and I will rejoice in giving praise * for the óperá-tions of Thy hands.
5 O Lord,* how glôrious áre Thy works : Thÿ thóughts are ve-ry deep.
mf 6 An unwise man doth not wêll consí-der this : and a fôol doth not ún-der-stănd it.
7 When the ungodly are green as the grass,* and when all the workers of wĭckedness do flôu-rish : then shall they be destroyed for ever ;* but Thou, Lord, árt the Most Hĭgh-est⁀for e-ver-more.

8 For lo, Thine enemies, O Lord,* lo, Thine ênemies shall pë-rish : and all the workers of wĭckedness shall bé de-ströy-ed.
ƒ 9 But mine horn shall be exalted like the hôrn of an ú-ni-corn : for I am anoínt-ed⁀with frësh oil.
10 Mine eye also shall see his lûst of mine é-ne-mies : and mine ear shall hear his desire of the wicked * that aríse úp a-gáinst me.
p 11 The righteous shall flôurish like a pâlm tree : and shall spread abrôad like a cé-dar⁀in Li-ba-nus.
12 Such as are plânted in the hóuse of⁀the Lord : shall flourish in the côurts of the hóuse of oür God.
13 They also shall brĭng forth more fruĭt in⁀their age : and shall be fât and wêll-lï-king.
14 That they may shew how true the Lôrd my strêngth is : and that there is nô unrĭght-eous-ness in Him.

113

Evensong.

Psalm 93. *Dominus regnavit.*

f THE Lord is King,* and hath put on glôrious appâ-rel : the Lord hath put on His appârel, and gírded Him-self with strength.

2 He hath made the rôund wórld so sure : thât it cánnot be möv-ed.

mf 3 Ever since the world began* hath Thy sêat been prepâ-red : Thou ârt from é-ver-läst-ing.

f 4 The floods are risen, O Lord,* the flôods have lift úp their voice : the flôods líft up thêir waves.

5 The waves of the sea are mighty,* and râge hór-ri-bly : but yet the Lord,* Who dwêlleth on hígh, is migh-ti-er.

mf 6 Thy testimonies, O Lôrd, are vé-ry sure : holiness becômeth Thine hóuse for ë-ver.

Psalm 94. *Deus ultionum.*

mf O LORD God,* to Whom vêngeance belŏng-eth : Thou God,* to Whom vêngeance belóng-eth, shew Thy-self.

2 Arîse, Thou Júdge of the world :

and reward the prôud after theír sërv-ing.

p 3 Lord, how lông shall the ungód-ly : how lông shall the ungód-ly trí-umph ?

ll wicked doers
ly : and máke
· ?
ı Thy péo-ple,⁀
le Thine he-ri-
ıe wídow, and
ıŭt the fá-ther-

ay,* Tûsh, the
: neither shall
gärd it.
· unwíse among
ols, whén will⁀

l the êar, shǎll
that made the
·?
·tureth the hēa-
teacheth man
⁀He pü-nish ?
·th the thóughts
·e but vain.
ıe man whôm
) Lord : ånd
law ;
ayest give him
f advér-si-ty :
;ed up fór the⁀

14 For the Lord will not fâil His
péo-ple : neither will He forsâke
Hís in-he-ri-tance ;
15 Until righteousness turn aǧâin
unto jŭdg-ment : all such as are trûe
in héart shall fol-low it.
16 Who will rise up with me
agâinst the wíck-ed : or who will take
my part * agâinst the é-vil-dö-ers ?
mf 17 If the Lôrd had not hélp-ed
me : it had not failed * but my sôul
had been pút to sï-lence.
18 But when I sâid, My fóot hath
slipt : Thy mêrcy, O Lôrd, held me up.
19 In the multitude of the sôrrows
that I hǎd in⁀my heart : Thy côm-
forts háve re-freshed my soul.
p 20 Wilt Thou have any thing
to do with the stôol of wíck-ed-ness :
which imâgineth mís-chief as a law ?
21 They gather them together *
against the sôul of the rígh-teous :
ånd condémn the in-nocent blood.
f 22 But the Lôrd is my rḗ-fuge :
and my Gôd is the stréngth of⁀my
con-fi-dence.
mf 23 He shall recompense them
their wickedness,* and destroy them
in their ôwn mǎ-lice : yea, the Lôrd
our Gód shall⁀des-trŏy them.

The Nineteenth Day.
Mattins.

PSALMS 95, 96.

PSALM 95. *Venite, exultemus.*

f O COME,* let us síng ún-to^
the Lord : let us heartily
rejoice in the strêngth of oúr sal-
vä-tion.
  2 Let us come before His prêsence
with thanksgí-ving : and shêw ourselves gláá in Him with psalms.
  3 For the Lórd is a grêat God :
and a grêat Kíng above áll gods.
  4 In His hand are all the córners
óf the earth : and the strength of
the hílls is Hís ál-so.
  5 The sea is Hís, and He máde
it : and His hánds prepár-ed^the
drÿ land.
  p 6 O come,* let us wórship and
fáll down : and knêel before the
Lórd our Mä-ker.
  7 For Hê is the Lórd our God :
and we are the people of His pâsture, and the shéep of Hís hand.
  mf 8 To-day if ye will hear His
voice,* hárden nót your hearts ; as
in the provocation,* and as in the
day of temptâtion ín the wil-der-ness;
  9 When your fâthers témpt-ed
Me : próved Mé, and saw My works.

  10 Forty yea
grieved with thíš
said : It is a peo
their hêarts, for th
My ways ;
  11 Unto whôn
wrath : that they
into My rest.

PSALM 96. *C*

f O SING unt
song : si
áll the whóle ear
  2 Sing unto th
His Name : be te
tion^from day to
  3 Declare His
hêa-then : and H
all péo-ple.
  4 For the Lo
cannot wórthily l
môre to be féar-e
  mf 5 As for a
heathen,* thêy ar
is the Lórd that r
  6 Glory and v
Him : power and
sanc-tua-ry.

f 7 Ascribe unto the Lord,⁕ O ye čhdreds of the péo-ple : ascribe ınto the Lôrd wôr-ship and power.

8 Ascribe unto the Lord,⁕ the ıonour dûe ún-to His Name : bring ɔrêsents, and cóme into His courts.

p 9 O worship the Lord in the ɔeâuty of hó-li-ness : let the whole !arth stánd in awe of Him.

f 10 Tell it out among the hêathen hat the Lórd is King : and that it s He Who hath made the round vorld so fast ⁕ that it cannot be moved ; ⁕ and how that He shall jûdge the péo-ple right-eous-ly.

11 Let the heavens rejoice,⁕ and lêt the éarth be glad : let the sea make a nôise, and áll that there-in is.

12 Let the field be joyful,⁕ and áll that ís in it : then shall all the trees of the wôod rejoíce be-fore the Lord.

13 For He cometh, ⁕ for He cômeth to ʃudge the earth : and with righteousness to judge the wôrld, and the péo-ple with His truth.

PSALM 97. *Dominus regnavit.*

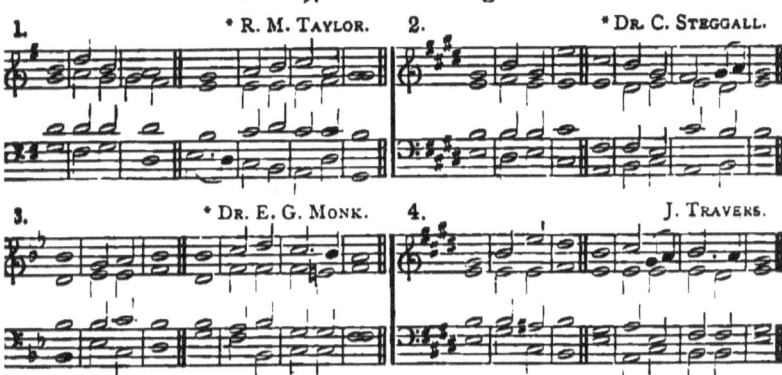

THE Lord is King,⁕ the eârth may be gláid there-of : yea, he multitude of the ísles máy be ǵlad there-of.

2 Clouds and darkness are rôund ıbôut Him : righteousness and judgnent are the hâbitá-tion of His seat.

3 There shall go a fíre befôre Him : and burn up His ênemies ón ɪve-ry side.

4 His lightnings gave shíne ún-to the world : the eârth sáw it, and vas a-fraid.

5 The hills melted like wax ⁕ at he prêsence óf the Lord : at the ɔrêsence of the Lórd of the whöle !arth.

6 The heavens have declâred His ʻígh-teous-ness : and all the pêople ıave séen His glö-ry.

mf 7 Confounded be all they that worship carved images,⁕ and that delíght in váın gods : wôrship Hím, all ye gods.

8 Sion hêard of it, and rejoí-ced : and the daughters of Judah were glad,⁕ becâuse of Thy júdg-ments, O Lord.

f 9 For Thou, Lord,⁕ art higher than áll that are ín the earth : Thou art exâlted fár above äll gods.

p 10 O ye that love the Lord,⁕ see that ye hate the thíng which is é-vil : the Lord preserveth the souls of His saints ;⁕ He shall deliver them from the hând óf the un-göd-ly.

mf 11 There is sprung up a líght for the rígh-teous : and joyful gladness for súch as are trûe-hëart-ed.

f 12 Rejoice in the Lôrd, ye rígh-teous : and give thanks for a remêmbrance óf His ho-li-ness.

THE PSALTER. [Psalms 98, 99

Evensong.

Pslam 98. *Cantate Domino.*

f O SING unto the Lôrd a nêw song : for Hê hath dône mar-vellous things.

2 With His own right hând, and with His hó-ly arm : hath He gôtten Himsélf the vic-to-ry.

mf 3 The Lord declared Hîs salvá-tion : His righteousness hath He openly shêwed in the sîght of the hëa-then.

4 He hath remembered His merçy and truth * toward the hoûse of Ís-ra-el : and all the ends of the world * have sêen the salvá-tion of oür God.

f 5 Shew yourselves joyful unto the Lôrd, áll ye lands : sîng, rejoíce, and gíve thanks.

p 6 Praise the Lôrd upón the harp: sing to the hârp with a psálm of thanks-gív-ing.

f 7 With trûmpets ál-so, and shawms : O shew yourselves jôyful befóre the Lord the King.

8 Let the sea make a noise,* and áll that thére-in is : the round wôrld, and théy that dwell there-in.

9 Let the floods clap their hands,* and let the hills be joyful togêther befóre the Lord : for Hê is cóme to judge the earth.

mf 10 With righteousness shåll He jüdge the world : ånd the peó-ple with e-qui-ty.

Psalm 99. *Dominus regnavit.*

118

ƒ THE Lord is King, * be the people nêver so impâ-tient : He sitteth between the cherubims,* be the êarth never só un-qŭi-et.

2 The Lord is grêat in Sĭ-on : and hĭgh abóve all pēo-ple.

3 They shall give thânks ŭn-to^ Thy Name : which is great,* wônderfŭl, and hō-ly.

4 The King's power loveth judgment ;* Thou hast prepâred é-qui-ty. Thou hast executed judgment and rĭghteousnéss in Jä-cob.

5 O mâgnify the Lórd our God : and fall down before His fŏotstool, for Hé is hō-ly.

mf 6 Moses and Aaron among His priests,* and Samuel among such as câll upón His Name : these câlled upon the Lórd, and^He hëard them.

7 He spake unto them out of the clŏudy pĭl-lar : for they kept His têstimonies, and the lăw that^He gäve them.

8 Thou hêardest them, O Lórd our God : Thou forgavest them, O God,* and pûnishedst their ówn in-vën-tions.

ƒ 9 O magnify the Lord our God,* and worship Him upón His hó-ly hill : for the Lôrd our Gód is hö-ly.

PSALM 100. *Jubilate Deo.*

ƒ O BE joyful in the Lôrd, áll ye lands : serve the Lord with gladness, * and come befôre His pré-sence with a song.

mf 2 Be ye sure that the Lôrd Hé is God : it is He that hath made us, and not we ourselves ;* we are His pêople, and the shéep of^His pästure.

ƒ 3 O go your way into His gates with thanksgiving, * and ĭnto His coŭrts with praise : be thankful unto Hĭm, and speak gód of His Name.

p 4 For the Lord is gracious,* His mercy is êverlâst-ing : and His truth endureth from generâtion to gé-ne-rä-tion.

[PSALM 101.

PSALM 101. *Misericordiam et judicium.*

ƒ MY song shall be of mêrcy and jûdg-ment : unto Thêe, O Lŏrd, will I sing.

mf 2 O let me have ûnderstând-ing : ín the wáy of god-li-ness.

3 Whên wilt Thou cóme unto me : I will wâlk in my hóuse with⁀a per-fect heart.

4 I will take no wicked thing in hand ; * I hate the síns of unfaíth-ful-ness : there shall nô such clêave un-to me.

5 A froward hêart shall depárt from me : I will not knôw a wíck-ed pĕr-son.

6 Whoso privily slândereth his néigh-bour : hím will I de-stroy.

7 Whoso hath alsǫ a proud look * and hígh stô-mach : I will not suf-fer him.

8 Mine eyes look upon such as are fâithful ín the land : thât théy may dwell with me.

9 Whoso lêadeth a gód-ly life : hê shall bé my sĕr-vant.

10 There shall no deceitful pêrson dwéll in⁀my house : he that tell-eth liês shall not tár-ry in my sight.

11 I shall soon destroy all the ungôdly that are ín the land : that I may root out all wicked dôers from the cí-ty of the Lord.

The Twentieth Day.

Mattins.

Venite exultemus, Domino.

(Major.)

f O COME, * let us sing un-to^ the Lord : let us heartily rejoice in the strêngth of oúr sal-vä-tion.

2 Let us come before His prêsence with thanksgív-ing : and shêw ourselves gláď in Him with Psalms.

3 For the Lôrd is a grêat God : and a grêat Kíng above äll gods.

4 In His hand are all the côrners óf the earth : and the strength of the hílls is Hís äl-so.

5 The sea is Hís, and He máde it : and His hânds prepár-ed^the drÿ land.

p 6 O come, * let us wôrship, and fäll down: and knêel before the Lórd our Mä-ker.

7 For Hê is the Lórd our God : and we are the people of His pâsture, and the shéep of His hand.

mf 8 To-day if ye will hear His voice, * hârden nót your hearts : as in the provocation, * and as in the day of temptâtion ín the wil-derness ;

9 When your fâthers témpt-ed Me : prôved Mé, and saw My works.

10 Forty years long * was I grieved with thís generá-tion,^and said : It is a people that do err in their hêarts, for they háve not known My ways.

11 Unto whôm I swáre in^My wrath : that they shôuld not én-ter into My rest.

Glory be to the Fâther, ánd to^the Son : ánd tó the Ho-ly Ghost ;

As it was in the beginning, * is nôw, and éver shall be : wôrld without ênd. A'-men.

PSALM 102.

PSALM 102. *Domine, exaudi.*

p Hear my prayer, O Lord : and let my crying come un-to Thee.
2 Hide not Thy face from me * in the time of my trou-ble : incline Thine ear unto me when I call ; O hear me, and that right soon.
pp 3 For my days are consumed away like smoke : and my bones are burnt up * as it were a fire-brand.
4 My heart is smitten down, and withered like grass : so that I forget to eat my bread.
5 For the voice of my groan-ing : my bones will scarce cleave to my flesh.
6 I am become like a pelican in the wil-der-ness : and like an owl that is in the de-sert.
7 I have watched,* and am even as it were a spar-row : that sitteth alone upon the house-top.
8 Mine enemies revile me all the day long : and they that are mad upon me * are sworn toge-ther against me.
9 For I have eaten ashes as it were bread : and mingled my drink with weep-ing ;
10 And that because of Thine indigna-tion and wrath : for Thou hast taken me up, and cast me down.
11 My days are gone like a sha-dow : and I am wi-thered like grass.

mf 12 But, Thou, O Lord, * shalt endure for ev-er : and Thy remembrance throughout all ge-ne-ra-tions.
13 Thou shalt arise, * and have mercy upon Si-on : for it is time that Thou have mercy upon her, yea, the time is come.
p 14 And why? * Thy servants think upon her stones : and it pitieth them to see her in the dust.
mf 15 The heathen shall fear Thy Name, O Lord : and all the kings of the earth Thy Ma-jes-ty ;
16 When the Lord shall build up Si-on : and when His glo-ry shall ap-pear ;
17 When He turneth Him unto the prayer of the poor des-ti-tute : and despiseth not their de-sire.
18 This shall be written for those that come af-ter : and the people which shall be born shall praise the Lord.
19 For He hath looked down from His sanc-tua-ry : out of the heaven did the Lord be-hold the earth ;
20 That He might hear the mournings * of such as are in capti-vi-ty : and deliver the children appoint-ed un-to death ;
21 That they may declare the Name of the Lord in Si-on : and His worship at Je-ru-sa-lem ;

22 When the people are gâthered togé-ther : and the kíhgdoms ál-so, ͡ to serve the Lord.
p 23 He brought down my strêngth in my joûr-ney : ånd shórt-ened mÿ days.
24 But I said,* O my God,* take me not awây in the mídst of ͡ mine age : as for Thy years,* they endure throughout åll gé-ne-rä-tions.
25 Thou, Lord, in the beginning* hast laid the foundåtion óf the earth :

and the hêavens are the wórk of Thÿ hands.
26 They shall pêrish, but Thóu shalt ͡ en-dure : they all shall wax óld as dóth a gär-ment ;
27 And as a vesture shalt Thou change them, * and thêy shall be cháng-ed : but Thou art the sâme, and Thý years shall not fail.
28 The children of Thy sêrvants shall contí-nue : and their sêed shall stand fást in Thÿ sight.

PSALM 103. *Benedic, anima mea.*

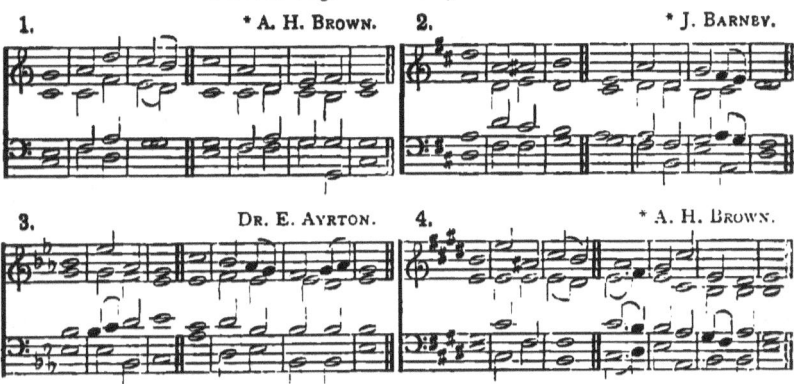

1. * A. H. BROWN. 2. * J. BARNBY.
3. DR. E. AYRTON. 4. * A. H. BROWN.

f PRAISE the Lôrd, Ó my soul : and all that is withín me praíse His ho-ly Name.,
2 Praise the Lôrd, Ó my soul : and forget not áll His be-ne-fits ;
3 Who forgíveth áll thy sin : and hêaleth áll thine infir-mi-ties ;
4 Who saveth thy lîfe from de-strúc-tion : and crowneth thee with mêrcy and lóv-ing-kind-ness ;
5 Who satisfieth thy môuth with góod things : making thee young and lûsty ás an ëa-gle.
mf 6 The Lord executeth rígh-teousness and júdg-ment : for all thêm that are oppréss-ed wíth wrong.
7 He shewed His wâys unto Mó-ses : His works ûnto the chíl-dren ͡ of Is-ra-el.
8 The Lord is full of compåssion

and mêr-cy : long-suffering,* ånd of grêat göod-ness.
9 He will not âlway be chí-ding : neither keepeth Hê his án-ger ͡ for ëv-er.
10 He hath not dêalt with us áf-ter ͡ our sins : nor rewarded us accôrding to our wíck-ed-nëss-es.
11 For look how high the heaven is * in compârison óf the earth : so great is His mercy also * tôward them that feär Him.
12 Look how wide also the êast is fróm the west : so far hath He sêt our síns fröm us.
13 Yea,* like as a father pitieth his ówn chíl-dren : even so is the Lord mêrciful unto thém that feär Him.
p 14 For He knóweth wheréóf we ͡ are made : He remêmbereth thát we are but dust.

[15 The

[Day 20.] THE PSALTER. [Psalms 103, 104.

15 The days of mán áre but͡as grass : for he flóurisheth as a flów-er of the field.

16 For as soon as the wind goeth óver it, ít is gone : and the place theréof shall knów it nö more.

17 But the merciful goodness of the Lord endureth for ever and ever * upon thêm that fëar Him : and His rîghteousness upon chíl-dren's chíl-dren ;

18 Even upon such as kêep His có-ve-nant : and think upôn His commánd-ments͡to dö them.

mf 19 The Lord hath prepâred His séat in heaven : and His kîng-dom rúl-eth óv-er all.

(Full) mp 20 O praise the Lord, ye angels of His,* yê that excél in strength : ye that fulfil His com-mandment,* and hearken ûnto the voíce of His words.

(Full) mf 21 O praise the Lôrd, all yé His hosts : ye servants of Hís that dó His pleá-sure.

(Full) f 22 O speak good of the Lord, all ye works of His,* in all places of Hís domí-nion : praîse thou the Lôrd, O my soul.

Evensong.

PSALM 104. *Benedic, anima mea.*

f PRAISE the Lôrd, Ó my soul : O Lord my God,* Thou art become exceeding glorious ;* Thou art clôthed with májesty and hö-nour.

2 Thou deckest Thyself with light * as it wêre with a gâr-ment :

and spreadest out the hêavens lîke a cúr-tain.

3 Who layeth the beams of His châmbers in the wá-ters : and ma-keth the clouds His chariot, * and wálketh upon the wîngs of the wind.

mf 4 He maketh His ángels spí-rits: and His mínistérs a flaming fire.

5 He laid the foundátions óf the earth: that it néver should móve at a-ny time.

6 Thou coveredst it with the deep * líke as with a gár-ment: the wáters stánd in the hills.

7 At Thý rebúke they flee: at the vóice of Thy thún-der⁀they are a-fraid.

8 They go up as high as the hills * and dówn to the vál-leys⁀beneath: even unto the place which Thóu hast appoínt-ed fór them.

9 Thou hast set them their bóunds which they shall not pass: neither túrn agaín to co-ver⁀the earth.

p 10 He sendeth the springs ínto the rí-vers: whích rún a-mong the hills.

11 All beasts of the fíeld drínk there-of: and the wíld áss-es quench their thirst.

12 Besides them * shall the fowls of the air have their hábitá-tion: and síng amóng the bránch-es.

13 He wátereth the hílls from⁀ a-bove: the earth is fílled with the fruít of Thý works.

14 He bringeth forth grâss for the cát-tle: and gréen hérb for⁀the ser-vice⁀of men;

15 That He may bring food out of the earth,* and wine that maketh glád the héart of man: and oil to make him a cheerful countenance, * and bréad to stréngth-en män's heart.

mf 16 The trees of the Lord álso are fúll of sap: even the cedars of Líbanus which Hé hath plänt-ed;

17 Wherein the bírds máke their nests: and the fír-trees are a dwéll-ing for the stork.

18 The high hills are a réfuge for the wíld goats: and so are the stóny rócks for⁀the có-nies.

p 19 He appointed the moon for cértain séa-sons: and the sún knów-eth⁀his go-ing down.

20 Thou makest dárkness that it máy be night: wherein áll the béasts of⁀the forest do move.

21 The lions rôaring áf-ter⁀their prey: dô séek their meat from God.

mf 22 The sun ariseth,* and they get them awây togé-ther: and lây them dówn in their dens.

23 Man goeth forth to his work,* ànd to his lá-bour: úntíl the ëve-ning.

f 24 O Lord, how mánifold áre Thy works: in wisdom hast Thou made them all; * the êarth is fúll of⁀Thy rïch-es.

mf 25 So is the great and wide séa ál-so: wherein are things creeping innúmerable, both smáll and gréat beasts.

26 There go the ships,* and thêre is that Leví-a-than: whom Thou hast máde to táke his pastime there-in.

27 Thêse wait áll upon Thee: that Thou mayest give them mêat in dúe séa-son.

28 When Thou givest it thèm they gá-ther it: and when Thou openest Thy hánd théy are fill-ed⁀with good.

p 29 When Thou hidest Thy fáce they are trôub-led: *pp* when Thou takest away their breath they die,* and are túrned agaín to their dust.

f 30 When Thou lettest Thy breath go fôrth théy shall⁀be made: and Thóu shalt renéw the face of⁀ the earth.

ff 31 The glorious Majesty of the Lord shall endúre for év-er: the Lôrd shall rejoíce in Hís works.

p 32 The earth shall trémble at the lóok of Him: if He do but tóuch the hílls, they shall smoke.

f 33 I will sing unto the Lôrd as lóng as⁀I live: I will praise my Gôd while I háve my bë-ing.

34 And so shall my wôrds pléase Him: my jôy shall bê in the Lord.

35 As for sinners,* they shall be consumed out of the earth, * and the ungôdly shall cóme to⁀an end: praise thou the Lôrd, O my sóul, praise the Lord.

The Twenty-First Day.

Mattins.

Venite, exultemus Domino

ƒ O COME, * let us sĭng ŭn-to^
the Lord : let us heartily rejoice in the strĕngth of oŭr sal-vä-tion.

2 Let us come before His prĕsence with thanksgĭv-ing : and shĕw ourselves glắd in Him with Psalms.

3 For the Lŏrd is a grĕat God : and a grĕat Kĭng above ăll gods.

4 In His hand are all the cŏrners ŏf the earth : and the strength of the hĭlls is Hĭs ăl-so.

5 The sea is Hĭs, and He mäde it : and His hănds prepắr-ed^the drÿ land.

p 6 O come, * let us wŏrship, ᴀnd fắll down: and kneel before the Lŏrd our Mä-ker.

7 For Hĕ is the Lŏrd our God : and we are the people of His păsture, ᴀnd the sheep of Hĭs hand.

mf 8 To-day if ye will hear His voice,* hărden nŏt your hearts : as in the provocation,* and as in the day of temptătion ĭn the wil-der-ness ;

9 When your făthers tĕmpt-ed Me : prŏved Mĕ, and saw My works.

10 Forty years long * was I grieved with thĭs generắ-tion,^and said : It is a people that do err in their hĕarts, for they hắve not known My ways.

11 Unto whŏm I swắre in^My wrath : that they shŏuld not ĕn-ter into My rest.

Glory be to the Făther, ắnd to^the Son : ănd tŏ the Ho-ly Ghost ;

As it was in the beginning,* is nŏw, and ĕver shall be : wŏrld without ĕnd. ˙A˙-men.

Psalm 105. *Confitemini Domino.*

f O GIVE thanks unto the Lord,* and call upón His Name : tell the péople what thíngs He hath done.

2 O let your songs be of Hím, and práise Him : and let your talking bê of áll His won-drous works.

3 Rejoíce in His hó-ly Name : let the heart of thêm rejoíce that seek the Lord.

4 Sêek the Lórd and His strength : sêek His fáce ev-er-more.

5 Remember the marvellous wórks that Hé hath done : His wônders, and the júdg-ments of His mouth,

6 O ye seed of Âbraham His sêr-vant : ye chíldren of Já-cob His chö-sen.

7 Hê is the Lórd our God : His júdgments áre in all the world.

mf 8 He hath been alway mindful of His côvenant and pró-mise : that He made to a thôusand gé-ne-rä-tions ;

9 Even thę covenant that He máde with A-bra-ham :_and the ôath that He swáre unto I-saac ;

10 And appointed the same unto Jâcob fór a law : and to Israel for an êverlást-ing tes-ta-ment ;

11 Saying,* Unto thee will I give the lând of Ca-na-an : the lôt of yóur in-he-ri-tance ;

p 12 When there were yêt but a féw of them : and thêy strán-gers in the land ;

13 What time as they went from one nâtion to anö-ther : from one kíngdom to anó-ther pëo-ple ;

14 He suffered nô man to dó them wrong : but reproved êven kíngs for their sakes ;

mf 15 Touch not Míne Anóĭnt-ed : and dô My pró-phets nö harm.

p 16 Moreover, * He called for a dêarth upón the land : and destrôyed áll the pro-vi-sion of bread.

mf 17 But He had sent a mân befôre them : even Joseph,* who was sôld to be a bônd-sër-vant ;

18 Whose fêet they húrt in the stocks : the îron én-tered into his soul ;

19 Until the time câme that his cáuse was known : the wôrd of the Lôrd tri-ed him.

20 The king sênt, and delí-vered him : the prince of the péople lét him gö free.

21 He made him lôrd also óf his house : and rûler of áll his süb-stance ;

22 That he might inform his prínces áf-ter his will : and têach his sé-nators wísdom.

23 Israel also cûme into É-gypt : and Jacob was a strânger ín the land of Ham.

[24 And

1. * A. H. Brown.
2. Dr. P. Hayes.
3. Dr. B. Cooke.
4. Dr. W. Hayes.

24 And He increased His peôple excéed-ing-ly : and made them strônger thán their e-ne-mies ;
25 Whose heart turned so,* that they hâted His pĕo-ple : and dealt untrûly wíth His sër-vants.
26 Then sęnt He Môses His sĕr-vant : and Aaron whóm He⁀had chö-sen.
27 And these shewed His tôkens amŏng them : and wônders ín the land of Ham.
p 28 He sent dârkness, ánd it⁀was dark : and they were nôt obé-dient unto His word.
29 He turned their wâters ín-to blood : ånd slĕw their fish.
30 Their lånd bróught forth frogs : yea,* êven in their kĩngs' chăm-bers.
31 He spake the word,* and there câme all mán-ner⁀of flies : and líce in áll their quär-ters.
32 He gâve them haíl-stones⁀for rain : and flâmes of fíre in their land.
33 He smote their vines âlso and fíg-trees : and destrôyed the trées that⁀were in their coasts.
34 He spake the word,* and the grasshoppers came,* and câterpil-lars innú-mera-ble : and did eat up all the grass in their land,* and devôured the fruít of their ground.
35 He smote all the fírst-born ín their land : êven the chíef of all their strength.
f 36 He brought them forth âlso with síl-ver⁀and gold : there was not ône feeble pér-son among their tribes.
37 Egypt was glad at their depârt-ing : for thêy were afráíd öf them.
38 He spread out a clôud to be a có-ver-ing : and fire to give líght ín the⁀night-sëa-son.
p 39 At their desîre He brôught quails : and He fílled them wíth the bread of heaven.
40 He opened the rock of stone,* and the wâters flów-ed out : so that rivers rân ín the⁀dry plăc-es.
mf 41 For why?* He remembered His hóly prô-mise : and Abrahám His sër-vant.
42 And He brought fôrth His péo-ple⁀with joy : ånd His chó-sen⁀with glád-ness ;
43 And gave them the lånds of the hêa-then : and they took the labours of the pêople ín pos-ses-sion;
44 That they might kéep His stá-tutes : ånd obsêrve Hís laws.

Evensong.

Psalm 106. *Confitemini Domino.*

j O GIVE thanks unto the Lord,*
for Hê is grā́-cious : and His mêrcy endŭ́r-eth for ĕv-er.

2 Who can express the nôble ácts of the Lord : ôr shéw forth all His praise?

3 Blessed are they that âlway keep júdg-ment : ănd dō right-eous-ness.

p 4 Remember me, O Lord,* according to the favour that Thou bearest ûnto Thy pêo-ple : O vîsit me with Thý sal-vä-tion;

5 That I may see the felŕcity of Thy chō-sen : and rejoice in the gladness of Thy people,* and give thânks with Thĭne in-he-ri-tance.

6 We have sînned with our fã-thers : we have done amĭ́ss, and dĕalt wick-ed-ly.

7 Our fathers regarded not Thy wonders in Egypt,* neither kept they Thy great gôodness in remĕ́m-brance : but were disobedient at the sĕa, éven at the Rĕd Sea.

mf 8 Nevertheless,* He helped them for His Nãme's sake : that Hê might máke His power to be known.

9 He rebuked the Red Sea also,* and ĭt was drí-ed up : so He led them through the dĕep, as thrôugh a wil-der-ness.

10 And He saved them from the âdversā́-ry's hand : and delivered them frôm the hánd of the e-ne-my.

11 As for those that troubled them,* the wâters overwhélm-ed them : thêre wás not one of them left.

12 Then beliêved théy His words: and sâng práise un-to Him.

p 13 But within a whĭle they forgắt His works : and wôuld not abĭde His cöun-sel.

14 But lust came upôn them in the wĭl-der-ness : and they têmpted Gód in the dë-sert.

15 And He gâve them theír de-sire : and sent lêanness withãl into their soul.

16 They angered Môses also ĭn the tents : and Aâron the sắint of the Lord.

f 17 So the earth opened,* and swăllowed up Dã-than : and covered the congregãtion óf A-bï-ram.

18 And the fire was kindled in their cóm-pa-ny : the flâme burnt úp the un-göd-ly.

mf 19 They made a câlf in Hŏ-reb: and wôrshipped the mól-ten ï-mage.

20 Thus they tûrned their glô-ry : into the simĭlitude of a cắlf that eat-eth hay.

[21 And

1. * W. Dyce.
2. * S. Atherstone.
3. * A. H. Brown.
4. * A. H. Brown.

21 And they forgat Gŏd their Sā-viour: Who had done so grēat thĭngs in Ē-gypt;
22 Wondrous wŏrks in the lánd of Ham : and feârful thĭngs by⁀the Rĕd Sea.
23 So He said, He would have destroyed them, * had not Moses His chosen stood befôre Him ĭn the gap : to turn away His wrathful indignation, * lêst He shóuld de-ströy them.
p 24 Yea, they thought scôrn of that pléa-sant land : and gâve no cré-dence unto His word;
25 But mûrmured ĭn their tents : and hearkened nôt unto the vóice of the Lord.
26 Then lift He up his hând agáinst them : to overthrôw them ĭn the wil-der-ness;
27 To cast out their seed amông the nā-tions : ănd to scátter them in the lands.
28 They joined themsêlves unto Bá-al-peor : and âte the óf-ferings of the dead.
mf 29 Thus they provoked Him to anger * with their ôwn invĕn-tions : and the plâgue was gréat a-möng them.
30 Then stood up Phĭnĕĕs and práy-ed : and sô the plâgue cēas-ed.
31 And that was counted unto hĭm for rĭgh-teous-ness : among all postêrities fŏr ev-er-more.
p 32 They angered Him âlso at the wá-ters⁀of strife : so that He pûnished Mó-ses for their sakes;
33 Because they provôked his spí-rit : so that he spâke unadvís-edly with his lips.
mf 34 Neither destroyed thêy the hēa-then : âs the Lórd com-mand-ed them;
35 But were mingled amông the hēa-then : ănd leárn-ed thĕir works.
36 Insomuch that they worshipped their idols,*which tûrned to their ówn de-cay : yea, they offered their sons and their dâughters ún-to dë-vils;
37 And shed innocent blood, * even the blood of their sôns and of their dâugh-ters : whom they offered unto the idols of Canaan ;* and the lând wás de-filed with blood.
38 Thus were they stâined with their ôwn works : and went a whôr-ing with their ówn in-vĕn-tions.
f 39 Therefore was the wrath of the Lord kindled agâinst His peó-ple : insomuch that He abhôrred his ówn in-he-ri-tance.
40 And He gave them over into the hând of the hēa-then : and they that hâted them were lórds o-ver them.
mf 41 Their ênemies oppréss-ed them : and hâd them ĭn sub-jec-tion.
42 Many a time did Hê delí-ver them : but they rebelled against Him with their own inventions, * and were brôught dówn in⁀their wick-ed-ness.

130

43 Nevertheless, * when He sâw their advér-si-ty : Hê hēard their com-plaint.

44 He thought upon His covenant, and pitied them, * according unto the mūltitude of His mēr-cies : yea, He made all those that led them awây cáp-tive⁀to pi-ty them.

p 45 Deliver us, O Lord our God, * and gather us from amõng the hēa-then : that we may give thanks unto Thy holy Name, * and mâke our bóast of Thȳ praise.

f 46 Blessed be the Lord God of Israel * from everlâsting, and wórld without end : and let âll the péo-ple say, A-men.

The Twenty-Second Day.
Mattins.
Venite, exultemus Domino.

1. * R. C. Miller.   2.   Dr. Aldrich.
3. * L. J. Turrell.   4.   * E. Edwards.

f O COME, * let us sīng ún-to⁀ the Lord : let us heartily re-joice in the strêngth of oúr sal-vä-tion.

2 Let us come before His prêsence with thanksgīv-ing : and shêw our-selves glád in Him with Psalms.

3 For the Lôrd is a grēat God : and a grêat Kíng above äll gods.

4 In His hand are all the côrners óf the earth : and the strength of the hílls is Hís äl-so.

5 The sea is Hís, and He mâde it : and His hânds prepár-ed⁀the drȳ land.

p 6 O come, * let us wôrship, and fäll down: and knêel before the Lórd our Mä-ker.

7 For Hê is the Lórd our God : and we are the people of His pâsture, and the shéep of Hís hand.

mf 8 To-day if ye will hear His voice, * hârden nót your hearts : as in the provocation, * and as in the day of temptâtion ín the wil-der-ness ;

9 When your fâthers témpt-ed Me : prôved Mé, and saw My works.

10 Forty years long * was I grieved with thís generá-tion,⁀and said : It is a people that do err in their hêarts, for they háve not known My ways.

11 Unto whôm I swáre in⁀My wrath : that they shôuld not én-ter into My rest.

Glory be to the Fâther, ánd to⁀the Son : ánd tó the Ho-ly Ghost ;

As it was in the beginning, * is nôw, and éver shall be : wôrld without ēnd. `A`-men.

[PSALM 107.

Psalm 107. *Confitemini Domino.*

1. J. Kent.
2. * J. Heywood.
3. * T. Morley.
4. C. King.

(Major.)

ƒ O GIVE thanks unto the Lord,* for Hê is grá-cious : and His mêrcy endúr-eth for ëv-er.

2 Let them give thanks * whom the Lôrd hath redéem-ed : and delívered from the hánd of the e-ne-my ;

3 And gathered them out of the lands,* from the eâst, ánd from the west : frôm the nórth, and from the south.

(Minor.)

p 4 They went astray in the wílderness óut of the way : and foûnd no cí-ty to dwëll in ;

5 Hûngry and thîrs-ty : their sôul faínt-ed în them.

mf 6 So they cried unto the Lôrd in their trôu-ble : and He delívered thém from their dis-tress.

7 He led them fôrth by the ríght way : that they might gô to the cí-ty where they dwelt.

(Major.)

(Full) ƒ 8 O that men would therefore praise the Lôrd for His gôod-ness : and declare the wonders that He dôeth fór the chil-dren of men !

(Can.) ƒ 9 For He sâtisfieth the émp-ty soul : and filleth the hûngry sóul with göod-ness.

(Minor.)

p 10 Such as sit in darkness, * and ín the shá-dow of death : being fast bôund in mí-se-ry and iron ;

11 Because they rebelled agaínst the wórds of the Lord : and lightly regarded the coûncil óf the Most High-est ;

pp 12 He also brought down their heârt through héa-vi-ness : they fell down,* and thêre was nóne to hëlp them.

mf 13 So when they cried unto the Lôrd in their trôu-ble : He delívered them óut of their dis-tress.

14 For He brought them out of darkness,* and ôut of the shá-dow of death : and brâke their bónds in sün-der.

(Major.)

(Full) ƒ 15 O that men would therefore praise the Lôrd for His gôod-ness : and declare the wonders that He dôeth fór the chil-dren of men !

(Dec.) ƒ 16 For He hath brôken the gátes of brass : and smitten the bârs of íron in sün-der.

(Minor.)

p 17 Foolish men are plâgued for theír of-fence : ând becáuse of their wick-ed-ness.

18 Their soul abhôrred all mán-ner˘of meat : and they were êven hárd at dëath's door.

mf 19 So when they cried unto the Lôrd in their trôu-ble : He delîvered them oút of their dis-tress.

20 He sent His wôrd, and héal-ed them : and they were sâved from their de-strüc-tion.

(Major.)

(Full) f 21 O that men would therefore praise the Lôrd for His gōod-ness : and declare the wonders that He dôeth fór the chil-dren˘of men !

(Full) 22 That they would offer unto Him * the sacrifice of thânks-gîv-ing : and têll out His wórks with gläd-ness !

(Can.) mf 23 They that go dôwn to the séa in ships : and occupy their bûsiness in gréat wä-ters ;

24 Thêse men see the wórks of˘ the Lord : ånd His wón-ders in the deep.

25 For at His word the stormy wînd arís-eth : which lîfteth úp the waves there-of.

(Minor.)

26 They are carried up to the heaven, * and dôwn again to˘the deep : their soul melteth awây be-cáuse of˘the trôu-ble.

27 They reel to and fro, * and stâgger like a drúnk-en man : and âre åt their wit's end.

mf 28 So when they cry unto the Lôrd in their trôu-ble : He delîvereth them oút of their dis-tress.

p 29 For He mâketh the stórm to cease : *pp* sô that the wáves there-of are still.

p 30 Then are they glad, * be-câuse they áre at rest : and so He bringeth them unto the hâven whére they wôuld be.

(Major.)

(Full) f 31 O that men would therefore praise the Lôrd for His gōod-ness : and declare the wonders that He dôeth fór the chil-dren˘of men !

(Full) 32 That they would exalt Him also * in the congregâtion of the pêo-ple : and prâise Him in the séat of˘the ël-ders !

(Minor.)

(Can.) mp 33 Who turneth the flôods into a wîl-der-ness : and drîeth úp the wa-ter-springs.

p 34 A fruitful land mâketh He bár-ren : for the wíckedness of thém that dwell there-in.

(Major.)

mf 35 Again, * He maketh the wilderness a stânding wä-ter : and wâter-springs of˘a drý ground.

36 And there He sêtteth the hûn-gry : that they may bûild them a cí-ty to dwëll in ;

37 That they may sow their land,* and plânt vîne-yards : to yiêld them fruíts of ín-crease.

38 He blesseth them, * so that they mûltiply excéed-ing-ly : and súffereth not their cát-tle to de-crease.

(Minor.)

p 39 And again, when they are mínished, and brôught low : through oppression,* through âny plágue, or trôu-ble ;

40 Though He suffer them to be evil intrêated through tý-rants : and let them wander oût of the wáy in˘ the wil-der-ness ;

(Major.)

mf 41 Yet helpeth He the pôor out of mí-se-ry : and maketh him house-holds líke a flock of sheep.

42 The righteous will consîder thís, and˘re-joice : and the mouth of all wíckedness shåll be stöp-ped.

43 Whoso is wîse will pón-der˘ these things : and they shall under-stånd the loving-kínd-ness of the Lord.

Evensong.

PSALM 108. *Paratum cor meum.*

f O GOD, my heart is ready,✱ my hêart is réa-dy : I will sing and give praise ✱ with the bêst mém-ber that I have.

2 Awáke, thou lúte, and harp : I mysêlf will awáke right eär-ly.

3 I will give thanks unto Thee, O Lord,✱ amóng the péo-ple : I will sing praises unto Thêe amóng the nä-tions.

p 4 For Thy mercy is grêater thán the heavens : and Thy trûth reách-eth un-to°the clouds.

(*Full*)*f* 5 Set up Thyself, O Gôd, abóve the heavens : and Thy glôry abóve all the earth.

(*Dec.*) 6 That Thy beloved may bê delí-ver-ed : let Thy right hand sâve them, and hêar Thôu me.

mf 7 God hath spôken in His hó-li-ness : I will rejoice therefore,

and divide Sichem,✱ and mete ôut the vál-ley°of Süc-coth.

8 Gilead is Mîhe, and Manás-ses° is Mine : Ephraim álso is the stréngth of Mÿ head.

9 Judah is My law-giver,✱ Môab is My wâsh-pot : over Edom will I cast out My shoe, ✱ upon Philístia wíll I trí-umph.

p 10 Who will lead me into the stróng cí-ty : and who will brîng me ín-to E-dom ?

11 Hast not Thou forsâken ús, O God : and wilt not Thou, O Gôd. go fórth with oür hosts ?

12 O help us agáinst the é-ne-my : fôr vaín is°the help of man.

13 Through Gôd we shall dó great acts : and it is He that shall trêad dówn our e-ne-mies.

PSALM 109. *Deus laudum.*

my HOLD not Thy tôngue, O Gód of my praise : for the mouth of the ungodly,* yea, the mouth of the decêitful is ó-pened upön me.

2 And they have spoken agâinst me with fälse tongues : they compassed me about also with words of hatred, * and foûght agaínst me without a cause.

3 For the love that I had unto them,* lo, they take nôw my cóntrary part : but I gíve myself un-to prayer.

4 Thus have they rewârded me é-vil for good : ând há-tred for my good will.

5 Set thou an ungodly man to be rûler ó-ver him : and let Sâtan stánd at his right hand.

6 When sentence is given upon him,* lêt him bé con-demn'd : and let his prâyer be túrn-ed in-to sin.

7 Lêt his dáys be few : and let anôther táke his öf-fice.

8 Let his chíldren be fá-ther-less : ând his wífe a wi-dow.

9 Let his children be vâgabonds, and bég their bread : let them seek it also ôut of dé-solate plä-ces.

10 Let the extortioner consûme áll that he hath : and let the strânger spoíl his lä-bour.

11 Let there be nô man to pí-ty him : nor to have compassion upôn his fá-therless chíl-dren.

12 Let his postêrity bé de-stroy'd : and in the next generâtion let his náme be clean put out.

13 Let the wickedness of his fathers be had in remêmbrance in the síght of the Lord: and let not the sín of his mó-ther be done a-way.

14 Let them âlway be befóre the Lord : that He may root out the memôrial of thém from off the earth;

15 And that, * because his mínd was nót to do good : but persecuted the poor helpless man, * that he might slay hím that was véx-ed at the heart.

16 His delight was in cursing,* and it shall hâppen ún-to him : he loved not blessing, * thêrefore sháll it be far from him.

17 He clothed himself with cursing,* líke as with a rái-ment : and it shall come into his bowels like water,* and líke óil in-to his bones.

18 Let it be unto him as the clôke that he háth upon him : and as the gírdle that he is ál-way gird-ed with-al.

19 Let it thus happen from the Lord * ûnto mine é-ne-mies : and to thôse that speak é-vil against my soul.

p 20 But deal Thou with me, O Lord God, * accôrding ún-to Thy Name : fôr swéet is Thy mër-cy.

21 O deliver me,* for I am hélpless and poor : and my hêart is woúnd-ed within me.

22 I go hence like the shâdow that depárt-eth : and am driven awây ás the grass-hop-per.

23 My knees are wêak through fást-ing : my flesh is dried ûp for wánt of fät-ness.

24 I became also a reprôach ún-to them : they that lôoked upón me shaked their heads.

25 Hêlp me, O Lórd my God : O save me accôrding tó Thy mër-cy.

mf 26 And they shall know,* how that thís is Thý hand : and that Thôu, Lórd, hast döne it.

27 Though they cûrse, yet bléss Thou : and let them be confounded that rise up against me ; * bût lét Thy ser-vant re-joice.

28 Let mine âdversaries be clóth-ed with shame : and let them cover themselves with their ôwn confú-sion, as with a cloke.

29 As for me,* I will give great thânks unto the Lórd with my mouth : and práise Him amóng the mul-ti-tude ;

30 For He shall stand at the ríght hánd of the poor : to save his sôul from unríght-eous judg-es.

135

The Twenty-Third Day.

Mattins.

Venite exultemus, Domino.

ƒ O COME, * let us sĭng ŭn-to͞ the Lord : let us heartily rejoice in the strêngth of oúr sal-vā-tion.

2 Let us come before His prĕsence with thanksgĭv-ing : and shĕw ourselves glád in Him with Psalms.

3 For the Lŏrd is a grêat God : and a grêat Kĭng above ãll gods.

4 In His hand are all the côrners ŏf the earth : and the strength of the hĭlls is Hĭs ãl-so.

5 The sea is Hĭs, and He mâde it : and His hânds prepár-ed͞ the drȳ land.

p 6 O come, * let us wôrship, and fãll down: and knêel before the Lŏrd our Mā-ker.

7 For Hê is the Lŏrd our God : and we are the people of His pâsture, and the shĕep of Hĭs hand.

mf 8 To-day if ye will hear His voice, * hârden nót your hearts : as in the provocation, * and as in the day of temptâtion ĭn the wil-derness ;

9 When your fâthers témpt-ed Me : prôved Mé, and saw My works.

10 Forty years long * was I grieved with thĭs generá-tion, ͞and said : It is a people that do err in their hêarts, for they háve not known My ways.

11 Unto whôm I swáre in͞ My wrath : that they shôuld not ĕn-ter into My rest.

Glory be to the Fâther, ánd to͞ the Son : ánd tó the Ho-ly Ghost ;

As it was in the beginning, * is nŏw, and éver shall be : wŏrld without ĕnd. ˙A˙-men.

PSALMS 110, 111.

PSALM 110. *Dixit Dominus.*

mf THE Lord sáid ún-to͞-my Lord : Sit Thou on My right hand, * until I máke Thine énemies Thy fo͞ot-stool.

2 The Lord shall send the rod of Thy pówer out of Sí-on : be Thou ruler, * even in the mídst amóng Thine e-ne-mies.

3 In the day of Thy power shall the people offer Thee free-will offerings * with an hóly wŏr-ship : the dew of Thy birth is of the wómb of the mōrn-ing.

f 4 The Lord swâre, and will not re-pent : Thou art a Príest for ever * after the ôrder óf Mel-chi-se-dech.

5 The Lôrd upon Thy right hand : shall wound even kĭngs in the dáy of His wrath.

mf 6 He shall judge among the heathen ; * He shall fill the places with the dêad bō-dies : and smite in sunder the hêads over dí-vers cōun-tries.

p 7 He shall drínk of the brŏok in the way : therefore shâll He lĭft up His head.

PSALM 111. *Confitebor Tibi.*

f I WILL give thanks unto the Lôrd with my whôle heart : secretly among the faithful, * ín the cón-gre-gā-tion.

2 The wŏrks of the Lórd are great : sought out of all them that have plea-sure͞ there-in.

3 His work is worthy to be praised, * and hâd in hō-nour : and His ríghteousness endúr-eth͞ for év-er.

4 The merciful and gracious Lord hath sô done His már-vellous works : that they óúght to be hád in remēm-brance.

mf 5 He hath given meat unto them that fēar Him : He shall ever be míndful óf His co-ve-nant.

6 He hath shewed His péople the pówer of His works : that He may give them the héritage óf the hēa-then.

7 The works of His hands are vērity and júdg-ment : âll His commānd-ments are true.

8 They stand fast for êver and év-er : and are dóne in trúth and e-qui-ty.

f 9 He sent redempt͝ion únto His péo-ple : He hath commanded His covenant for ever, * hôly and ré-verend is His Name.

mf 10 The fear of the Lord is the beginning of wís-dom : a good understanding have all they that do thereafter, * the praĭse of it endúr-eth͞ for ēver.

[PSALM 112.

Psalms 112, 113.

1. Bishop Medley. 2. T. Purcell.
3. *Dr. C. Steggall. 4. *A. H. Brown.

Psalm 112. *Beatus vir.*

mf BLESSED is the man that fear-eth⌢the Lord : he hath great delight in His com-mändments.

2 His seed shall be mighty upón earth : the generation of the faithful shall be bléss-ed.

3 Riches and plénteousness shall be in⌢his house : and his righteousness endúr-eth⌢for ë-ver.

4 Unto the godly there ariseth up light in the dárk-ness : he is mérciful, lóv-ing,⌢and right-eous.

p 5 A good man is mérciful, and lénd-eth : and will gúide his wórds with discrë-tion.

6 For hê shall néver be mov'd : and the righteous shall be hâd in everlást-ing remëm-brance.

7 He will not be afraid of any êvil tí-dings : for his heart standeth fâst, and belíev-eth in the Lord.

8 His heart is estâblished, and will not shrink : until he see his desíre upón his e-ne-mies.

9 He hath dispersed abroad, * and gíven tó the poor : and his righteousness remaineth for ever ; * his hórn shall be exált-ed⌢with hö-nour.

10 The ungodly shall see it, * and it shall gríeve him : he shall gnash with his teeth, and consume away ; * the desíre of the ungód-ly⌢shall pë-rish.

Psalm 113. *Laudate, pueri.*

f PRAISE the Lôrd, ye sér-vants : O práise the Náme of the Lord.

2 Blêssed be the Náme of⌢the Lord : from thís time fórth for e-vermore.

3 The Lord's Náme is práis-ed : from the rising up of the sun * únto the gó-ing down of⌢the same.

4 The Lord is high abôve all heá-then : ând His gló-ry above the heavens.

mf 5 Who is like unto the Lord our God, * That hâth His dwélling⌢so high : and yet humbleth Himself to behold the thíngs that áre in heaven and earth ?

6 He taketh up the símple oút of⌢the dust : and lífteth the póor out of⌢the mire ;

7 That He may sêt him with the prín-ces : even with the prínces óf His pëo-ple.

8 He maketh the barren wôman to kêep house : and to be a jôyful mó-ther⌢of chíl-dren.

Evensong.

Psalms 114, 115.

1. T. Kelway.
2. * Dr. E. G. Monk.
3. * A. H. Brown.
4. * A. H. Brown.

Psalm 114. *In exitu Israel.*

mf WHEN Israel came ôut of Ē-gypt : and the house of Jacob * from amŏng the strănge pëo-ple.
  2 Jŭdah was his sắnc-tua-ry : and Ĭsrael hís do-mĭ-nion.
  3 The sêa saw thắt, and fled : Jôrdắn was driv-en back.
  4 The môuntains skĭp-ped⁀like rams : and the lĭttle hĭlls like yŏung sheep.
  p 5 What aileth thee, O thou sêa, that thou flēd-dest : and thou Jôrdan, that thóu wast driv-en back?
  6 Ye môuntains, that ye skĭp-ped⁀like rams : and ye lĭttle hĭlls, like yŏung sheep?
  mf 7 Tremble, thou earth, * at the prêsence ŏf the Lord : at the prêsence of the Gód of Jä-cob;
  8 Who turned the hard rock in-to a stănding wä-ter : and the flĭnt-stone ĭn-to⁀a spring-ing well.

Psalm 115. *Non nobis, Domine.*

f NOT unto us, O Lord, not unto us, * but untu Thy Nâme gíve the praise : for Thy loving mêrcy, ǎnd for⁀Thy trŭth's sake.

2 Whêrefore shall the hếa-then say : Whếfe is now their God;
  3 As for oûr God, Hê is⁀in heaven : He hath dône whatsoế-ver pleas-ed Him.
  mf 4 Their îdols are sĭl-ver⁀and gold : êven the wórk of mĕn's hands.
  5 They have môuths, and spêak not : êyes háve they⁀and sëe not.
  6 They have eârs and hêar not : nôses háve they,⁀and smëll not.
  7 They have hands, and handle not; * fêet have they, and wălk not : nêither spêak they through their throat.
  8 They that mâke them are lĭke unto them : and so are all sûch as pŭt their trust in them.
  9 But thou, house of Israel,* trûst thŏu in⁀the Lord : Hê is their sŭc-cour and de-fence.
  10 Ye house of Aaron, * pŭt your trŭst in⁀the Lord : He is their hêlper ánd de-fĕnd-er.
  11 Ye that fear the Lord, * pŭt your trûst in⁀the Lord : He is their hêlper ánd de-fĕnd-er.
  p 12 The Lord hath been mindful of us, * and Hê shall blĕss us : even He shall bless the house of Israel, * He shall blĕss the hóuse of Aä-ron.

13 He shall bless thêm that féar the Lord : bôth smãll ãnd great.
14 The Lord shall incrêase you móre and more : yôu ánd your chïl-dren.
15 Ye are the blêssed óf the Lord : whô mãde heaven and earth.
mf 16 All the whole hêavens áre the Lord's : the earth hath He gíven tó the chil-dren of men.
p 17 The dêad praise not Thée, O Lord : neither all thêy that go dówn into sï-lence.
f 18 But wê will praíse the Lord : from this time forth for êvermôre. Praise the Lord.

The Twenty-Fourth Day.
Mattins.
Venite, exultemus Domino.

f O COME,* let us síng ún-to the Lord : let us heartily rejoice in the strêngth of oúr sal-vã-tion.

2 Let us come before His prêsence with thanksgív-ing : and shêw ourselves glãd in Him with Psalms.

3 For the Lôrd is a grĕat God : and a grêat Kíng above äll gods.
4 In His hand are all the cŏrners óf the earth : and the strength of the hîlls is Hís ïl-so.
5 The sea is Hís, and He mãde it : and His hânds prepár-ed⌒the drÿ land.
p 6 O come,* let us wôrship, and fãll down : and knêel before the Lórd our Mã-ker.
7 For Hê is the Lórd our God : and we are the people of His pâsture, and the shéep of His hand.
mf 8 To-day if ye will hear His voice,* hârden nót your hearts : as in the provocation,* and as in the day of temptâtion ín the wil-der-ness ;
9 When your fâthers témpt-ed Me : prôved Mé, and saw My works.
10 Forty years long * was I grieved with thís generá-tion,⌒and said : It is a people that do err in their hêarts, for they háve not known My ways.
11 Unto whôm I swáre in⌒My wrath : that they shôuld not én-ter into My rest.
f Glory be to the Fâther, ánd to⌒ the Son : ánd tó the Ho-ly Ghost ;
As it was in the beginning,* is nôw, and éver shall be : wôrld without énd. 'A'-men.

PSALMS 116, 117.

1. *A. H. BROWN.
2. L. J. TURRELL.
3. *W. DYCE.
4. T. KELWAY.

PSALM 116. *Dilexi, quoniam.*

I AM well pléas-ed : that the Lord hath hêard the voíce of mÿ prayer ;
2 That He hath inclined His eâr ún-to me : therefore will I câll upon Him as lŏng as I live.
p 3 The snares of death cŏm-passed me rŏund a-bout : and the pains of hêll gat hóld up-ŏn me.
4 I shall find trouble and heavi-ness,* and I will câll upon the Náme of⌒the Lord : O Lord, I besêech Thee, delí-ver mÿ soul.
mf 5 Gracious is the Lŏrd, and rígh-teous : yêa, our Gód is mer-ci-ful.

6 The Lord presêrveth the sím-ple: I was in mísery, ánd He help-ed me.
p 7 Turn again then unto thy rêst, Ó my soul : fôr the Lórd hath⌒ re-ward-ed thee.
8 And why ? Thou hast delívered my sóul from death : mine eyes from têars, and my féet from fãll-ing.
9 I will wâlk befóre the Lord : ín the lánd of⌒the lîv-ing.
10 I believed, and therefore will I speak ;* but I was sôre trôub-led : I said in my hâste, All men⌒are lï-ars.
11 What reward shall I gíve ún-to⌒the Lord : for all the benefits that Hê hath dóne un-to me ?

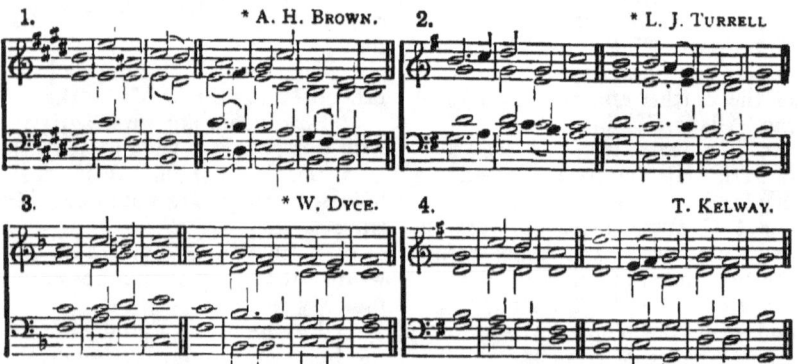

f 12 I will receive the cûp of salvā-tion : and câll upon the Nāme of the Lord.
13 I will pay my vows now in the presence of âll His pēo-ple : right dear in the sight of the Lôrd is the déath of Hïs saints.
p 14 Behold, O Lord,* how that Î am Thy sēr-vant : I am Thy servant, and the son of Thine handmaid ; * Thou hast brôken my bónds in sün-der.
15 I will offer to Thee the sacrifice of thânksgī-ving : and will câll upon the Nāme of the Lord.

mf 16 I will pay my vows unto the Lord, * in the sight of âll His pēo-ple : in the courts of the Lord's house, * even in the midst of thee, O Jerûsalem. Prāise the Lord.

PSALM 117. *Laudate Dominum.*

f O PRAISE the Lord, * âll ye hēa-then : prâise Him, âll ye nä-tions.
2 For His merciful kindness is ever more and môre tôwards us : and the truth of the Lord endureth for êver. Prāise the Lord.

PSALM 118. *Confitemini Domino.*

f O GIVE thanks unto the Lord,* for Hê is grācious : *(full)* because His mêrcy endúr-eth ⁀ for ëv-er.

(Dec.) 2 Let Israel now confess, that Hê is grā-cious : *(full)* and that His mêrcy endúr-eth ⁀ for ëv-er.

(Can.) 3 Let the house of Aâron nŏw con-fess : *(full)* that His mêrcy endŭr-eth⁀for ĕv-er.

(Dec.) 4 Yea, let them now that fêar the Lŏrd con-fess : *(full)* that His mêrcy endŭr-eth⁀for ĕv-er.

(Can.) p 5 I called upon the Lôrd in trŏu-ble : and the Lôrd heãrd me at large.

6 The Lôrd is on mÿ side : I will not fear what mân dŏ-eth un-to me.

7 The Lord taketh my part with thêm that hêlp me : therefore shall I see my desîre upŏn mine e-ne-mies.

8 It is bêtter to trŭst in⁀the Lord : than to pût any côn-fi-dence in man.

9 It is bêtter to trŭst in⁀the Lord : than to put any cônfidénce in prïn-ces.

10 All nations cômpassed me rŏund a-bout : *(full) mf,* but in the Name of the Lôrd will I des-trŏy them.

(Can.) p 11 They kept me in on every side,* they kept me in, I sây, on ĕve-ry side : *(full) mf,* but in the Name of the Lôrd will I des-trŏy them.

(Dec.) p 12 They came about me like bees, * and are extinct even as the fîre amŏng the thorns : *(full) mf* for in the Name of the Lôrd I' will destrŏy them.

(Can.) p 13, Thou hast thrust sôre at me, that I might fall : bût the Lŏrd was mÿ help.

mf 14 The Lôrd is my strĕngth, and⁀my song : and is becôme mÿ sal-vä-tion.

15 The voice of joy and health is in the dwêllings of the rĭgh-teous : the right hand of the Lôrd bringeth mĭgh-ty things to pass.

f 16 The right hand of the Lord,* hâth the pre-ĕ-mi-nence : the right hand of the Lôrd bringeth mĭgh-ty things to pass.

mf 17 I shall not dĭe, but live : and declâre the wŏrks of the Lord.

18 The Lord hath châstened and corrĕct-ed me : but He hath not gĭven me ŏ-ver un-to death.

f 19 Open me the gâtes of rĭgh-teous-ness : that I may go into them, * and gĭve thãnks un-to⁀the Lord.

20 Thĭs is the gâte of⁀the Lord : the rĭghteous shall ĕn-ter in-to it.

21 I will thank Thee, * for Thoû hast heãrd me : and art becôme mÿ sal-vä-tion.

22 The same stone which the bûilders refŭs-ed : is become the hêad-stone ĭn the cör-ner.

23 Thĭs is the Lôrd's doing : ănd it is mắr-vellous in our eyes.

(Full) 24 This is the dây which the Lŏrd hath made : wê will rejoĭce and⁀be glad in it.

(Can.) mf 25 Hêlp me nŏw, O Lord : O Lord, sênd us nŏw pros-pe-ri-ty.

f 26 Blessed be He that cômeth in the Nắme of⁀the Lord : we have wished you good luck,* ye that âre of the hôuse of the Lord.

mf 27 God is the Lôrd who hath shĕw-ed⁀us light : bind the sacrifice with cords,* yea, êven unto the hŏrns of⁀the äl-tar.

f 28 Thou art my God, * and Î will thãnk Thee : Thou art my Gôd, and I will praïse Thee.

(Full) 29 O give thanks unto the Lord,* for Hê is grã-cious : and His mêrcy endŭr-eth⁀for ĕv-er.

Evensong.

PSALM 119.

1. * L. J. Turrell.
2. R. Farrant.
3. W. Savage.
4. * W. Dyce.

Beati immaculati.
(Major.)

mf BLESSED are those that are undefïled ín the way : and wâlk in the lãw of the Lord.

2 Blessed are they that kêep His tés-timo-nies : and sêek Him wíth their whŏle heart.

3 For they who dô no wíck-ed-ness : wâlk ín His ways.

4 Thôu hast chärg-ed : that we shall dîligently kéep Thy commänd-ments.

p 5 O that my wâys were made so di-rect : that Î might keép Thy stä-tutes !

6 So shall I nôt be confŏund-ed : while I have respĉct unto áll Thy commänd-ments.

7 I will thânk Thee with an unfeígn-ed heart : when I shall have learned the jûdgments ôf Thy right-eous-ness.

8 I will kêep Thy cé-remo-nies : Ô forsáke me͡not ut-ter-ly.

In quo corriget?

p WHEREWITHAL shall a yôung man cleánse his way: even by rûling himsêlf after Thy word.

10 With my whole heârt have I sôught Thee : O let me not go wrông out of Thý com-mänd-ments.

11 Thy words have I hĭd withín my heart : that I shôuld not sín a-gäinst Thee.

mf 12 Blêssed art Thóu, O Lord : Ô teách me͡Thy stä-tutes.

13 With my lips have Î been tĕl-ling : of âll the júdg-ments of Thy mouth.

14 I have had as great delight in the wây of Thy tés-timo-nies : as in âll mán-ner͡of rĭch-es.

15 I will talk of Thý commänd-ments : and hâve respéct unto Thy ways.

16 My delight shall bê in Thy stä-tutes : and I will nót for-get Thy word.

*⁂ when Major.

Retribue servo Tuo.
(Major.)
mp O DO well únto Thy sêr-vant :
that I may líve, and keep Thy word.

18 Ópen Thóu mine eyes : that I may see the wôndrous thíngs of Thÿ law.

p 19 I am a stránger upôn earth : O hide not Thÿ commánd-ments fröm me.

20 My soul breaketh out * for the vêry fér-vent⁀de-sire : that it hath álway ún-to⁀Thy júdg-ments.

21 Thôu hast rebúk-ed⁀the proud : and cursed are they that do êrr from Thÿ com-mänd-ments.

22 O tûrn from me sháme and⁀ re-buke : for I have képt Thy tes-timo-nies.

23 Princes also did sit and spêak agáinst me : but Thy servant is óccupied ín Thy stä-tutes.

24 For Thy têstimonies are mý de-light : ánd mÿ coun-sel-lors.

Adhæsit pavimento.
(Minor.)
p MY soul clêaveth tó the dust : O quicken Thou mê, accórd ing⁀to Thÿ word.

26 I have acknowledged my wáys, and Thou héard-est me : O téach me⁀Thy stä-tutes.

27 Make me to understand the way of Thÿ commánd-ments : and sô shall I tálk of⁀Thy won-drous works.

28 My soul melteth away for vêry héa-vi-ness : comfort Thou mê accórd-ing unto Thy word.

29 Take from me the wáy of lÿ-ing : and cause Thou mê to make múch of Thÿ law.

30 I have chôsen the wáy of truth : and Thy jûdgments have I laid be-före me.

31 I have stúck unto Thy tés-timo-nies : Ô Lórd, con-found me not.

32 I will run the way of Thÿ commánd-ments : when Thou hast sêt my héart at li-ber-ty.

K   145

The Twenty-Fifth Day.

Mattins.

Venite, exultemus Domino.

f O COME, * let us sĭng ún-to^ the Lord : let us heartily rejoice in the strĕngth of oúr sal-vā-tion.

2 Let us come before His prĕsence with thanksgĭv-ing : and shĕw ourselves glád in Him with Psalms.

3 For the Lôrd is a grĕat God : and a grĕat Kĭng above ăll gods.

4 In His hand are all the côrners óf the earth : and the strength of the hĭlls is Hĭs ăl-so.

5 The sea is Hĭs, and He máde it : and His hânds prepár-ed^the drÿ land.

p 6 O come, * let us wôrship, and făll down : and knĕel before the Lórd our Mä-ker.

7 For Hĕ is the Lórd our God : and we are the people of His pâsture, and the shĕep of Hĭs hand.

mf 8 To-day if ye will hear His voice, * hârden nót your hearts : as in the provocation, * and as in the day of temptâtion ĭn the wil-der-ness ;

9 When your fâthers témpt-ed Me : prôved Mé, and saw My works.

10 Forty years long * was I grieved with tl̆.ĭs generá-tion,^and said : It is a people that do err in their hêarts, for they háve not known My ways.

11 Unto whôm I swáre in^My wrath : that they shôuld not én-ter into My rest.

Glory be to the Fâther, ánd to^the Son : ănd tó the Ho-ly Ghost ;

As it was in the beginning, * is nôw, and éver shall be : wôrld without ĕnd. ˙A˙-men.

PSALM 119.—*(Continued.)*

Legem pone.

mf TEACH me, O Lord,⁕ the wây of Thy stā-tutes : and Î shall kéep it un-to͡the end.

⌃ 34 Give me understanding,⁕ and Î shall kéep Thy law : yea, I shall kêep it wíth my whŏle heart.

35 Make me to go in the path of Thŷ commānd-ments : fôr therefn is my de-sire.

36 Incline my hêart unto Thy téstimo-nies: ândnót to co-vetous-ness.

p 37 O turn away mine eyes,⁕ lest they behŏld vá-ni-ty : and qûicken Thou mé in Thÿ way.

38 O stablish Thy wôrd in Thy sêr-vant : thât I may fëar Thee.

39 Take away the rebuke that Î am afráid of : fôr Thy jûdg-ments äre good.

40 Behold, my delight is in Thŷ commānd-ments : O qûicken me ín Thy righ-teous-ness.

Et veniat super me.

mf LET Thy loving mercy come âlso unto mé, O Lord : even Thy salvâtion, accórd-ing unto Thy word.

42 So shall I make answer unto mŷ blasphē-mers : fôr my trúst is in Thy word.

43 O take not the word of Thy truth ûtterly óut of͡my mouth : for my hôpe is ín Thy jûdg-ments.

44 So shall I âlway kéep Thy law : yêa, for év-er͡and ëv-er.

⌃ 45 And I will wâlk at lí-ber-ty : for Î séek Thy commänd-ments.

46 I will speak of Thy testimonies also,⁕ êven befôre kings : ând will nót be͡a-shäm-ed.

47 And my delight shall þe in Thŷ commānd-ments : whích I have löv-ed.

48 My hands also will I lift up ụnto Thy commandments,⁕ which I have lŏv-ed : and my study shall bê ín Thy stä-tutes.

Memor esto servi Tui.

mf O THINK upon Thy sêrvant, as concérn-ing͡Thy word : wherein Thou hast caûsed mé to put my trust.

50 The same is my cômfort in my trôu-ble : fôr Thy wórd hath quickened me.

51 The proud have had me excêedingly in derí-sion : yêt have I not shrínk-ed from Thy law.

52 For I remember Thine everlâsting jûdg-ments, ͡O Lord : ând recefv-ed côm-fort.

p 53 I am hôrriblý a-fraid : for the ungôdly thát for-sake Thy law.

mf 54 Thy stâtutes have béen my songs : ín the hóuse of͡my pil-grim-age.

55 I have thought upon Thy Name, O Lord,⁕ in the nfghtsêa-son : âṇd have képt Thy law.

56 Thís I had : becâuse I képt Thy commānd-ments.

[*Portio mea.*

Portio mea, Domine.

p THOU art my pór-tion⁀O Lord :
I have prômised to kêep Thÿ law.

58 I made my humble petition in Thy presence * wĭth my whôle heart : O be merciful unto mê, accórd-ing⁀to Thÿ word.

59 I called mine own wâys to remêm-brance : and turned my fêet ún-to⁀Thy tes-ti-mo-nies.

60 I made haste,* and prolônged nót the time : tô kéep Thy commănd-ments.

61 The congregations of the ungôdly have rób-bed me : but I have nót for-got-ten⁀Thy law.

62 At midnight I will rĭse to give thánks unto Thee : becâuse of Thy rígh-teous jŭdg-ments.

63 I am a companion of all thêm that fĕar Thee : ănd kéep Thy commănd-ments.

mf 64 The earth, O Lord,* is fŭll of Thy mĕr-cy : Ô téach me⁀Thy stă-tutes.

Bonitatem fecisti.

mf O LORD,* Thou hast dealt graciously wĭth Thy sĕr-vant : ăccórd-ing unto Thy word.

66 O learn me true under-stânding and knôw-ledge : for I have beliêved Thý com-mănd-ments.

67 Before I was trôubled, I wĕnt wrong : bût nów have⁀I kept Thy word.

68 Thou art gôod and gră-cious : Ô teăch me⁀Thy stă-tutes.

69 The proud have imagined a lĭe agăinst me : but I will keep Thy commăndments wĭth my whôle heart.

70 Their hêart is as fắt as brawn : but my delĭght hath béen in Thy law.

71 It is good for me that I have bêen in trôu-ble : that I may leărn Thy stă-tutes.

72 The law of Thy mouth is dêarer ún-to me : than thôusands of góld and sĭl-ver.

Evensong.

1. B. Lamb.   2. R. Langdon.
3. Dr. P. Hayes.   4. A. H. Brown.

Manus Tuæ fecerunt me.

mf THY hands have mâde me and fásh-ioned me : O give me understanding, * that I may leárn Thy commänd-ments.

74 They that fear Thee will be glâd when they sẽe me : because I have pût my trúst in Thy̆ word.

75 I know, O Lôrd, that Thy júdg-ments are right : and that Thou of very faithfulness * hast cáused me tó be tröu-bled.

76 O let Thy merciful kíndness be my cóm-fort : according to Thy wôrd ún-to Thy sër-vant.

77 O let Thy loving mercies come unto mê, that I may live : fôr Thy láw is my de-light.

78 Let the proud be confounded, * for they go wickedly abôut to destróy me : but I will be ôccupied in Thy̆ com-mänd-ments.

79 Let such as fear Thee, * and have knôwn Thy tés-timo-nies : bê túrn-ed un-to me.

80 O let my heart be sôund in Thy stā-tutes : that I bé not ashäm-ed.

Defecit anima mea.

mf MY soul hath longed for Thy̆ salvā-tion : and I have a good hôpe, becaúse of Thy̆ word.

82 Mine eŷes long sóre for Thy word : sâying, O whén wilt Thou com-fort me?

83 For I am become like a bôttle ín the smoke : yet do I nôt forgét Thy stā-tutes.

84 How many are the dâys of Thy sër-vant : when wilt Thou be avênged of thém that per-secute me?

85 The proud have dígged píts for me : whích áre not after Thy law.

86 All Thy commánd-ments are true : they persecute me fâlsely ; O be Thou my help.

87 They had almost made an end of mê upőn earth : but I forsôok not Thy̆ com-mänd-ments.

88 O quicken me after Thy lôving-kínd-ness : and so shall I kêep the tésti-monies of Thy mouth.

[*In æternum.*

In æternum, Domine.

mf O LORD, Thy word : endûreth for év-er‿in hëa-ven.
90 Thy truth also remaineth * from one generâtion to anô-ther : Thou hast laid the foundation of the earth, and ít a-bíd-eth.
91 They continue this day * accórding to Thine ór-di-nance : fôr áll things sërve Thee.
92 If my delight hâd not beén in‿ Thy law : I should have pêrished ín my tröu-ble.
93 I will never forgêt Thy com-mándments : fôr with thém Thou‿ hast quick-ened me.
94 I am Thîne, O sãve me : for Î have soúght Thy commánd-ments.
95 The ungodly laid wait for mê to destrôy me : but I will consí-der‿ Thy tes-ti-mo-nies.
96 I see that áll things cóme to‿ an end : but Thy commándment ís ex-ceed-ing broad.

Quomodo dilexi!

mf LORD, what lôve have I ún-to‿Thy law : all the day lông is my stú-dy ïn it.
98 Thou through Thy commánd-ments * hast made me wîser than mine é-ne-mies : for thêy are év-er with me.
99 I have more understãndin:̌ than my têach-ers : for Thy têsti-monies áre my stü-dy.
100 I am wîser than the ã-ged : be-câuse I kéep Thy commänd-ments.
101 I have refrained my feet from êvery é-vil way : thât I may keep Thy word.
102 I have not shrünk from Thy jûdg-ments : fôr Thôu teach-est me.
103 O how sweet are Thy wôrds ún-to‿my throat : yea, swêeter than hó-ney unto my mouth.
104 Through Thy commandments I gêt understánd-ing : thêrefore I háte all e-vil ways.

The Twenty-Sixth Day

Mattins.

Venite, exultemus Domino.

f O COME, * let us sĭng ŭn-to⁀ the Lord : let us heartily rejoice in the strĕngth of oŭr sal-vä-tion.

2 Let us come before His prêsence with thanksgĭv-ing : and shĕw ourselves glăd in Him with Psalms.

3 For the Lôrd is a grêat God : and a grêat Kĭng above äll gods.

4 In His hand are all the côrners ŏf the earth : and the strength of the hĭlls is Hĭs äl-so.

5 The sea is Hĭs, and He mâde it : and His hânds prepăr-ed⁀the drÿ land.

p 6 O come, * let us wôrship, and fäll down: and knêel before the Lŏrd our Mä-ker.

7 For Hê is the Lŏrd our God : and we are the people of His pâsture, and the shĕep of Hĭs hand.

mf 8 To-day if ye will hear His voice, * hârden nŏt your hearts : as in the provocation, * and as in the day of temptâtion ĭn the wil-derness ;

9 When your fâthers tĕmpt-ed Me : prôved Mĕ, and saw My works.

10 Forty years long * was I grieved with thĭs generă-tion,⁀and said : It is a people that do err in their hêarts, for they hăve not known My ways.

11 Unto whôm I swăre in⁀My wrath : that they shôuld not ĕn-ter into My rest.

Glory be to the Fâther, ănd to⁀the Son : ănd tŏ the Ho-ly Ghost ;

As it was in the beginning, * is nôw, and ĕver shall be : wôrld without ĕnd. ˙A˙-men.

PSALM 119.—*(Continued.)*

Lucerna pedibus meis.
(Major.)
mf THY word is a lăntern ŭn-to⁀ my feet : ănd a lĭght unto my paths.
106 I have sworn, * and am stĕdfastly pŭr-pos-ed : to kĕep Thy rĭght-eous jŭdg-ments.
p 107 I am trŏubled above mĕa-sure : quicken me, O Lŏrd, accŏrd-ing⁀to Thў word.
108 Let the free-will offerings of my mŏuth plĕase Thee,⁀O Lord : ănd tĕach me⁀Thy jŭdg-ments.
109 My soul is ălway ĭn my hand : yĕt do I nŏt for-get Thy law.
110 The ungodly have lăid a snăre for me : but yet I swerved nŏt from Thў com-mănd-ments.
111 Thy testimonies have I claimed * as mine hĕritage for ĕv-er : and why ? * they are the vĕry jŏy of mў heart.
112 I have applied my heart * to fulfil Thy stătutes ăl-way : ĕven ŭn-to the end.

Iniquos odio habui.
(Minor.)
mf I HATE them that imăgine ĕv-il things : bŭt Thў law do I love.
114 Thŏu art my defĕnce and shield : ănd my trŭst is in Thy word.

115 Awăy from me, ye wĭck-ed : I will kĕep the commănd-ments of my God.
116 O stablisḥ me according to Thy wŏrd, that I may live : and let me nŏt be disappoĭnt-ed of my hopᵉ.
117 Hold Thou me ŭp, and I shall⁀be safe : yea, my delight shall be ĕver ĭn Thy stă-tutes.
118 Thou hast trodden down all them that depărt from Thy stă-tutes : fŏr they imă-gine but de-ceit.
119 Thou puttest away all the ungŏdly of the eărth like dross : thĕrefore I lŏve Thy tes-timo-nies.
p 120 My flesḥ trĕmbleth for fĕar of Thee : and I am afraĭd of⁀Thy judg-ments.

Feci judicium.
(Major.)
mf I DEAL with the thĭng that is lăw-ful⁀and right : O give me not ŏver unto mĭne op-prĕs-sors.
122 Make Thou thy servant to delĭght in thăt which⁀is good : that the prŏud dŏ me nŏ wrong.
123 Mine eyes are wasted away with lŏoking fŏr Thy health : ănd for the wŏrd of⁀Thy righ-teous-ness.
124 O deal with Thy servant * according unto Thy lŏving mĕr-cy : ănd teăch me⁀Thy stă-tutes.

125 I am Thy servant,* O grant me ŭnderstǎnd-ing : that I may knŏw Thy tes-ti-mo-nies.
126 It is time for Thee, Lord,* to lây tŏ Thine hand : for thêy have destrŏy-ed Thȳ law.
127 For I lôve Thy commǎnd-ments : abôve gŏld and pre-cious stone.
128 Therefore hold I straight ǎll Thy commǎnd-ments : and all false wâys I ŭt-ter-ly ab-hor.

Mirabilia.

mf THY têstimonies are wŏn-der-ful : thêrefore doth my sôul këep them.

130 When Thy wôrd gŏ-eth forth : it giveth light and understǎnding ŭn-to⌢the sǐm-ple.

131 I opened my môuth, and drĕw in⌢my breath : for my delǐght was in Thȳ com-mänd-ments.

132 O lok Thou upon me,* and be mêrciful ŭn-to me : as Thou usest to dô uṇto thŏse that love Thy Name.

133 Order my stĕps in⌢Thy word : and so shall no wickedness hâve domǐ-nion o-ver me.

134 O deliver me from the wrông-ful dĕal-ings⌢of men : and sô shall I këep Thy commǎnd-ments.

135 Shew the light of Thy counte-nance upôn Thy sĕr-vant : ǎnd tĕach me⌢Thy stä-tutes.

136 Mine eyes gush ôut with wä-ter : because mên këep not Thȳ law.

Justus es, Domine.

mf RÎGHTEOUS art Thŏu, O Lord : ǎnd trŭe is⌢Thy jŭdg-ment.

138 The testimonies that Thôu hast commǎnd-ed : âre excĕed-ing right-eous⌢and true.

139 My zeal hath êven consŭm-ed me : because mine ênemies have forgŏt-ten Thȳ words.

140 Thy word is trǐed to the ŭt-ter-most ǎnd Thy sĕr-vant lov-eth it.

141 I am small,* and of nô reputǎ-tion : yet do I nôt forgĕt Thy commänd-ments.

142 Thy righteousness is an everlâsting rǐgh-teous-ness : ǎnd Thȳ law is the truth.

p 143 Trouble and heaviness have tâken hŏld upon me : yet is my delǐght in Thȳ com-mänd-ments.

144 The righteousness of Thy tes-timonies * is êverlâst-ing : O grǎnt me understǎnd-ing,⌢and I shall live.

Evensong.

Clamavi in toto corde meo.
(Major.)

mf I CALL with my whole heart: hear me, O Lord, I will keep Thy sta-tutes.

146 Yea, even unto Thee do I call : help me, and I shall keep Thy tes-timo-nies.

147 Early in the morning do I cry unto Thee : for in Thy word is my trust.

148 Mine eyes prevent the night-watch-es : that I might be oc-cupied in Thy words.

p 149 Hear my voice, O Lord,* according unto Thy loving-kind-ness : quicken me, accord-ing as Thou art wont.

150 They draw nigh that of malice per-secute me : and are far from Thy law.

151 Be Thou nigh at hand, O Lord : for all Thy command-ments are true.

152 As concerning Thy testimo-nies,* I have known long since : that Thou hast grounded them for ev-er.

Vide humilitatem.
(Minor.)

p O CONSIDER mine adversity, and deli-ver me : for I do not for-get Thy law.

154 Avenge Thou my cause, and deli-ver me : quicken me, accord-ing to Thy word.

155 Health is far from the un-god-ly : for they regard not Thy sta-tutes.

156 Great is Thy mer-cy, O Lord : quicken me, as Thou art wont.

157 Many there are that trouble me, and per-secute me : yet do I not swerve from Thy tes-timo-nies.

158 It grieveth me when I see the transgres-sors : because they keep not Thy law.

159 Consider, O Lord, * how I love Thy command - ments : O quicken me, * according to Thy lov-ing-kindness.

160 Thy word is true from ever-last-ing : all the judgments of Thy righteousness endure for ev-er-more.

Principes persecuti sunt.
(*Minor.*)

mf PRINCES have pêrsecuted me withóut a cause : but my heart stândeth in áwe of Thÿ word.

162 I âm as glád of ⌒Thy word : as ône that fínd-eth grëat spoils.

163 As for lies,* I hâte and abhôr them : bût Thý law do I love.

164 Seven times a dây do I praíse Thee : becaúse of Thy rîght-eous jüdg-ments.

165 Great is the peace that thêy have who lóve Thy law : and they are nôt offénd-ed ât it.

166 Lord,* I have lôoked for Thy sáv-ing health : and dône after Thý com-mänd-ments.

167 My soul hath kêpt Thy tés-timo-nies : and lôved thém ex-ceed-ing-ly.

168 I have kept Thy commând-ments and tés-timo-nies : for âll my wáys are befóre Thee.

Appropinquet deprecatio.
(*Major.*)

mf LET my compláint come befóre Thee,⌒O Lord : give me understânding, accórd - ing⌒to Thÿ word.

170 Let my supplicâtion cóme before Thee : delíver me, accórd-ing⌒to Thÿ word.

171 My lîps shall spéak of⌒Thy praise : whên thou hast taúght me⌒ Thy stä-tutes.

172 Yea, my tôngue shall síng of⌒ Thy word : for âll Thy commánd-ments⌒are rîgh-teous.

173 Let Thine hând hëlp me : for I have chôsen Thý com-mánd-ments.

174 I have longed for Thy sâving héalth, O Lord : and în Thy láw is my de-light.

175 O let my soul live,* and ît shall praíse Thee : ând Thy júdg-ments⌒shall hëlp me.

176 I have gone astrây like a shéep that⌒is lost : O seek Thy servant,* for I dô not forgét Thy commánd-ments.

The Twenty-Seventh Day.

Mattins.

Venite exultemus, Domino.

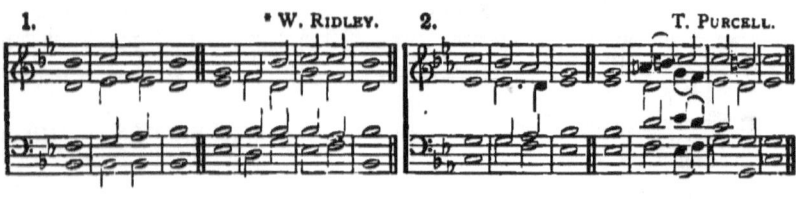

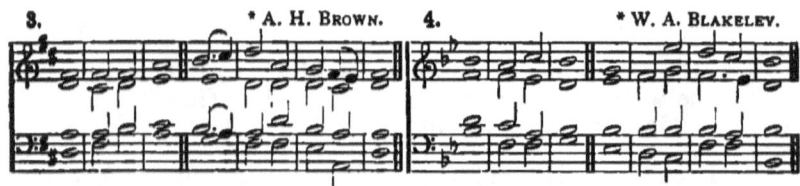

f O COME,✶ let us sing ún-to⁀ the Lord : let us heartily rejoice in the strength of our sal-vä-tion.

2 Let us come before His présence with thanksgív-ing : and shew ourselves glád in Him with Psalms.

3 For the Lórd is a gréat God : and a great Kíng above äll gods.

4 In His hand are all the córners óf the earth : and the strength of the hills is Hís äl-so.

5 The sea is Hís, and He made it : and His hánds prepár-ed⁀the drÿ land.

p 6 O come,✶ let us wôrship, and fáll down: and knêel before the Lórd our Mä-ker.

7 For Hê is the Lórd our God : and we are the people of His pâsture, and the shéep of His hand.

mf 8 To-day if ye will hear His voice,✶ hárden nót your hearts : as in the provocation,✶ and as in the day of temptâtion ín the wil-der-ness ;

9 When your fâthers témpt-ed Me : próved Mé, and saw My works.

10 Forty years long✶ was I grieved with thís generá-tion,⁀and said : It is a people that do err in their hêarts, for they háve not known My ways.

11 Unto whóm I swáre in⁀My wrath : that they shôuld not én-ter into My rest.

Glory be to the Fâther, ánd to⁀the Son : ánd tó the Ho-ly Ghost ;

As it was in the beginning,✶ is nôw, and éver shall be : wôrld without énd. ˙A˙-men.

156

PSALMS 120, 121.

PSALM 120. *Ad Dominum.*

mf WHEN I was in trouble I
called upón the Lord:
ånd Hē heård me.

2 Deliver my soul, O Lôrd, from
lý-ing lips : ånd fróm a^de-ceit-ful
tongue.

3 What reward shall be given or
done unto thêe, thou fålse tongue :
even mighty and sharp årrows, with
hōt burn-ing coals.

p 4 Wo is me,* that I am con-
strained to dwêll with Mē-sech :
and to have my habitation amóng
the ténts of Kë-dar.

5 My sôul hath long dwélt among
them : thåt are é-nemies un-to
peace.

6 I labour for peace,* but when I
spêak unto thém there-of : they
måke them réady to båt-tle.

PSALM 121. *Levavi oculos.*

mf I WILL lift up mine êyes ún-
to^the hills : fróm whênce
cometh my help.

2 My help cometh êven fróm the
Lord : Whô hath måde heaven and
earth.

3 He will not suffer thy fôot to be
mōv-ed : and Hê that kéep-eth^thee
will not sleep.

4 Behold, Hê that keepeth Ís-ra-
el : shall nêither slúm-ber nör sleep.

5 The Lord Himsêlf is thy kêep-er:
the Lord is thy defênce upón thy
right hand ;

6 So that the sūn shall not búrn
thee^by day : nêither the mōon by
night.

7 The Lord shall preserve thee
from åll é-vil : yea, it is êven Hé
that^shall keep thy soul.

8 The Lord shall preserve thy
going ôut, and thy cóm-ing in : from
thís time fórth for e-ver-more.

157 [PSALM 122.

Psalms 122, 123.

Psalm 122. *Lætatus sum.*

mf I WAS glâd when they saíd unto me : We will gô into the hoúse of the Lord.

2 Oụr fêet shall stánd in ͡ thy gates : O Je-ru-sa-lem.

3 Jerusalem is bûilt as a cí-ty : that ís at ú-nity in it-self.

4 For thither the tribes go up, * êven the tríbes of ͡ the Lord : to testify unto Israel, * to give thânks unto the Nâme of the Lord.

5 For there is the sêat of ſudg-ment : even the sêat of the hoúse of Dä-vid.

p 6 O pray for the peâce of Jerú-sa-lem : thêy shall prós-per ͡ that löve thee.

7 Pêace be withín thy walls : and plêntcousness withín thy pa-la-ces.

8 For my brẹ́thren and compá-nions' sakes : I will wísh thee ͡ pros-pe-ri-ty.

9 Yea, because of ͜ the hoûse of the Lórd our God : I will séek to do thee good.

Psalm 123. *Ad Te levavi oculos meos.*

mp UNTO Thêe lift I úp mine eyes : O Thôu that dwéll-est in the heavens.

2 Behold, * even as the eyes of servants look unto the hand of their masters, * and as the eyes of a maiden unto the hând of her mís-tress : even so our eyes wait upon the Lord our God, * untîl He have mér-cy upön us.

p 3 Have mercy upon us, O Lord, * have mêrcy upön us : for we are ûtterlý de-spís-ed.

4 Our soul is filled with the scorn-ful reprôof of the wêal-thy : and with the despíte-fulness of the proud.

PSALMS 124, 125.

PSALM 124. *Nisi quia Dominus.*

mf IF the Lord Himself had not been on our side,* nôw may Ís-rael say : if the Lord Himself had not been on our side, * when mên róse up against us ;

2 They had swâllowed ús up quick : when they were so wrâthfully displéas-ed ät us.

p 3 Yea, the wâters had drówn-ed us : and the strêam had gone ó-ver oür soul.

4 The deep wâters óf the proud : had gone êven ó-ver oür soul.

mf 5 But prâised bé the Lord : Who hath not given us ôver for a prêy unto their teeth.

6 Our soul is escaped * even as a bird out of the snâre of the fôwl-er : the snare is brôken, and wé are deli-ver-ed.

(Full) f 7 Our help stândeth in the Náme of the Lord : Whô hath mâde heaven and earth.

PSALM 125. *Qui confidunt.*

mf THEY that put their trust in the Lord * shall be even as the môunt Sí-on : which may not be removed, * but stândeth fást for ëv-er.

2 The hills stand abôut Jerú-salem : even so standeth the Lord round about His people, * from thís time fórth for ev-er-more.

3 For the rod of the ungodly * cometh not into the lôt of the righteous : lest the righteous pût their hánd unto wick-ed-ness.

p 4 Dô wéll, O Lord : unto thôse that are góod and true of heart.

5 As for such as turn back * unto their ôwn wíck-ed-ness : the Lord shall lead them forth with the evildoers ; * but pêace shall bé upon Is-ra-el.

Evensong.

PSALMS 126, 127.

PSALM 126. *In convertendo.*

f WHEN the Lord turned again the captívity of Síon : thén were we líke unto them that dream.

2 Then was our mouth fílled with láugh-ter : áñd our tongue with joy.

3 Then said they amóng the héa-then : The Lord hath dóne gréat things for them.

4 Yea, the Lord hath done great things for ús alréa-dy : whéreóf we re-joice.

mf 5 Túrn our captí-vity,⁀O Lord : ás the rí-vers in the south.

6 Théy that sów in tears : sháll réap iñ joy.

7 He that now goeth on his way weeping, ✶ and béareth fórth good seed : shall doubtless come agáin with joy, ✶ and brǐng his she͞aves with him.

PSALM 127. *Nisi Dominus.*

mf EXCEPT the Lórd búild the house : their lábour is but lóst that búild it.

2 Except the Lórd keep the cí-ty : the wátchman wák-eth but in vain.

3 It is but lost labour that ye haste to rise up early, ✶ and so late take rest, ✶ and eat the bréad of cáre-ful-ness : for so He gíveth Hís be-lov-ed sleep.

p 4 Lo, chíldren and the frúit of⁀ the womb : are an heritage and gíft that cóm-eth of the Lord.

5 Like as the arrows in the hánd of the gí-ant : even sô are the yoŭng chíl-dren.

6 Happy is the man that hath his qúiver fúll of them : they shall not be ashamed ✶ when they spêak with their é-nemies in the gate.

PSALM 128. *Beati omnes.*

mf BLESSED are all théy that féar the Lord : ånd wálk in Hïs ways.

2 For thou shalt eat the lâbours óf thine hands : O well is thêe, and háp-py shalt thou be.

3 Thy wife shall bê as the fruít-ful vine : upôn the wálls of thíhe house.

4 Thy children like the ôlive-brånch-es : rôund abóut thy tä-ble.

f 5 Lo, thûs shall the mán be bless'd : thât fe'ar-eth the Lord.

6 The Lord from out of Sîon shall * só bless thee : that thou shalt see Jerusalem in prospêrity áll thy lïfe long.

7 Yea, that thou shalt see thy children's chíl-dren : ånd péace upon Is-ra-el.

PSALMS 129, 130.

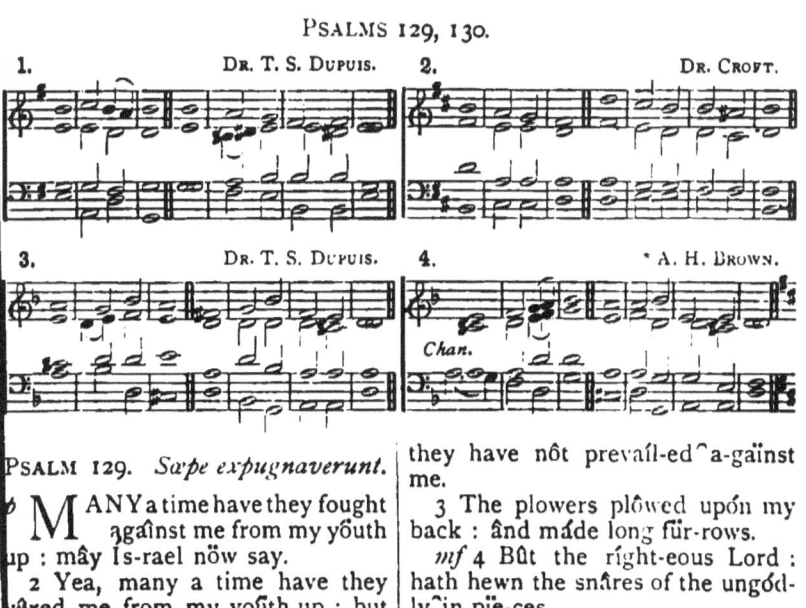

PSALM 129. *Sæpe expugnaverunt.*

MANY a time have they fought against me from my yóuth up : mây Is-rael nöw say.

2 Yea, many a time have they véxed me from my yoûth up : but

they have nôt prevaíl-ed ͡ a-gaínst me.

3 The plowers plôwed upón my back : ånd máde long fúr-rows.

mf 4 Bût the ríght-eous Lord : hath hewn the snáres of the ungódly ͡ in pïe-ces.

L   161   [*mp* 5 Let

mp 5 Let them be confounded and turned back-ward : as many as have evil will at Si-on.

6 Let them be even as the grass * growing upon the house-tops : which withereth afore it be pluck-ed up ;

7 Whereof the mower filleth not his hand : neither he that bind th up the sheaves his bö-som.

8 So that they who go by * say not so much as,The Lord pros-per you : we wish you good luck in the Name of the Lord.

PSALM 130. *De profundis.*

p OUT of the deep have I called unto Thee, O Lord : Lord hear my voice.

2 O let Thine ears consi-der well : the voice of my com-plaint.

3 If Thou, Lord, wilt be extreme * to mark what is done a-miss : O Lord who may abide it?

4 For there is mer-cy with Thee : therefore shalt Thou be fear-ed.

5 I look for the Lord ; * my soul doth wait for Him : in His word is my trust.

6 My soul fleeth un-to the Lord : before the morning watch, * I say, before the mor-ning watch.

7 O Israel, trust in the Lord, * for with the Lord there is mer-cy : and with Him is plen-teous re-demp-tion.

8 And He shall redeem Is-ra-el : from all his sins.

PSALM 131. *Domine, non est.*

VENITE.] MATTINS. [DAY 28.

mf LORD, I am not hígh-mínd-ed : I have nó próud looks.
2 I do not exercise mysêlf in great mät-ters : whĭch are tóo high fõr me.
p 3 But I refrain my soul, and keep it low, * like as a child that is wêaned from his mō-ther : yea, my soul is even ás a wean-ed child.
4 O Ísrael, trústin^the Lord : from thĭs time fórth for e-ver-more.

The Twenty-Eighth Day.
Mattins.

Venite, exultemus Domino.

1. * W. A. BLAKELEY. 2. * DR. E. G. MONK.
3. * L. J. TURRELL. 4. W. RUSSELL.

f O COME, * let us síng ún-to^ the Lord : let us heartily re-joice in the strêngth of oúr sal-vä-tion.
2 Let us come before His prêsence with thanksgív-ing : and shêw our-selves gláð in Him with Psalms.
3 For the Lôrd is a grêat God : and a grêat Kíng above äll gods.
4 In His hand are all the côrners óf the earth : and the strength of the hĭlls is Hĭs äl-so.
5 The sea is Hĭs, and He máde it : and His hânds prepár-ed^the drÿ land.
p 6 O come, * let us wôrship, and fäll down: and knêel before the Lórd our Mä-ker.
7 For Hê is the Lórd our God : and we are the people of His pâsture, and the shéep of Hĭs hand.

mf 8 To-day if ye will hear His voice, * hârden nót your hearts : as in the provocation, * and as in the day of temptâtion ín the wil-der-ness ;
9 When your fâthers témpt-ed Me : prôved Mé, and saw My works.
10 Forty years long * was I grieved with thĭs generá-tion,^and said : It is a people that do err in their hêarts, for they háve not known My ways.
11 Unto whôm I swáre in^My wrath : that they shôuld not én-ter into My rest.
Glory be to the Fâther, ánd to^the Son : ánd tó the Ho-ly Ghost ;
As it was in the beginning, * is nów, and éver shall be : wôrld without ênd. ˙A˙-men.

163 [PSALM 132.

PSALM 132. *Memento, Domine.*

mf LORD, remêmber Dā́-vid :
ănd áll his tròu-ble ;
2 How he swâre ún-to͡ the Lord :
and vowed a vow unto the Almī́ghty
Gód of Jä-cob ;
3 I will not come within the
tâbernacle óf mine house : nôr clímb
up into my bed ;
4 I will not suffer mine eyes to
sleep, * nor mine êye-lids to slū́mber: neither the temples of my
hêad to tā́ke a-ny rest ;
5 Until I find out a place for the
têmple óf the Lord : an habitation
or the mī́ghty Gód of Jä-cob.
6 Lo, we heard of the sâme at
Ĕph-ra-ta : ănd fóund it in the wood.
7 We will gô into His tá-berna-cle :
and fall low on our knêes befóre
His fôot-stool.
8 Arise, O Lôrd, into Thy rést-ing-place : Thôu, and the árk of
Thy strength.
9 Let Thy priests be clôthed with
rī́gh-teous-ness : and let Thy saínts
sī́ng with joy-ful-ness.
p 10 For Thy sêrvant Dá-vid's
sake : turn not away the prêsence of
Thíne A-noïnt-ed.
mf 11 The Lord hath made a
faithful ôath unto Dā́-vid : ănd He
shall not shrink from it ;

12 Of the frúït of thy bô-dy : shall
Î sét up-on thy seat.
13 If thy children will keep My
çovenant,* and My testimonies that
Î shall lēarn them : their children
also shall sít upon thy séat for ev-er-more.
14 For the Lord hath chosen
Sion * to be an habitâtion fór
Him-self : Hê hath lóng-ed för her.
(Full) mf 15 This shall be My
rêst for ēv-er : here will I dwêll, for
I háve a͡ de-light there-in.
(Dec) mf 16 I will bless her
vī́ctuals with ín-crease : and will
sâtisfý her poor with bread.
f 17 I will dêck her príests with
health : ănd her saínts shall͡ re-joice
and sing.
18 There shall I make the horn
of Dâvid to flôu-rish : I have
ordained a lântern for Míne A-noïnt-ed.
19 As for his enemies, * I shall
clôthe thém with shame : but upon
himsêlf shall his crôwn flôu-rish.

PSALM 133. *Ecce, quam bonum!*

mf BEHOLD, how good and
jôyful a thī́ng it is :
brethren, * to dwêll togé-ther͡ in
u-ni-ty !

2 It is like the precious ointment upon the head, * that ran dôwn ún-to^the beard : even unto Aaron's beard, * and went dôwn to the skírts of^his clöth-ing.

3 Like as the dêw of Hĕr-mon : which fĕll upon the hîll of Sï-on.
4 For there the Lord prômised His blĕs-sing : ând lífe for e-ver-more.

PSALM 134. *Ecce nunc.*

ƒ BEHÔLD now, praíse the Lord : âll ye sĕr-vants of the Lord ;
2 Ye that by night stând in the hóuse of^the Lord : even in the coûrts of the hóuse of oür God.
3 Lift up your hânds in the sánc-tua-ry : ând praíse the Lord.
4 The Lôrd that made heáven and earth : give thee blĕssing oút of Sï-on.

PSALM 135. *Laudate Nomen.*

ƒ O PRAISE the Lord,* lâud ye the Náme of^the Lord : praíse it, O ye sĕr-vants of the Lord ;
2 Ye that stând in the hóuse of^ the Lord : in the coûrts of the hóuse of oür God.
3 O praise the Lord, * for the Lôrd is grä-cious : O sing praises unto His Náme, for ít is löve-ly.
mf 4 For why ? * the Lord hath çhosen Jâcob úp-to^Him-self : and Israel for His Own pos-sĕs-sion.
ƒ 5 For I knôw that the Lórd is great : ând that our Lórd is above all gods.
6 Whatsoever the Lord pleased,* that dîd He in heáven, and^in earth : and in the sêa, and in âll deep plä-ces.
7 He bringeth forth the clôuds from the énds of^the world : and sendeth forth lightnings with the rain, * bringing the wînds óut of^ His trëa-sures.
mf 8 He smote the fîrst-born of É-gypt : bŭth of man and beast.
9 He hath sent tokens and wonders intǫ the midst of thee,* O thou lând of É-gypt : upon Phâraoh, and áll his sĕr-vants.
10 He smote dîvers nä-tions : ând slĕw migh-ty kings ;
11 Sehon king of the Amorites,* and Og the kîng of Bä-san : and âll the kíng-doms^of Cä-naan ;
12 And gave their land to bê an hé-ri-tage : even an heritage unto Israél His pëo-ple.
(Full) ƒ 13 Thy Name, O Lord,* endûreth for ĕv-er : so doth Thy memorial, O Lord, * from one generâtion tó an-ö-ther.

[*(Dec.)* *mf* 14 For

(*Dec.*) *mf* 14 For the Lord will avênge His pē̇-ple: and be grâcious ún-to͡ His sĕr vants.
p 15 As for the images of the heathen, * thêy are but sĭl-ver͡and gold: thē wǒrk of mēn's hands.
16 They have môuths, and spēak not: eyes have they, bŭt they sëe not.
17 They have ears,* and yêt they hēar not: neither is there âny brēath in thëir mouths.

18 They that mâke them are lĭke unto them: and so are all thêy that pŭt their trust in them.
f 19 Praise the Lord, ye hôuse of Ĭs-ra-el: praise the Lôrd, ye hóuse of Aä-ron.
20 Praise the Lord, ye hôuse of Lē-vi: ye that fêar the Lôrd, praise the Lord.
(*Full*) *f* 21 Praised be the Lôrd, out of Sĭ̇-on: Who dwêlleth ăt Je-ru-sa-lem.

Evensong.

PSALM 136. *Confitemini.*

f O GIVE thanks unto the Lord,* for Hê is grā-cious: †(*full*) and His mêrcy endŭr-eth͡for ëv-er.
2 O give thânks unto the Gód of͡ all gods: for His mêrcy endŭr-eth͡ for ëv-er.
3 O thânk the Lórd of͡ all lords: for His mêrcy endŭr-eth͡for ëv-er.

† The second half of each verse to be sung full.

4 Who only dôeth great wŏn-ders : for His mêrcy endúr-eth⁀for ëv-er.

mf 5 Who by His excellent wís-dom máde the heavens : for His mêrcy endúr-eth⁀for ëv-er.

6 Who laid out the earth abŏve the wā-ters : for His mêrcy endúr-eth⁀for ëv-er.

7 Who hath mâde grēat lights : for His mêrcy endúr-eth⁀for ëv-er ;

8 The sûn to rúle the day : for His mêrcy endúr-eth⁀for ëv-er ;

9 The moon and the stârs to gó-vern⁀the night : for His mêrcy endúr-eth⁀for ëv-er.

10 Who smote Êgypt with their fïrst-born : for His mêrcy endúr-eth⁀ for ëv-er.

11 And brought out Îsrael from amŏng them : for His mêrcy endúr-eth⁀for ëv-er ;

12 With a mighty hând, and strétch-ed⁀out arm : for His mêrcy endúr-eth⁀for ëv-er.

f 13 Who divided the Rêd Séa in⁀two parts : for His mêrcy endúr-eth⁀for ëv-er.

14 And made Israel to go thrôugh the mídst of it : for His mêrcy endúr-eth⁀for ëv-er.

15 But as for Pharaoh and his host, * He overthrew thêm in the Rêd Sea : for His mêrcy endúr-eth⁀ for ëv-er.

16 Who led His people thrôugh the wíl-der-ness : for His mêrcy endúr-eth⁀for ëv-er.

mf 17 Whô smóte great kings : for His mêrcy endúr-eth⁀for ëv-er.

18 Yea, and slêw mígh-ty kings : for His mêrcy endúr-eth,̂for ëv-er ;

19 Sehon kíhg of the Á-mo-rites : for His mêrcy endúr-eth⁀for ëv-er.

20 And Og the kíng of Bā-san : for His mêrcy endúr-eth⁀for ëv-er.

21 And gave away their lând for an hé-ri-tage : for His mêrcy endúr-eth⁀for ëv-er ;

22 Even for an heritage unto Ísrael His sêr-vant : for His mêrcy endúr-eth⁀for ëv-er.

mp 23 Who remembered us whên we were in trôu-ble : for His mêrcy endúr-eth⁀for ëv-er.

24 And hath delivered us frôm our é-ne-mies : for His mêrcy endúr-eth⁀for ëv-er.

25 Who gíveth fóod to⁀all flesh : for His mêrcy endúr-eth⁀for ëv-er.

f 26 O give thânks unto the Gód of heaven : for His mêrcy endúr-eth⁀for ëv-er.

27 O give thânks unto the Lórd of lords : for His mêrcy endúr-eth⁀ for ëv-er.

PSALM 137. *Super flumina*

p BY the waters of Babylon we sât dówn and wept : when we remêmbered thée, O Sï-on.

2 As for our hârps, we háng-ed⁀ them up : upôn the trées that are there-in.

3 For they that led us away captive * required of us then a song, and melody, ĭn our héa-vi-ness : Sing us ône of the sóngs of Sï-on.
pp 4 How shall we sĭng the Lôrd's song : ĭn a strànge land ?
5 If I ĭorget thêe, O Jerŭ-sa-lem: let my right hånd forgét her cün-ning.
6 If I do not remember thee, * let my tongue clêave to the róof of my mouth : yea, if I prefêr not Jerŭ-salem in my mirth.

mp 7 Remember the children of Edom, O Lord, * in the dây of Jerŭ-sa-lem : how they said, Down with it, * dôwn with it, é-ven to the ground.
p 8 O daughter of Babylon, * wâsted with mĭ-se-ry : yea, happy shall he be that rewardeth thêe, as thóu hast serv-ed us.
9 Blessed shall he be that tâketh thy clĭil-dren : and thróweth thém a-gainst the stones.

PSALM 138. *Confitebor Tibi.*

f I WILL give thanks unto Thee, O Lôrd, with my whôle heart : even before the gôds will I sing prafse un-to Thee.
2 I will worship toward Thy holy temple, and praise Thy Name, * because of Thy lôving-kĭnd-ness and truth : for Thou hast magnified

Thy Nâme, and Thy Wórd, above äll things.
3 When I called upôn Thee, Thou heárd-est me : and endûedst my sóul with mŭch strength.
4 All the kings of the eârth shall praĭse Thee, O Lord : for they have heârd the wórds of Thÿ mouth.

5 Yea, they shall sĭng in the wáys of the Lord : that grêat is the gló-ry of the Lord.

p 6 For though the Lord be high, * yet hath He respect ûnto the lŏw-ly ; as for the proud, * He behŏldeth thĕm a-fär off.

7 Though I walk in the midst of trouble, * yet shalt Thôu refrĕsh me : Thou shalt stretch forth Thy hand upon the furiousness of mine enemies, * and Thy rĭght hánd shall säve me.

8 The Lord shall make good His loving-kĭndness tŏward me : yea, Thy mercy, O Lord, endureth for ever, * despise not thên the wórks of Thine ŏwn hands.

The Twenty-Ninth Day.
Mattins.
Venite, exultemus Domino.

f O COME, * let us sĭng ŭn-to˘ the Lord : let us heartily rejoice in the strêngth of oŭr sal-vä-tion.

2 Let us come before His prêsence with thanksgĭv-ing : and shêw ourselves glăd in Him with Psalms.

3 For the Lôrd is a grêat God : and a grĕat Kĭng above äll gods.

4 In His hand are all the côrners ŏf the earth : and the strength of the hĭlls is Hĭs äl-so.

5 The sea is Hĭs, and He mäde it : and His hânds prepár-ed˘the drў land.

p 6 O come, * let us wôrship, and fäll down : and knêel before the Lórd our Mä-ker.

7 For Hê is the Lórd our God : and we are the people of His pâsture, and the shéep of Hĭs hand.

mf 8 To-day if ye will hear His voice, * hârden nŏt your hearts : as in the provocation, * and as in the day of temptâtion ĭn the wil-der-ness ;

9 When your fâthers témpt-ed Me : próved Mé, and saw My works.

10 Foity years long * was I grieved with tĭ.ĭs generá-tion,˘and said : It is a people that do err in their hêarts, for they háve not known My ways.

11 Unto whôm I swáre in˘My wrath : that they shôuld not ĕn-ter into My rest.

Glory be to the Fâther, ánd to˘the Son : ánd tó the Ho-ly Ghost ;

As it was in the beginning, * is nôw, and éver shall be : wôrld without ĕnd. 'A'-men.

[PSALM 139.

PSALM 139. *Domine, probasti.*

mf O LORD Thou hast searched me ôut, and knôwn me : Thou knowest my down-sitting, and mine up-rising * Thou under-stândest my thôughts long be-fore.

2 Thou art about my pâth, and abôut my bed : ând spíest out all my ways.

3 For lo, * there is nôt a wórd in my tongue : but Thou, O Lord,* knôwest it ál-to-gë-ther.

4 Thou hast fâshioned me behínd and be-fore : and laîd Thine hánd up-ôn me.

mp 5 Such knowledge is too wonderful * and êxcellent fôr me : I cânnot attaín un-to it.

6 Whither shall I gô then from Thy Spí-rit : or whither shall I gô then fróm Thy prë-sence ?

7 If I climb up into heâven, Thóu art there : if I go down to hêll, Thou art thére äl-so.

8 If I take the wíngs of the mörn-ing : and remain in the ûttermost párts of the sea ;

9 Even there also shall Thy hând léad me : and Thy ríght hánd shall höld me.

10 If I say, * Peradventure the dârkness shall có-ver me : thên shall my níght be turn-ed to day.

11 Yea, the darkness is no dark- ness with Thee, * but the níght is as cléar as the day : the darkness and líght to Théе are both a-like.

12 Fôr my reíns are Thine : Thou hast côvered me ín my mo-ther's womb.

13 I will give thanks unto Thee,* for I am feârfully and wón-derfully made : marvellous are Thy works,* and thât my soul knów-eth right well.

14 My bônes are not híd from Thee : though I be made secretly, * and fâshioned benëath in the earth.

15 Thine eyes did see my sub-stance, * yet bêing impêr-fect : and in Thy book were âll my mém-bers writ-ten ;

16 Which day by dây were fásh-ion-ed : whên as yét there was none of them.

mf 17 How dear are Thy côunsels unto mé, O God : Ô how gréat is the sum of them !

18 If I tell them, * they are more in nûmber thán the sand : when I wake ûp I am pré-sent with Thee.

mp 19 Wilt Thou not slây the wíck-ed, O God ; depârt from me, ye blóod-thirs-ty men.

20 For they speak unríghteously agaínst Thee : and Thine ênemies táke Thy Name in vain.

21 Do not I hate them, O Lôrd, that háte Thee : and am not I grieved with thôse that ríse up against Thee?
22 Yêa, I háte ͡ them right sore : even as thôugh they wére mine e-ne-mies.

p 23 Try me, O God, * and sêek the gróund of ͡ my heart : prôve me, and exá-mine mÿ thoughts.
24 Look well * if there be any way of wíckedness ín me : and lead me in the wây év-er-läst-ing.

PSALM 140. *Eripe me, Domine.*

mf DELIVER me, O Lôrd, from the é-vil man : and pre-sêrve me fróm the wick-ed man.
2 Who imagine míschief ín their hearts : and stír up strífe all ͡ the däy long.
3 They have sharpened their tôngues like a sér-pent : adder's pôison is ún-der theïr lips.
4 Keep me, O Lord, * from the hánds of the ungód-ly : preserve me from the wicked men, * who are pûrposed to overthrów my gö-ings.
5 The proud have laid a snare for me,* and spread a nêt abróad with cords : yêa, and set tráps in mÿ way.
p 6 I said unto the Lôrd, Thóu art ͡ my God : hêar the voíce of ͡ my prayers, O Lord.
7 O Lord Gôd, Thou stréngth of ͡ my health : Thou hast covered my hêad in the dáy of bät-tle.

8 Let not the ungodly hâve his desíre, O Lord : let not his mis-chievous imagination prôsper, lést they be too proud.
mf 9 Let the mischief of their own lips * fáll upon the héad of them : thât cóm-pass me a-bout.
10 Let hot burning côals fáll upon them : let them be cast into the fire, and into the pit, * that they nêver ríse up a-gain.
11 A man full of words * shall not prôsper upón the earth : evil shall hunt the wicked pêrson to ó-ver-thröw him.
12 Sure I am * that the Lôrd will avénge the poor : and maintâin the caúse of ͡ the hëlp-less.
13 The righteous also shall give thânks ún-to ͡ Thy Name : and the jûst shall contí-nue in Thy sight.

[PSALM 141.

Psalm 141. *Domine, clamavi.*

p LORD, I call upon Thee, * hâste Thee ún-to me : and consider my vôice when I crý un-to Thee.

2 Let my prayer be set forth in Thy síght as the ín-cense : and let the lifting up of my hânds be an éve-ning sa-cri-fice.

3 Set a watch, O Lôrd, befóre my mouth : and kêep the dóor of my̆ lips.

4 O let not mine heart be inclíned to any é-vil thing : let me not be occupied in ungodly works * with the men that work wickedness,* lest I êat of such thíngs as plëase them.

5 Let the righteous rather smíte me frínd-ly : ánd re-pröve me.

6 But let not their precious bâlms bréak my head : yea, I will prây yet agaínst their wick-ed-ness.

mp 7 Let their judges be overthrown in stôny plá-ces : that they may hêar my wórds, for they are sweet.

8 Our bones lie scâttered befóre the pit : like as when one breaketh and hêweth wóod up-on the earth.

mf 9 But mine eyes look unto Thêe, O Lôrd God : in Thee is my trûst, O cást not out my soul.

p 10 Keep me from the snâre that they have laíd for me : ånd from the tráps of^the wick-ed doers.

11 Let the ungodly fall into their own nêts tog͡e-ther : and lêt me év-er^es-cäpe them.

Evensong.
Psalms 142, 143.

Psalm 142.

Voce mea ad Dominum.

p 1 I CRÎED unto the Lórd with͡ my voice: yea, even unto the Lord did I mâke my súp-pli-cä-tion.

2 I poured out my compláints befōre Him: and shêwed Him óf my tröu-ble.

3 When my spirit was in heâvi-ness Thou knéw-est͡my path: in the way wherein I walked ✳ have they prívily laíd a snare for me.

4 I looked âlso upon my ríght hand: and saw there was nô man thát would knöw me.

5 I had nô place to flée un-to: and nô man cár-ed for my soul.

6 I cried unto Thêe, O Lórd, and said: Thou art my hope, ✳ and my pôrtion in the lánd of͡the lïv-ing.

7 Consîder mý com-plaint: for Î am brôught ve-ry low.

8 O delíver me from my pér-secu-tors: for thêy are tóo strong for me.

mf 9 Bring my soul out of prison,✳ that I may give thânks ún-to͡Thy Name: which thing if Thou wilt grant me, ✳ then shall the righteous resôrt ún-to͡my com-pa-ny.

Psalm 143. *Domine, exaudi.*

p HEAR my prayer, O Lord, ✳ and consîder mý de-sire: hearken unto mê for Thy trúth and right-eousness' sake.

2 And enter not into jûdgment with Thy sēr-vant: for in Thy sight shall nô man líving be jus-ti-fied.

3 For the enemy hath persecuted my soul; ✳ he hath smitten my lîfe dówn to͡the ground: he hath laid me in the darkness,✳ as the mên thát have been long dead.

4 Therefore is my spirit vêxed witkín me: and my heârt withín͡ me is de-so-late.

mp 5 Yet do I remember the time past; ✳ I mûse upon áll Thy works: yea, I exercise mysêlf in the wórks of Thÿ hands.

6 I stretch fôrth my hánds unto Thee: my soul gâspeth unto Thée as͡a thirs-ty land.

p 7 Hear me, O Lord, and that soon,✳ for my spírit wáx-eth faint: hide not Thy face from me.✳ lest I be like unto thêm that go dōwn in-to͡ the pit.

8 O let me hear Thy loving-kindness betimes in the môrning, for in Thée is͡my trust: shew Thou me the way that I should walk in,✳ for I lîft up my sôul un-to Thee.

9 Deliver me, O Lôrd, from mine é-ne-mies: for I flêe unto Thée to hïde me.

10 Teach me to do the thing that pleaseth Thêe, for Thóu art͡my God: let Thy loving Spirit lead me fôrth into the lánd of right-eous-ness.

mf 11 Quicken me, O Lôrd, for Thy Nãme's sake: and for Thy righteousness' sake ✳ brîng my sóul out͡of tröu-ble.

12 And of Thy goodness slây mine é-ne-mies: and destrọy all them that vex my sôul; for I am͡ Thy sër-vant.

173

The Thirtieth Day.

Mattins.

Venite, exultemus Domino.

f O COME,* let us síng ún-to˄ the Lórd : let us heartily rejoice in the strêngth of oúr salvä-tion.

2 Let us come before His prêsence with thanksgív-ing : and shêw ourselves gláđ in Him with Psalms.

3 For the Lôrd is a grêat God : and a grêat Kíng above äll gods.

4 In His hand are all the côrners óf the earth : and the strength of the hîlls is Hís äl-so.

5 The sea is Hís, and He mãde it : and His hânds prepár-ed˄the drÿ land.

p 6 O come,* let us wôrship and fäll down : and knêel before the Lórd our Mä-ker.

7 For Hê is the Lórd our God : and we are the people of His pâsture, and the shéep of His hand.

mf 8 To-day if ye will hear His voice,* hârden nót your hearts : as in the provocation,* and as in the day of temptâtion ín the wil-derness ;

9 When your fâthers témpt-ed Me : prôved Mé, and saw My works.

10 Forty years long * was I grieved with thís generá-tion,˄and said : It is a people that do err in their hêarts, for they háve not known My ways.

11 Unto whôm I swáre in˄My wrath : that they shôuld not én-ter into My rest.

Glory be to the Fâther, ánd to˄ the Son : ánd tó the Ho-ly Ghost ;

As it was in the beginning, * is nôw, and éver shall be : wôrld without ênd. 'A˙-men.

Psalm 144. *Benedictus Dominus.*

f BLÊSSED be the Lórd my strength : Who teacheth my hânds to wár, and⌢my fin-gers⌢to fight ;

2 My hope and my fortress,⁕ my castle and deliverer, ⁕ my defênder in Whóm I trust : Who subdueth my pêople thát is un-der me.

p 3 Lord, what is man,⁕ that Thou hast sûch respéct unto him : or the son of man,⁕ that Thôu só re-gard-est him ?

pp 4 Mân is like a thíng of nought : his time pâsseth awáy like⌢a shä-dow.

f 5 Bow Thy hêavens, O Lórd, and⌢come down : toûch the móun-tains⌢and they shall smoke.

6 Cast forth Thy líghtning, and teâr them : shoot out Thine ârrows, ánd con-süme them.

mf 7 Send dôwn Thine hánd from⌢ a-bove : deliver me, and take me out of the great wâters, from the hánd⌢ of strange chíl-dren ;

8 Whose mouth tâlketh of vá-ni-ty : and their right hând is a ríght hand⌢of wick-ed-ness.

f 9 I will sing a new sông unto Thée, O God : and sing praises unto Thêe upon a tên-string-ed lute.

10 Thou hast given víctory ún-to kings : and hast delivered David Thy sêrvant from the pé-ril of the sword.

mf 11 Save me,⁕ and deliver me from the hând of strange chíl-dren : whose mouth talketh of vanity, ⁕ and their right hând is a right hánd of⌢in-i-qui-ty.

12 That our sons may grow ûp as the yôung plants : and that our daughters may be as the polished côrners óf the tëm-ple.

13 That our garners may be full and plênteous with all mán-ner⌢of store : that our sheep may bring forth thôusands and tén thousands in our streets.

14 That our oxen may be strong to labour ;⁕ that thêre be nó de-cay : no leading into captivity,⁕ and nô complaín-ing in our streets.

15 Happy are the pêople that are in súch a case : yea, blessed are the pêople who have the Lórd for theír God.

PSALM 145. *Exaltabo Te, Deus.*

f 1 I WILL magnify Thêe, O Gŏd, my King : and I will praise Thy Nâme for év-er⁀and ĕv-er.
2 Every dây will I give thánks unto Thee : and praise Thy Nâme for év-er⁀and ĕv-er.
(Full) f 3 Great is the Lord, and marvellous,⁕ wôrthy to be práis-ed : thére is no énd of⁀His greätness.
(Dec.) f 4 One generation shall praise Thy wôrks unto anŏ-ther : ănd declâre Thÿ power.
5 As for me,⁕ I will be tâlking of Thy wŏr-ship : Thy glŏry, Thy praíse, and won-drous works ;
6 So that men shall speak of the mĭght of Thy már-vellous acts : and I will âlso téll of⁀Thy greätness.
7 The memorial of Thine abundant kĭndness shall be shĕw-ed : and mĕn shall sĭng of⁀Thy right-eousness.
p 8 The Lord is grâcious, and mér-ci-ful : long-suffering ⁕ ănd of grĕat gŏod-ness.
9 The Lord is lŏving unto éve-ry man : and His mĕrcy is ŏ-ver all His works.
f 10 All Thy wŏrks praíse Thee,⁀ O Lord : and Thy saínts give thănks un-to Thee.

11 They shew the glŏry of Thy kĭng-dom : ănd tálk of Thÿ power ;
12 That Thy power, Thy glory,⁕ and mıghtiness of Thy kĭng-dom : mĭght be knŏwn un-to men.
13 Thy kingdom is an everlâsting kĭng-dom : and Thy dominion endûreth throughŏut all á-ges.
p 14 The Lord uphôldeth all sŭch as fall : and lifteth ûp all thŏse that are down.
15 The eyes of all wâit upon Thée, O Lord : and Thou givest them their mêat in dŭe sĕa-son.
16 Thou ôpenest Thíne hand : and fillest âll things lĭving with plen-teous-ness.
mf 17 The Lord is rĭghteous in âll His ways : ănd hŏ-ly⁀in all His works.
18 The Lord is nigh unto all thĕm that cáll upon Him : yea, all such as câll upŏn Him faith-ful-ly.
19 He will fulfil the desire of thĕm that féar Him : He also will hêar their crý, and⁀will hĕlp them.
20 The Lord preservcth all thĕm that lŏve Him : but scattereth abrŏad âll the⁀un-gŏd-ly.
f 21 My mouth shall spĕak the praíse of⁀the Lord : and let all flesh give thanks unto His holy Nâme for év-er⁀and ĕv-er.

PSALM 146. *Lauda, anima mea.*

f PRAISE the Lord, O my soul;∗ while I live will I praise the Lord : yea, as long as I have any being,∗ I will sîng praís-es unto my God.

2 O put not your trust in princes,∗ nor in âny chíld of man : fôr there is nô help in them.

p 3 For when the breath of man goeth forth ∗ he shall tûrn agaín to⁀ his earth : and then âll his thôughts pē-rish.

mf 4 Blessed is he that hath the God of Jâcob fór his help: and whose hôpe is ín the Lord his God ;

5 Who made heaven and earth,∗ the sea, and âll that thére-in is : Who kêepeth His pró-mise⁀for ëv-er;

6 Who helpeth them to ríght that súf-fer wrong : Whô féed-eth⁀the hün-gry.

mp 7 The Lord looseth mên out of prí-son : the Lôrd giveth síght to the blind.

8 The Lord helpeth thêm that are fäl-len : the Lord câreth fór the right-eous.

9 The Lord careth for the stran-gers ;∗ He defendeth the fâtherless and wí-dow : as for the way of the ungôdly, He tûrn-eth⁀it up-side down.

f 10 The Lord thy God, O Sion, ∗ shall be Kíng for év-er-more : and throughôut all gé-ne-rā-tions.

Evensong.

PSALMS 147, 148.

PSALM 147. *Laudate Dominum.*

f O PRAISE the Lord,* for it is a good thing to sing praises ŭn-to͡our God : yea, a joyful and pleasant thĭng it ĭs to͡be thănk-ful.

2 The Lord doth bŭild up Jerú-sa-lem : and gather togêther the oŭt-casts͡of Is-ra-el.

p 3 He healeth thôse that are brŏk-en͡in heart : and giveth mêdi-cine to hĕal their sĭck-ness.

4 He telleth the nŭmber óf the stars : and câlleth them áll by theír names.

(Full) f 5 Great is our Lôrd, and greát is͡His power : yêa, and His wĭs-dom͡is in-fi-nite.

(Dec.) mf 6 The Lord sêtteth úp the meek : and brĭngeth the ungód-ly down to͡the ground.

f 7 O sing unto the Lôrd with thanksgĭv-ing : sing prâises upon the hărp unto our God ;

mf 8 Who covereth the heaven with clouds,* and prepâreth raín for͡the earth : and maketh the grass to grow upon the môuntains, and hĕrb for͡the use of men ;

9 Who giveth fodder ŭnto the căt-tle : and feedeth the young râvens that cáll up-ön Him.

10 He hath no pleâsure in the strĕngth of͡an horse : neither de-lĭghteth Hé in any man's legs.

p 11 But the Lord's delight is in thĕm that feâr Him : and pŭt their trúst in͡His mër-cy.

f 12 Praise the Lôrd, O Jerú-sa-lem : praîse thy Gód, O Sï-on.

13 For He hath made fâst the bárs of͡thy gates : and hath blêssed thy chĭl-dren withĭn thee.

p 14 He maketh pêace in thy bôr-ders : and fĭlleth thee wĭth the flour of wheat.

15 He sendeth forth His com-mândment upŏn earth : and His wôrd runneth vĕ-ry swĭft-ly.

16 He gĭveth snŏw like wool : and scattereth the hôar-fróst like ăsh-es.

17 He casteth forth His ĭce like môr-sels : who is âble tó a-bide His frost?

18 He sendeth out His wôrd, and mĕlt-eth them : He blôweth with His wĭnd, and͡the wa-ters flow.

19 He sheweth His wôrd unto Jă-cob : His statutes and ŏrdinances ŭn-to Is-ra-el.

20 He hath not dealt so with ăny nă-tion : neither have the hêathen knów-ledge of His laws.

Psalm 148. *Laudate Dominum.*

f O PRAISE the Lórd of heaven: praísé Him in the height.
2 Praise Him, âll ye án-gels⁀of His : praíse Him, all His host.
3 Prâise Him, sún and moon : prâise Him áll ye stars and light.
4 Prâise Him, áll ye heavens : and ye wâters that áre a-bove the heavens.
5 Let them prâise the Náme of⁀ the Lord : for He spake the word, and they were made ; * He com-mânded, and théy were⁀cre-ä-ted.
6 He hath made them fast for êver and êv-er : He hath given them a lâw which shall nót be brö-ken.
mf 7 Prâise the Lórd upon earth: yê drágons, and äll deeps ;

8 Fire and hail, * snôw and vâ-pours : wind and stôrm, fulfíll-ing His word ;
9 Môuntains and âll hills : fruit-ful trêes and âll cë-dars ;
10 Bêasts and all cät-tle : wôrms and fea-thered fowls ;
11 Kings of the êarth and all péo-ple : prínces and all júd-ges of the world ;
f 12 Young men and maidens, * old men and children, * prâise the Náme of⁀the Lord : for His Name only is excellent, * and Hís praíse above heaven and earth.
13 He shall exalt the horn of His people ; * all His sâints shall prâise Him : even the children of Israel, * êven the péo-ple⁀that ser-veth Him.

Psalm 149. *Cantate Domino.*

1.   * A. H. Brown.   2.   * J. Turle.

3.   * W. A. Blakeley.   4.   Dr. B. Cooke.

f O SING unto the Lôrd a nêw song : let the congregâtion of sâints praise Him.
2 Let Israel rejoice in Hím that mâde him : and let the children of Síon be jóy-ful in their King.
3 Let them prâise His Náme in⁀ the dance : let them sing prâises unto Hím with tabret and harp.
mf 4 For the Lord hath plêasure in His péo-ple : and hêlpeth the mêek-heárt-ed.

5 Let the saints be jôyful with glô-ry: lêt them rejoíce in their beds.
6 Let the praises of Gôd bé in⁀ their mouth : and a twô-edged swórd in their hands ;
f 7 To be avênged of the hêa-then : ánd to rebúke the pëo-ple ;
8 To bínd their kíngs in chains : ánd their nóbles with links of iron.
9 That they may be avenged of them, * ás it is writ-ten : Súch hó-nour⁀have all His saints.

PSALM 150. *Laudate Dominum.*

f O PRAISE Gôd in His hó-liness : prâise Him in the fír-mament of His power.

2 Prâise Him in His nó-ble acts : praise Him accôrding to His éxcellent grëat-ness.

3 Praise Him in the sôund of the trúm-pet : prâise Him upón the lute and harp.

4 Praise Him in the cÿmbals and dãn-ces : prâise Him upón the strings and pipe.

5 Praise Him upon the wêll-tuned cÿm-bals : praise Him upôn the loûd cÿm-bals.

(Full) f 6 Let êvery thing thát hath breath : pfâïse the Lord.

PROPER PSALMS FOR THE FOUR GREAT FESTIVALS,

AND THE FASTS OF ASH-WEDNESDAY AND GOOD-FRIDAY: ALSO THE *MISERERE* FOR USE DURING LENT.

―•―

Christmas-Day.
𝔐attins.
Venite, exultemus Domino.

1. * C Fisher.   2.   * L. J. Turrell.

f O COME, * let us síng ún-to^
the Lord : let us heartily rejoice in the stréngth of oúr sal-vä-tion.
2 Let us come before His présence with thanksgív-ing : and shéw ourselves gláú in Him with Psalms.
3 For the Lórd is a gréat God : and a grêat Kíng above äll gods.
4 In His hand are all the córners óf the earth : and the strength of the hílls is Hís äl-so.
5 The sea is Hís, and He máde it : and His hânds prepár-ed^the drÿ land.
p 6 O come, * let us wórship, and fäll down: and knêel before the Lórd our Mä-ker.
7 For Hê is the Lórd our God : and we are the people of His pâsture, and the shéep of Hís hand.

mf 8 To-day if ye will hear His voice, * hârden nót your hearts : as in the provocation, * and as in the day of temptâtion ín the wil-der-ness ;
9 When your fâthers témpt-ed Me : próved Mé, and saw My works.
10 Forty years long * was I grieved with thís generá-tion,^and said : It is a people that do err in their héarts, for they háve not known My ways.
11 Unto whóm I swáre in^My wrath : that they shóuld not én-ter into My rest.
Glory be to the Fâther, ánd to^the Son : ánd tó the Ho-ly Ghost ;
As it was in the beginning, * is nôw, and éver shall be : wôrld without ênd. 'A'-men.

181   PSALM 19.

CHRISTMAS-DAY.] *THE PSALTER.* [PSALMS 19, 45.

PROPER PSALMS, 19, 45, 85.

PSALM 19. *Cæli enarrant.*

1. J. CORFE.   2. R. BELLAMY.

f THE heavens declâre the glô-ry⌃ of God : and the fîrmament shéweth His han-dy work.

2 One day télleth anô-ther : and one night cêrtiffeth an-ö-ther.

3 There is neither spêech nor lân-guage : but their vôices are heárd a-möng them.

4 Their sound is gone oût into âll lands : and their wôrds into the ênds of the world.

5 In them hath He set a tâber-nacle fôr the sun : which cometh forth as a bridegroom out of his chamber,⁕ and rejôiceth as a gíant to run his course.

6 It goeth forth from the utter-most part of the heaven, ⁕ and runneth about unto the ênd ôf it⌃ a-gain : and there is nôthing hîd from⌃the heat there-of.

mf 7 The law of the Lord is an undefiled lâw, convérting the soul : the testimony of the Lord is sure,⁕ and giveth wîsdom ún-to⌃the sim-ple.

8 The statutes of the Lord are rîght, and rejoíce the heart : the commandment of the Lord is pure,⁕ and gíveth lîght un-to⌃the eyes.

9 The fear of the Lord is clean,⁕ and endûreth for év-er : the judg-ments of the Lord are true,⁕ and rîghteous ál-to-gë-ther.

10 More to be desired are they than gold,⁕ yêa, than much fîne gold : sweeter also than hôney, ánd the hon-ey-comb.

11 Moreover, by thêm is Thy sér-vant taught : and in kêeping of them thére is great re-ward.

p 12 Who can tell how ôft he offénd-eth : O cleânse Thou me fróm my se-cret faults.

13 Keep Thy servant also from presumptuous sins,⁕ lest they get the domîhion ó-ver me : so shall I be undefiled,⁕ and ínnocent fróm the great of-fence.

14 Let the words of my mouth,⁕ and the meditâtion ôf my heart : be âlway accépt-able in Thy sight,

15 Ô⌃ Lord : my strêngth, and mý Re-dëem-er.

PSALM 45. *Eructavit cor meum.*

1. ⁕ A. H. BROWN.   2. ⁕ I. J. TURRELL.

mf MY heart is inditing of a gôod mât-ter : I speak of the thîngs which I have máde un-to⌃the King.

2 Mý tóngue is⌃the pen : ôf a réa-dy wri-ter.

3 Thou art faîrer than the chîl-dren⌃of men : full of grace are Thy lips,⁕ because God hath blêssed Thée for ëv-er.

f 4 Gird Thee with Thy sword upon Thy thigh,⁕ O Thôu Most Mîgh-ty : accôrding to Thy wôr-ship and re-nown.

[PSALMS 45, 85.] MATTINS. [CHRISTMAS-DAY.

5 Good luck have Thôu with Thine hô-nour : ride on, because of the word of truth,* of meekness, and righteousness,* and Thy right hând shall teách Thee ter-rible things.
6 Thy arrows are very sharp,* and the people shall be subdûed ún-to Thee : even in the midst amông the Kíng's e-ne-mies.
7 Thy seat, O God,* endûreth for ĕv-er : the sceptre of Thy kíng-dom is a rîght scëp-tre.
8 Thou hast loved righteousness,* and hâted iní-qui-ty : wherefore God, even Thy God,* hath anointed Thee with the oil of glâdness abóve Thy fĕl-lows.
p 9 All Thy garments smell of myrrh, * âloes, and cás-si-a : out of the ivory pâlaces, whereby̆ they͡ have made Thee glad.
10 Kings' daughters were among Thy hônourable wö́-men : upon Thy right hand did stand the queen in a vesture of gold,* wrought abôut with dí-vers cö-lours.
11 Hearken, O daughter,* and consíder, inclíne thine ear : forget

also thine own pêople, ánd thy fa-ther's house.
12 So shall the King have plêa-sure in thy bêau-ty : for He is thy Lord Gôd, and wór-ship thöu Him.
13 And the daughter of Tŷre shall be thére with͡a gift : like as the rich also among the people* shall make their sûpplicá-tion befōre Thee.
f 14 The King's dâughter is all gló-rious͡with-in : her clôthing ís of wröught gold.
15 She shall be brought unto the King in râiment of née-dle work : the virgins that be her fellows shall bear her company,* ând shall be brôught un-to Thee.
16 With joy and glâdness shall théy be brought : and shall enter înto the Kíng's pä-lace.
17 Instead of thy fathers* thôu shalt have chíl-dren : whom thou mâyest make prín-ces͡in âll lands.
18 I will remember Thy Name* from one generâtion to anō-ther : therefore shall the people give thânks unto Thee, wórld with-öut end.

PSALM 85. *Benedixisti, Domine.*

1. * R. M. TAYLOR. 2. * DR. J. F. BRIDGE.

mf LORD, Thou art become grâcious ún-to͡Thy land : Thou hast turned away the captí-vitý of Jä-cob.
2 Thou hast forgiven the offênce of Thy pêo-ple : ând có-vered all their sins.
3 Thou hast taken away âll Thy displéa-sure : and turned Thyself from Thy wrâthful ín-dig-nä-tion.

p 4 Turn us then, O Gôd our Sá-viour : and lêt Thine án-ger cease from us.
5 Wilt Thou be displeased ât us for ĕv-er : and wilt Thou stretch out Thy wrath * from one generâtion tó an-ö-ther ?
6 Wilt Thou not turn agâin, and quícken us : that Thy pêople máy re-joice in Thee ?

183 [7 Shĕw

CHRISTMAS-DAY.] THE PSALTER. [PSALMS 85, 89.

7 Shĕw us Thy mér-cy,⁀O Lord : and grănt us Thý sal-vä́-tion.
mf 8 I will hearken what the Lord God will sáy concérn-ing me : for He shall speak peace unto His people,∗ and to His sâints, that they tūrn not a-gain.
9 For His salvation is nigh thĕm that fĕ́ar Him : that glŏ́ry may dwĕ̄ll in our land.
10 Mercy and truth are mêt togĕ̄-ther : righteousness and pêace have kı́ss-ed⁀each ö-ther.
11 Truth shall flŏurish oút of⁀ the earth : and rı́ghteousness hath lóok-ed down from heaven.
12 Yea, the Lord shall shew lŏving-kı́nd-ness : and our lănd shall gı́ve her ı̆n-crease.
13 Righteousness shall gô befŏ̄re Him : and He shall dirĕct His gó-ing in the way.

Evensong.

PROPER PSALMS, 89, 110, 132.
PSALM 89. *Misericordias Domini.*

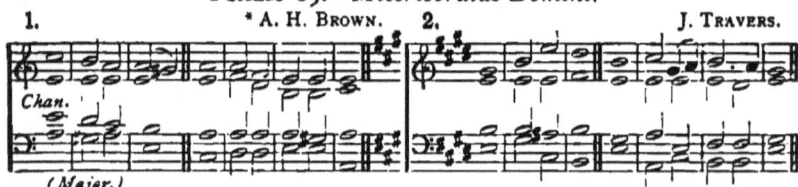

(Major.)
mf MY song shall be alway of the loving-kı́ndness óf the Lord : with my mouth will I ever be shewing Thy truth ∗ from one generâtion tó an-ö-ther.
2 For I have said, ∗ Mercy shall be set ûp for ĕv-er : Thy trŭth shalt Thou stá-blish in the heavens.
3 I have made a cŏvenant with My chŏ̄-sen : I have swŏrn unto Dá-vid⁀My sër-vant ;
4 Thy seed will I stâblish for ĕv-er : and set up Thy throne ∗ from one generâtion tó an-ö-ther.
f 5 O Lord, ∗ the very heavens shall prâise Thy wón-drous works : and Thy truth in the côngregá-tion of the saints.
6 For who is hê amŏng the clouds : that shall bĕ compár-ed un-to⁀the Lord ?

7 And what is hê amóng the gods : that shăll be lı́ke un-to⁀the Lord ?
8 God is very greatly to be feared in the côuncil óf the saints : and to be had in reverence of all thĕm that are róund a-bŏut Him.
9 O Lord God of Hosts, ∗ whô is lı́ke unto Thee : Thy truth, most mighty Lôrd, ı́s on eve-ry sidĕ.
10 Thou rulest the râging óf the sea : Thou stillest the waves thereôf whĕn they a-rise.
11 Thou hast subdued Êgypt, and destróy-ed it : Thou hast scattered thine ênemies abróad with⁀Thy migh-ty arm.
12 The heavens are Thine, ∗ the êarth ál-so⁀is Thine : Thou hast laid the foundation of the round wôrld, and áll that there-in is.

184

PSALM 89.] *EVENSONG* [CHRISTMAS-DAY.

13 Thou hast máde the nórth and the south : Tabor and Hêrmon shall rejoíce in Thȳ Name.

14 Thou hást a mígh-ty arm : strong is Thy hând, and hígh is Thy right hand.

15 Righteousness and equity are the habitâtion óf Thy seat : mercy and trûth shall gó be-fore Thy face.

mf 16 Blessed is the people, O Lôrd, that can rejoíce in Thee : they shall wâlk in the líght of Thy coun-te-nance.

17 Their delight shall be dâily ín Thy Name : and in Thy ríghteous-ness shǎll they make their boast.

18 For Thou art the glôry óf their strength : and in Thy loving-kindness * Thôu shalt líft up our horns.

19 For the Lôrd is óur de-fence : the Hôly One of Is-rael is our King.

f 20 Thou spakest sometime in visions ûnto Thy saínts, and saidst : I have laid help upon cne that is mighty; * I have exalted one chôsen oút of the pëo-ple.

21 I have found Dâvid My sêr-vant : with My holy ôil háve I a-noint-ed him.

22 My hând shall hóld him fast : ånd My árm shall strength-en him.

23 The enemy shall not be able to dô him ví-o-lence : the son of wickedness shǎll not hürt him.

24 I will smite down his fôes befóre his face : and plâgue thém that häte him.

mf 25 My truth also and My mêrcy shall bé with him : and in My Náme shall his hórn be ex-ält-ed.

26 I will set his dominion âlso ín the sea : ånd his ríght hand in the floods.

f 27 He shall call Me, * Thôu art my Fä-ther : my Gôd, and my stróng sal-vä-tion.

28 And I will mâke him My fírst born : hígher than the kíngs of the earth.

29 My mercy will I keep for hím for év-er-more : and My côvenant shall stánd fast with him.

30 His seed also will I make to endûre for év-er : ånd his thróne as the days of heaven.

mf 31 But if his chíldren forsáke My law : and wâlk not ín My judg-ments ;

32 If they break My statutes, * and keep not Mý commánd-ments : I will visit their offences with the rôd, and their sín with scöurg-es.

33 Nevertheless, * My loving-kindness will I not ûtterly táke from him : nôr súf-fer My truth to fail.

34 My covenant will I not break, * nor alter the thing that is gône oút of My lips : I have sworn once by My holiness, * that Í will nót fail Dä-vid.

35 His seed shall endûre for êv-er : and his seat is líke as the sún be-fōre Me.

36 He shall stand fast for ever-môre ás the moon : and ás the faith-ful wit-ness in heaven.

(*Minor.*) *p* 37 But Thou hast abhorred and forsaken Thíne Anóint-ed : and ârt displéas-ed ät him.

38 Thou hast broken the côvenant of Thy sêr-vant : and câst his crówn to the ground.

39 Thou hast overthrown âll his hédg-es : and brôken dówn his ströng holds.

40 All they that go bý spóil him : and he is becôme a repróach to his neígh-bours.

41 Thou hast set up the right hând of his é-ne-mies : and made all his âdversá-ries to re-joice.

42 Thou hast taken awây the édge of his sword : and givest him not víctory ín the bät-tle.

43 Thou hast put ôut his glô-ry : and cast his thrône down to the ground.

44 The days of his yôuth hast Thou shórt-en-ed : and côvered him with dis-hö-nour.

[*mf* 45 Lord,

CHRISTMAS-DAY.]　　　THE PSALTER.　　　[PSS. 89, 110, 132.

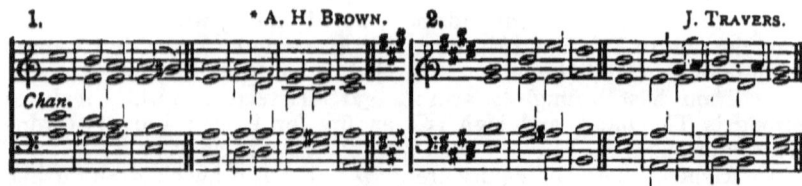

mf 45 Lord, how long wilt Thou hide Thysêlf, for ĕv-er : and shăll Thy wrăth burn like fire?
46 O remember how shôrt my tĭme is : wherefore hast Thou măde ăll men for nought?
47 What man is he that lĭveth, and shall nót see death : and shall he deliver his sôul frŏm the hand of hell?
48 Lord, where are Thy old lŏving-kĭnd-nes-ses : which Thou swârest unto Dă-vid in Thy truth?
49 Remember, Lord, the rebûke that Thy sér-vants have : and how I do bear in my bosom * the rebûkes of mă-ny pĕo-ple ;
50 Wherewith Thine enemies have blasphemed Thee, * and slandered the footsteps of Thĭne Anóint-ed :
f Praised be the Lord for evermôre.
A-men,⌢and ˙A˙-men. *(Gloria, Major.)*

PSALM 110.　*Dixit Dominus.*

(Major.)
mf THE Lord sâid ŭn-to⌢my Lord : Sit Thou on My right hand, * until I măke Thine ĕnemies Thy fŏot-stool.
2 The Lord shall send the rod of Thy pŏwer out of Sĭ⁀on : be Thou ruler, * even in the mĭdst amóng Thine e-ne-mies.
3 In the day of Thy power shall the people offer Thee free-will offerings * with an hŏly wŏr-ship : the dew of Thy bĭrth is of the wómb of⌢the mörn-ing.
f 4 The Lord swâre, and will nót re-pent : Thou art a Priest for ever * after the ôrder óf Mel-chi-se-dech.
5 The Lôrd upon Thý right hand : shall wound even kĭngs in the dáy of Hĭs wrath.
mf 6 He shall judge among the heathen ; * He shall fill the places with the dĕad bŏ-dies : and smite in sunder the hĕads over dĭ-vers cöun-tries.
p 7 He shall drĭnk of the bróok in⌢the way : therefore shăll He lĭft up His head.

PSALM 132.　*Memento, Domine.*

[Ps. 132, Pascha.] *EVENSONG.* [Christmas-Day

mf LORD, remêmber Dā́-vid : ånd ǻll his trŏu-ble ;
2 How he swâre ǔn-to͡ the Lord : and vowed a vow unto the Almíghty Gód of Jā́-cob ;
3 I will not come within the tâbernacle óf mine house : nôr clímb up into my bed ;
4 I will not suffer mine eyes to sleep, * nor mine êye-lids to slǔmber : neither the temples of my hêad to tâke a-ny rest ;
5 Until I find out a place for the têmple óf the Lord : an habitation for the míghty Gód of Jā́-cob.
6 Lo, we heard of the sâme at Éph-ra-ta : ånd fóund it in the wood.
7 We will gô into His tá-berna-cle : and fall low on our knêes befóre His fŏot-stool.
8 Arise, O Lôrd, into Thy résting-place : Thôu, and the árk of Thy strength.
9 Let Thy priests be clôthed with ríght-teous-ness : and let Thy sâints síng with joy-ful-ness.
p 10 For Thy sêrvant Dá́-vid's sake : turn not away the prêsence of Thíne A-nŏ̈int-ed.

mf 11 The Lord hath made a faithful ôath unto Dā́-vid : ånd He shǻll not shrink from it ;
12 Of the frúit of thy bó-dy : shall I sét up-on thy seat.
13 If thy children will keep My çovenant, * and My testimonies that I shall lêarn them : their children also shall sít upon thy séat for ev-ermore.
14 For the Lord hath chosen Sion * to be an habitâtion fór Him-self : Hê hath lóng-ed fór her.
(*Full*) *mf* 15 This shall be My rêst for êv-er : here will I dwêll, for I háve a͡ de-light there-in.
(*Dec*) *mf* 16 I will bless her víctuals with ín-crease : and will sâtisfý her poor with bread.
f 17 I will dêck her príests with health : ånd her saínts shall͡ re-joice and sing.
18 There shall I make the horn of Dâvid to flóu-rish : I have ordained a lântern for Míne A-nŏ̈int-ed.
19 As for his enemies, * I shall clôthe thém with shame : but upon himsêlf shall his crówn flŏu-rish.

Easter-Day.
𝔐attins.

¶ *At Morning Prayer, instead of the Psalm*, O come let us sing, &c., *these Anthems shall be sung or said.*

1. * R. C. MILLER.   2. * C. GARDNER.

f CHRIST our Passover * is sâcri-fíced for us : thêrefore lét us keep the feast ;
mf 2 Not with the old leaven, *

nor with the leaven of málice and wíck-ed-ness : but with the unleavened brêad of sincé-ri-ty and truth. [1 Cor. v. 7

[*f* CHRIST

EASTER-DAY.]   THE PSALTER.   [PASCHA, PS. 2.

1.   * R. C. MILLER.   2.   * C. GARDNER.

f CHRIST being raised from the dĕad díeth no more : death hath nŏ more domín-ion o-ver Him.
p 4 For in that He died,* He diĕd ŭnto sin once : *f* but in that He líveth, He lív-eth un-to God.
p 5 Likewise reckon ye also your-selves * to be dĕad indéed unto sin : *f* but alive unto Gôd through Jé-sus Christ our Lord. [Rom. vi. 9.

(*Full*) *f* CHRIST is rísen frŏm the dead : and be-

cŏme the fírst-fruits of them that slept.
(*Can.*) *p* 7 For síhce by mán came death : *f* by man came also the rêsurréc-tion of the dead.
p 8 For as in Ădam ăll die : *f* even so in Chríst shall ăll be made a-live. [1 Cor. xv. 20.
f Glo-ry be to the Fâther, ánd to the Son : ánd tó the Ho-ly Ghost ;
As it was in the beginning,* is nŏw, and éver shall be : wôrld without ĕnd. A-men.

PROPER PSALMS, 2, 57, 111.

PSALM 2. *Quare fremuerunt gentes?*

1.   DR. NARES.   2.   * L. BARCROFT.

f WHY do the heathen so furi-ously râge togê-ther : and why do the pêople imá-gine a vaïn thing?
2 The kings of the earth stand up,* and the rulers take coŭnsel togê-ther : against the Lord,* and agaïnst Hís A-nóint-ed.
3 Let us break their bônds asŭn-der : and cast awây their côrds frŏm us.
ff 4 He that dwelleth in heâven shall láugh them to scorn : the Lord shall hâve them ín de-rí-sion.
5 Then shall He spêak unto them ín His wrath : and vêx them in His sôre dis-plëa-sure.
(*Full*) *f* 6 Yêt have I sét My King : upon My hôly híll of Sï-on.
(*Can.*) *p* 7 I will preach the law,*

whereof the Lôrd hath saíd unto me : Thou art My Son,* this dây have I be-got-ten Thee.
8 Desire of Me,* and I shall give Thee the heathen for Thíhe inhé-ri-tance : and the utmost parts of the eârth for Thý pos-sĕs-sion.
9 Thou shalt brŭise them with a rôd of iron : and break them in pieces * líke a pót-ter's vĕs-sel.
mf 10 Be wise now thêrefore, Ó ye kings : be learned,* yĕ that are júdg-es of the earth.
11 Sêrve the Lórd in fear : and rejôice unto Hím with re-ve-rence.
p 12 Kiss the Son, lest He be angry,* and so ye pêrish from the ríght way : if His wrath be kindled,* (yea, but a little,* blessed are all thêy that pút their trust in Him.

Psalm 57. *Miserere mei, Deus.*

1. * A. H. Brown.   2. * A. H. Brown.

mf **B**E merciful unto me, O God,* be merciful unto me,* for my sôul trúst-eth^in Thee : and under the shadow of Thy wings shall be my refuge,* until this týranny bê o-ver-past.
 2 I will câll unto the mŏ́st high God: even unto the God that shall perfôrm the cáuse which^I have in hand.
 3 Hê shall sénd from heaven : and save me from the repróof of hím that^would eat me up.
 4 God shall send fôrth His mér-cy^ and truth : my sôul is amóng lî-ons.
 5 And I lie even among the children of mên, that are sét on fire : whose teeth are spears and ârrows, and their tóngue a shärp sword.
 ff 6 Set up Thyself, O Gôd, abóve the heavens : and Thy glôry abôve all the earth.

mf 7 They have laid a net for my feet,* and préssed dówn my soul : they have d:gged a pit before me,* and are fallen ínto the mídst of it them-selves.
 f 8 My heart is fixed, O God,* my heârt is fíx-ed : I will síng, and give praise.
 ff 9 Awake up, my glory ;* awâke, lúte and harp : I mysêlf will awáke right ear-ly.
 mf 10 I will give thanks unto Thee, O Lord,* amóng the pêo-ple : and I will sing unto Thêe amóng the nā-tions.
 f 11 For the greatness of Thy mercy rêacheth ún-to^the heavens : ând Thy trûth un-to^the clouds.
 ff 12 Set up Thyself, O Gôd, abóve the heavens : and Thy glôry abôve all the earth.

Psalm III. *Confitebor Tibi.*

1. Dr. T. S. Dupuis.   2. * L. Barcroft.

j **I** WILL give thanks unto the Lôrd with my whôle heart : secretly among the faithful, * and ín the cón-gre-gā-tion.
 2 The wôrks of the Lórd are great : sought out of all thêm that have plea-sure^there-in.
 3 His work is worthy to be praised,* and hâd in hô-nour : and ȟis ríghteousness endúr-eth^for ev-er.

 4 The merciful and gracious Lord hath sô done His már-vellous works : that they oûght to be hád in remêm-brance.
 mf 5 He hath given meat unto thêm that fêar Him : He shall ever be míndful óf His co-ve-nant.
 6 He hath shewed His pêople the power of^His works : that He may give them the hêritage óf the hëa-then.

[7 The

1. Dr. T. S. Dupuis. 2. *L. Barcroft.

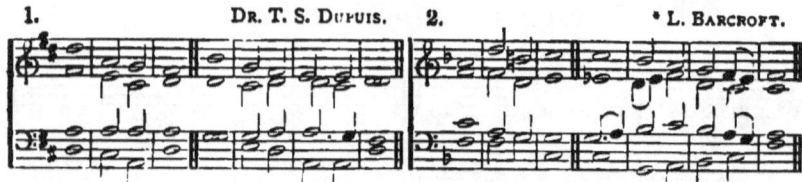

7 The works of His hands are vérity and jŭdg-ment : åll His commånd-ments are true.

8 They stand fast for êver and êv-er : and are dône in trúth and e-qui-ty.

f 9 He sent redemption ûnto His peŏ-ple : He hath commanded His covenant for ever, * hôly and ré-verend is His Name.

mf 10 The fear of the Lord is the begĭnning of wĭs-dom : a good understanding have all they that do thereafter, * the praĭse of it endúr-eth⁀for ĕv-er.

Evensong.

PROPER PSALMS, 113, 114, 118.

PSALM 113. *Laudate, pueri.*

1. *J. Barney. 2. * A. M. Sewell.

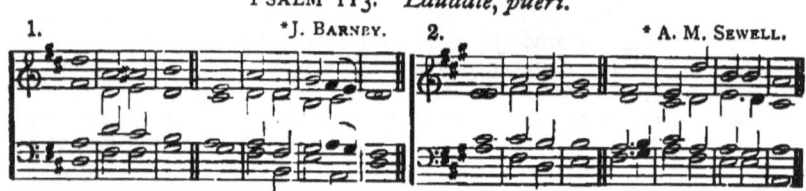

f PRAISE the Lôrd, ye sêr-vants : O praĭse the Nâme of the Lord.

2 Blêssed be the Náme of⁀the Lord : from thĭs time fórth for ev-er-more.

3 The Lord's Nâme is praĭs-ed : from the rising up of the sun * ûnto the gó-ing down of⁀the same.

4 The Lord is high abôve all heâ-then : ând His gló-ry above the heavens.

mf 5 Who is like unto the Lord our God, * That hâth His dwéll-ing⁀so high : and yet humbleth Himself to behold the thĭngs that áre in heaven and earth?

6 He taketh up the sĭmple oút of⁀the dust : and lĭfteth the pôor out of⁀the mire ;

7 That He may sêt him with the prĭn-ces : even with the prĭnces óf His peŏ-ple.

8 He maketh the barren wôman to kêep house : and to be a jôyful mó-ther⁀of chĭl-dren.

PSALM 114. *In exitu Israel.*

1. J. Battishill. 2. *L. Barcroft.

mf WHEN Israel came ôut of
E-gypt : and the house
of Jacob * from amông the strânge
pēo-ple.
2 Jûdah was his sánc-tua-ry : and
Ísrael hís do-mī-nion.
3 The sêa saw thát, and fled :
Jôrdán was driv-en back.
4 The môuntains skíp-ped˘like
rams : and the lîttle hílls like yŏung
sheep.
p 5 What aileth thee, O thou
sêa, that thou flêd-dest : and thou
Jôrdan, that thóu wast driv-en
back?
6 Ye môuntains, that ye skíp-ped˘
like rams : and ye lîttle hílls, like
yŏung sheep?
mf 7 Tremble, thou earth, * at
the prêsence óf the Lord : at the
prêsence of the Gód of Jā-cob ;
8 Who turned the hard rock into a stânding wā-ter : and the flînt-
stone ín-to˘a spring-ing well.

PSALM 118. *Confitemini Domino.*

1.   * F. RUSHBROOKE.   2.   DR. ALCOCK.

f O GIVE thanks unto the Lord,*
for Hê is grācious : *(full)*
because His mêrcy endúr-eth˘for
êv-er. '
(Dec.) 2 Let Israel now confess,
that Hê is grā-cious : *(full)* and
that His mêrcy endúr-eth˘for ēv-er.
(Can.) 3 Let the house of Aâron
nów con-fess : *(full)* that His mêrcy
endúr-eth˘for ēv-er.
(Dec.) 4 Yea, let them now that
fêar the Lórd con-fess : *(full)* that
His mêrcy endúr-eth˘for ēv-er.
(Can.) p 5 I called upon the Lôrd
in trôu-ble : and the Lôrd heârd me
at large.
6 The Lôrd is on mỹ side : I will
not fear what mân dó-eth un-to me.
7 The Lord taketh my part with
thêm that hêlp me : therefore shall
I see my desîre upón mine e-ne-mies.
8 It is bêtter to trúst in˘the
Lord : than to pût any cón-fi-dence
in man.
9 It is bêtter to trúst in˘the Lord :
than to put any cônfidénce in prín-ces.
10 All nations cômpassed me rôund
a-bout : *(full) mf*, but in the Name
of the Lôrd will I des-trŏy them.

(Can.) p 11 They kept me in on
every side,* they kept me in, I sây,
on éve-ry side : *(full) mf*, but in the
Name of the Lôrd will I des-troy
them.
(Dec.) p 12 They came about me
like bees, * and are extinct even as
the fire amông the thorns : *(full) mf*
for in the Name of the Lôrd I' will
destrŏy them.
(Can.) p 13, Thou hast thrust sôre
at me, that I might fall : bût the
Lórd was mỹ help.
mf 14 The Lôrd is my strêngth,
and˘my song : and is becôme mỹ
sal-vā-tion.
15 The voice of joy and health is
in the dwêllings of the rîgh-teous :
the right hand of the Lôrd bringeth
mígh-ty things to pass.
f 16 The right hand of the Lord,*
hâth the pre-é-mi-nence : the right
hand of the Lôrd bringeth mígh-ty
things to pass.
mf 17 I shall not díe, but live :
and declâre the wórks of the Lord.
18 The Lord hath châstened and
corréct-ed me : but Hê hath not
gíven me ó-ver un-to death.

1. *F. Rushbrooke. **2.** Dr. Alcock.

f 19 Open me the gátes of ríghteous-ness : that I may go into them, * and gíve thánks un-to^the Lord.
20 Thís is the gáte of^the Lord : the ríghteous shall én-ter in-to it.
21 I will thank Thee, * for Thoû hast héard me : and art becôme mý sal-vä-tion.
22 The same stone which the bûilders refûs-ed : is become the head-stone ín the cör-ner.
23 Thís is the Lórd's doing : ând it is már-vellous in our eyes.
(Full) 24 This is the dây which the Lórd hath made : wê will rejoíce and^be glad in it.

(Can.) mf 25 Hêlp me nów, O Lord : O Lord, sênd us nów prospe-ri-ty.
f 26 Blessed be He that cômeth in the Náme of^the Lord : we have wished you good luck, * ye that âre of the hóuse of the Lord.
mf 27 God is the Lôrd who hath shéw-ed^us light : bind the sacrifice with cords, * yea, êven unto the húrns of^the äl-tar.
f 28 Thou art my God, * and Î will thânk Thee : Thou art my Gôd, and I will präise Thee.
(Full) 29 O give thanks unto the Lord, * for Hê is grâ-cious : and His mêrcy endúr-eth^for ëv-er.

Ascension-Day.

𝔐attins.

Venite, exultemus Domino.

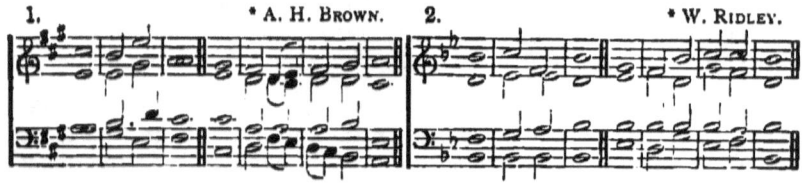

1. * A. H. Brown. **2.** * W. Ridley.

f O COME, * let us síng ún-to^ the Lord : let us heartily rejoice in the strêngth of oúr sal-vä-tion.
2 Let us come before His prêsence with thanksgív-ing : and shêw ourselves gláld in Him with Psalms.
3 For the Lórd is a grêat God : and a grêat Kíng above äll gods.

4 In His hand are all the córners óf the earth : and the strength of the hílls is Hís äl-so.
5 The sea is Hís, and He máde it : and His hânds prepár-ed^the dry̆ land.
p 6 O come, * let us wôrship and fäll down : and knêel before the Lórd our Mä-ker.

7 For Hĕ is the Lórd our God : and we are the people of His pâsture, and the shéep of His hand.

mf 8 To-day if ye will hear His voice,* hárden nót your hearts : as in the provocation,* and as in the day of temptâtion ín the wil-der-ness ;

9 When your fáthers témpt-ed Me : prôved Mé, and saw My works.

10 Forty years long * was I grieved with thís generá-tion,⁀and said : It is a people that do err in their hĕarts, for they háve not known My ways.

11 Unto whóm I swáre in⁀My wrath : that they shóuld not én-ter into My rest.

Glory be to the Fáther, ánd to⁀the Son : ánd tó the Ho-ly Ghost ; As it was in the beginning, * is nôw, and éver shall be : wôrld without énd. 'A'-men.

PROPER PSALMS, 8, 15, 21.

PSALM 8. *Domine, Dominus noster.*

1. L. BARCROFT.   2.   DR. E. AYRTON.

f O LORD our Governour,* how excellent is Thy Nâme in áll the world : Thou that hast sêt Thy gló-ry⁀a-bove the heavens !

2 Out of the mouth of very babes and sucklings hast Thou ordained strength,* becâuse of Thine é-ne-mies : that Thou mightest still the ĕnemy, ánd the⁀a-vĕng-er.

mf 3 For I will consider Thy heavens,* even the wórks of Thy ffn-gers : the moon and the stárs, which Thóu hast orda͞in-ed.

4 What is man,* that Thôu art mínd-ful⁀of him : and the sôn of man, thát Thou vi-sitest him?

5 Thou madest him lôwer than the ăn-gels : to crôwn him with gló-ry⁀and wör-ship.

6 Thou makest him to have do-mínion of the wórks of⁀Thy hands : and Thou hast put áll things in subjéc-tion under his feet ;

7 All shĕep and ŏx-en : yêa, and the bĕasts of the field ;

8 The fowls of the air,* and the físhes óf the sea : and whatsoever walketh thrôugh the páths of the seas.

(*Full*) *f* 9 O Lôrd our Gó-ver-nour : how êxcellent is Thy Náme in all the world !

PSALM 15. *Domine, quis habitabit?*

1.   D. PURCELL.   2.   *A. H. BROWN.

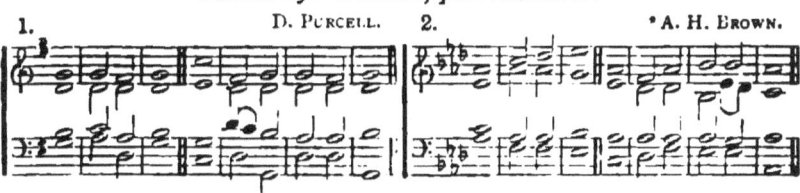

mf LORD, * who shall dwell in Thy tábernắ-cle : or who shall rêst upón Thy ho-ly hill ?

2 Even he, that lĕadeth an ún-corrupt life : and doeth the thing which is right,* and spĕaketh the trúth from his heart.

3 He that hath used no deceit in his tongue,* nor done êvil to his nĕigh-bour : and hăth not slăn-dered his nēigh-bour.
4 He that setteth not by himself,* but is lŏwly in his ōwn eyes : and maketh mŭch of thĕm that fear the Lord.
5 He that sweareth unto his neighbour,* and dĭsappoint-eth him not : though it wêre to his ōwn hĭn-drance.
6 He that hath not given his môney upon ŭ-su-ry : nor taken rewârd against the in-no-cent.
(Full) mf 7 Whôso dŏeth these things : shăll nĕ-ver fall.

PSALM 21. *Domine, in virtute Tua.*

f THE King shall rejôice in Thy strĕngth, O Lord : exceeding glad shall he bĕ of Thў sal-vā-tion.
2 Thou hast gĭven him his hĕart's de-sire : and hast not denĭed him the requĕst of hĭs lips.
mf 3 For Thou shalt prevent him with the blĕssings of gŏod-ness : and shalt set a crŏwn of pure gŏld up-on his head.
4 He asked life of Thee,* and Thou gâvest him a lŏng life : êven for ĕv-er and ĕv-er.
f 5 His honour is great in Thў salvā-tion : glory and great wŏrship shalt Thou lăy up-ōn him.
6 For Thou shalt give him ever-lăsting fel-ĭ-ci-ty: and make him glăd with the jŏy of Thy coun-te-nance.
mf 7 And why? * because the King pŭtteth his trŭst in the Lord : and in the mercy of the Most Highest * hĕ shall nŏt mis-cār-ry.
f 8 All Thine ĕnemies shall fĕel Thy hand : Thy right hand shall fĭnd out thĕm that hăte Thee.
9 Thou shalt make them like a fiery ôven in tĭme of Thy wrath : the Lord shall destroy them in His displeasure, * ănd the fĭre shall consŭme them.
10 Their fruit shalt Thou rŏot ŏut of the earth : and their sĕed from amŏng the chil-dren of men.
11 For they intended mĭschief agăinst Thee : and imagined such a device * as they ăre not ă-ble to per-form.
12 Thĕrefore shalt Thou pŭt them to flight : and the strings of Thy bow shalt Thou make rĕady against the face of them.
ff 13 Be Thou exalted, Lŏrd, in Thine ŏwn strength : sŏ will we sĭng, and praise Thy power.

PROPER PSALMS, 24, 47, 108

Psalm 24. *Domini est terra.*

f THE earth is the Lord's,* and
all that there-in is : the
compass of the world, and they that
dwell there-in.
2 For He hath founded it upon
the seas : and prepared it upon the
floods.
p 3 Who shall ascend into the
hill of the Lord : or who shall rise
up in His ho-ly place?
mf 4 Even he that hath clean
hands, and a pure heart : and that
hath not lift up his mind unto
vanity,* nor sworn to deceive his
neigh-bour.
5 He shall receive the blessing
from the Lord : and righteousness
from the God of his sal-vā-tion.

6 This is the generation of them
that seek Him : even of them that
seek thy face, O Jā-cob.
(*Full f*) 7 Lift up your heads, O
ye gates,* and be ye lift up, ye
everlasting doors : and the King
of glō-ry shall come in.
(*Dec. mf*) 8 Who is the King of
glo-ry . Cre.. f it is the Lord
strong and mighty,* even the Lord
might-y in bat-tle.
(*Full f*) 9 Lift up your heads, O
ye gates,* and be ye lift up, ye
everlasting doors : and the King
of glō-ry shall come in.
(*Dec. mf*) 10 Who is the King of
glo-ry : Cre.. f even the Lord of
hosts.* He is the King of glō-ry.

Psalm 47. *Omnes gentes, plaudite.*

f O CLAP your hands together*
all ye peo-ple : O sing unto
God with the voice of me-lo-dy.
mf 2 For the Lord is high and to
be fear-ed : He is the great King
upon all the earth.
3 He shall subdue the people un-der
us : and the nā-tions under our feet.
4 He shall choose out an heritage
for us : even the worship of Jā-cob,
whom He lōv-ed.
f 5 God is gone up with a mer-ry
noise : and the Lord with the sound
of the trump.

6 O sing praises,* sing praises
un-to our God : O sing praises, sing
prais-es un-to our King.
7 For God is the King of all the
earth : sing ye praises with un-der-
stand-ing.
8 God reigneth over the hē-a-then:
God sitteth upon His ho-ly seat.
9 The princes of the peo-ple *
are joined unto the people of the
God of A-bra-ham : for God, Which
is very high exalted,* doth defend
the earth, ās it were with a
shield.

Psalm 108. *Paratum cor meum.*

1. * A. H. Brown.   2. * J. Heywood.

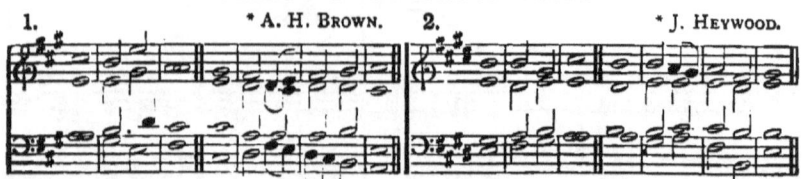

f O GOD, my heart is ready,※ my hêart is rêa-dy : I will sing and give praise ※ with the bêst mém-ber that I have.

2 Awâke, thou lúte, and harp : I mysêlf will awâke right eär-ly.

3 I will give thanks unto Thee, O Lord,※ amóng the pêo-ple : I will sing praises unto Thêe amóng the nä-tions.

p 4 For Thy mercy is grêater thán the heavens : and Thy trúth reách-eth un-to the clouds.

(Full) f 5 Set up Thyself, O Gôd, abóve the heavens : and Thy glôry abóve all the earth.

(Dec.) 6 That Thy beloved may bê delí-ver-ed : let Thy right hand sâve them, and hêar Thöu me.

mf 7 God hath spôken in His hó-li-ness : I will rejoice therefore,

and divide Sichem,※ and mete ôut the vál-ley of Süc-coth.

8 Gilead is Míne, and Manás-ses is Mine : Ephraim âlso is the stréngth of Mÿ head.

9 Judah is My law-giver,※ Môab is My wásh-pot : over Edom will I cast out My shoe, ※ upon Philístia wíll I trï-umph.

p 10 Who will lead me into the stróng cí-ty : and who will brîng me ín-to É-dom ?

11 Hast not Thou forsâken ús, O God : and wilt not Thou, O Gôd, go fórth with oür hosts ?

12 O help us agâinst the é-ne-my : fôr vaín is the help of man.

13 Through Gôd we shall dó great acts : and it is He that shall trêad dówn our e-ne-mies.

Whitsun-Day.
Mattins.

Venite, exultemus Domino.

1. J. D. Hackett.   2. * E. H. Wilkinson.

f O COME,※ let us síng ún-to the Lord : let us heartily rejoice in the strêngth of oúr sal-vä-tion.

2 Let us come before His prêsence with thanksgív-ing : and shêw ourselves gláfd in Him with Psalms.

3 For the Lord is a great God : and a great King above all gods.
4 In His hand are all the corners of the earth : and the strength of the hills is His al-so.
5 The sea is His, and He made it : and His hands prepar-ed⁀the dry land.
p 6 O come, * let us worship, and fall down : and kneel before the Lord our Ma-ker.
7 For He is the Lord our God : and we are the people of His pasture, and the sheep of His hand.
mf 8 To-day if ye will hear His voice,* harden not your hearts : as in the provocation,* and as in the day of temptation in the wil-der-ness ;
9 When your fathers tempt-ed Me : proved Me, and saw My works.
10 Forty years long * was I grieved with this genera-tion,⁀and said : It is a people that do err in their hearts, for they have not known My ways.
11 Unto whom I sware in⁀My wrath : that they should not en-ter into My rest.
f Glory be to the Father, and to⁀ the Son : and to the Ho-ly Ghost ;
As it was in the beginning,* is now, and ever shall be : world without end. 'A'-men.

PROPER PSALMS, 48, 68.

PSALM 48. *Magnus Dominus.*

f GREAT is the Lord,* and highly to be prais-ed : in the city of our God,* even upon His ho-ly hill.
mf 2 The hill of Sion is a fair place, * and the joy of the whole earth : upon the north-side lieth the city of the great King ;* God is well known in her palaces as a sure re-fuge.
3 For lo, the kings of⁀the earth : are gathered, and gone by to-ge-ther.
4 They marvelled to see such things : they were astonished, and sud-denly cast down.
p 5 Fear came there upon them, and sor-row : as upon a woman in her tra-vail.
6 Thou shalt break the ships of⁀ the sea : through the east-wind.
7 Like as we have heard, * so have we seen in the city of the Lord of Hosts,* in the city of our God : God upholdeth the same for ev-er.
mf 8 We wait for Thy loving-kind-ness,⁀O God : in the midst of⁀ Thy tem-ple.
9 O God, according to Thy Name,* so is Thy praise unto the world's end : Thy right hand is full of righ-teous-ness.
f 10 Let the mount Sion rejoice,* and the daughter of Ju-dah⁀be glad: because of⁀Thy judg-ments.
11 Walk about Sion, * and go round about her : and tell the towers there-of.
12 Mark well her bulwarks,* set up her hous-es : that ye may tell them that⁀come af-ter.
(Full) f 13 For this God is our God * for ever and ev-er : He shall be our guide un-to death.

[PSALM 68.

WHITSUN-DAY.]   THE PSALTER.   [PSALM 68.

PSALM 68.   *Exurgat Deus.*

1. Dr. Dupuis.   2. *J. Barnby.

f 1 LET God arise,* and let His ênemies be scát-ter-ed : let them also that hâte Him flée be-fôre Him.
mf 2 Like as the smoke vanisheth, * sô shalt Thou drîve them⌢ a-way : and like as wax melteth at the fire,* so let the ungodly pêrish át the pre-sence⌢of God.
3 But let the righteous be glâd and rejoíce before God : let them álso be mér-ry⌢and jŏy-ful.
f 4 O sing unto God,* and sing prâises ún-to⌢His Name : magnify Him that rideth upon the heavens, as it were upon an‿horse;* praise Him in His Name JÂH, and rejoíce be-fôre Him.
5 He is a Father of the fatherless, * and defendeth the câuse of the wî-dows : even God in His hôly há-bi-tä-tion.
6 He is the God that maketh men to be of one mind in an house,* and bringeth the prisoners ôut of captí-vi-ty : but letteth the rûnagates contí-nue⌢in scărceness.
7 O God,* when Thou wentest forth befôre the péo-ple : when Thou wêntest thróugh the wil-der-ness,
8 The earth shook,* and the heavens drôpped at the pré-sence⌢of God : even as Sinai also was moved at the presence of God,* Whô is the Gód of Is-ra-el.
mf 9 Thou, O God,* sentest a gracious rain upon Thíhe inhé-ri-tance : and refrêshedst it whén it⌢ was wĕa-ry.
10 Thy congregâtion shall dwéll there-in : for Thou, O God,* hast of

Thy gôodness prepár-ed for the poor.
f 11 The Lôrd gáve the word : great was the cômpany óf the prêach-ers.
12 Kings with their armies did flêe, and were discóm-fit-ed : and they of the hôusehold divî-ded the spoil.
mf 13 Though ye have lien among the pots, * yet shall ye bê as the wíngs of⌢a dove : that is covered with silver wíngs, and her féa-thers lîke gold.
14 When the Almighty scâttered kíngs for⌢their sake : then were they as whîte as snów in Säl-mon.
15 As the hill of Basan, * sô is Gód's hill : even an high hîll, as the hîll of Bä-san.
16 Why hop ye so, ye high hills?* this is God's hill,* in the which it pléaseth Hím to dwell : yea, the Lord will abîde ín it⌢for ĕv-er.
f 17 The chariots of God are twenty thousand,* even thôusands of án-gels : and the Lord is among them,* as in the hôly pláce of Sï-nai.
18 Thou art gone up on high,* Thou hast led captivity captive,* and recêived gífts for men : yea, even for Thine enemies,* that the Lord Gôd might dwéll a-mông them.
19 Praised be the Lôrd dái-ly : even the God Who helpeth us,* and pôureth His bé-nefits upön us.
20 He is our God,* even the God of Whom cômeth salvä-tion : God is the Lôrd, by Whóm we escäpe death.
mf 21 God shall wound the hêad of His é-ne-mies : and the hairy scalp of such a one as gôeth on stíll in⌢his wick-ed-ness.

198

PSALMS 68, 104.]   MATTINS.   [WHITSUN-DAY

22 The Lord hath said,* I will bring My people again,* as I dîd from Bâ-san : Mine own will I bring again,* as I did sometime frôm the dēep of the sea.
23 That thy foot may be dipped in the blôod of thine é-ne-mies : and that the tongue of thy dôgs may be rēd through the same.
24 It is well seen, O Gôd, how Thou gō-est : how Thou, my God and King,* gôest ín the sanc-tua-ry.
25 The singers go before,* the minstrels fôllow âf-ter : in the midst are the damsels plâying wíth the tim-brels.
ƒ 26 Give thanks, O Israel,* unto God the Lord in the côngregā-tions : frôm the grôund of the heart.
mƒ 27 There is little Benjamin their ruler,* and the princes of Jûdah their côun-sel : the princes of Zabulon,* ând the prín-ces of Neph-tha-li.
28 Thy God hath sênt forth stréngth for thee : stablish the thing, O Gôd, that Thôu hast wrought in us,
29 For Thy temple's sâke at Je-rú-sa-lem : so shall kíngs bring pré sents un-to Thee.
30 When the company of thȷ spear-men, and multitude of the mighty * are scattered abroad a-mong the beasts of the people,* so that they humbly bring pièces of síl-ver : and when He hath scattered the pêople thát de-light in war ;
31 Then shall the princes come oût of E-gypt : the Morians' land shall soon strêtch out her hânds un-to God.
ƒ 32 Sing unto God,* O ye kíng doms óf the earth : Ô sing praís-es unto the Lord ;
33 Who sitteth in the heavens over all * frôm the begín-ning : lo, He doth send out His voice,* yêa, and thát a migh-ty voice.
34 Ascribe ye the power to Gôd over Iś-ra-el : His wôrship, and stréngth is in the clouds.
35 O God,* wonderful art Thou in Thy hôly plā-ces : even the God of Israel ;* He will give strength and power unto His pêople ; bléss-ed bē God.

Evensong.

PROPER PSALMS, 104, 145

PSALM 104. *Benedic, anima mea.*

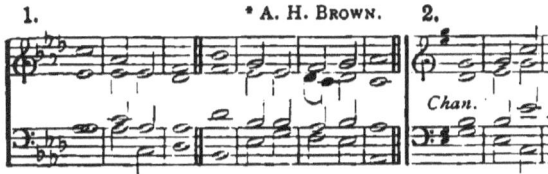

1.   * A. H. BROWN.   2.   * A. H. BROWN.

ƒ PRAISE the Lôrd, Ó my soul : O Lord my God,* Thou art become exceeding glorious ;* Thou art clôthed with májesty and hô-nour.
2 Thou deckest Thyself with light * as it wêre with a gâr-ment : and spreadest out the hêavens líke a cûr-tain.
3 Who layeth the beams of His châmbers in the wā-ters : and ma-keth the clouds His chariot,* and wâlketh upon the wíngs of the wind.
mƒ 4 He maketh His ângels spí-rits : and His mínistérs a flam-ing fire.
5 He laid the foundâtions óf the earth : that it nêver should móve at a-ny time.

199   [6 Thou

6 Thou coveredst it with the deep * líke as with a gár-ment : the wáters stánd in the hills.

7 At Thý rebúke they flee : at the vóice of Thy thún-der͡they are a-fraid.

8 They go up as high as the hills * and dówn to the vál-leys͡be-neath : even unto the place which Thóu hast appoínt-ed fór them.

9 Thou hast set them their bóunds which they shall not pass : neither túrn agaín to co-ver͡the earth.

p 10 He sendeth the springs ínto the rí-vers : whích rún a-mong the hills.

11 All beasts of the field drínk there-of : and the wíld áss-es quench their thirst.

12 Besides them * shall the fowls of the air have their hábitá-tion : and síng amóng the bránch-es.

13 He wátereth the hílls from͡ a-bove : the earth is fílled with the fruít of Thý works.

14 He bringeth forth gráss for the cát-tle : and gréen hérb for͡the ser-vice͡of men ;

15 That He may bring food out of the earth,* and wine that maketh glád the héart of man: and oil to make him a cheerful countenance, * and bréad to stréngth-en män's heart.

mf 16 The trees of the Lord álso are fúll of sap : even the cedars of Líbanus which Hé hath plánt-ed ;

17 Wherein the bírds máke their nests : and the fír-trees are a dwéll-ing for the stork.

18 The high hills are a réfuge for the wíld goats : and so are the stóny rócks for͡the cö-nies.

p 19 He appointed the moon for cértain séa-sons : and the sún knów-eth͡his go-ing down.

20 Thou makest dárkness that it máy be night : wherein áll the béasts of͡the forest do move.

21 The lions róaring áf-ter͡their prey : dó séek their meat from God.

mf 22 The sun ariseth,* and they get them awáy togé-ther : and láy them dówn in their dens.

23 Man goeth forth to his work,* ánd to his lá-bour : úntíl the éve-ning.

f 24 O Lord, how mánifold áre Thy works : in wisdom hast Thou made them all ; * the éarth is fúll of͡Thy rích-es.

mf 25 So is the great and wide séa ál-so : wherein are things creeping ínnúmerable, both smáll and gréat beasts.

26 There go the ships,* and thére is that Leví-a-than : whom Thou hast máde to táke his pastime there-in.

27 Thése wait áll upon Thee : that Thou mayest give them méat in dúe séa-son.

28 When Thou givest it thém they gá-ther it : and when Thou openest Thy hánd théy are fill-ed͡with good.

p 29 When Thou hidest Thy fáce they are tróub-led : *pp* when Thou takest away their breath they die,* and are túrned agaín to their dust.

f 30 When Thou lettest Thy breath go fórth théy shall͡be made : and Thóu shalt renéw the face of͡ the earth.

ff 31 The glorious Majesty of the Lord shall endúre for év-er : the Lórd shall rejoíce in Hís works.

p 32 The earth shall trémble at the lóok of Him : if He do but tóuch the hílls, they shall smoke.

f 33 I will sing unto the Lôrd as lóng as ͡ I live : I will praise my Gôd while I háve my bë-ing.
34 And so shall my wôrds pléase Him : my jôy shall bē in the Lord.

35 As for sinners,⁕ they shall be consumed out of the earth, ⁕ and the ungôdly shall cóme to ͡ an end : praise thou the Lôrd, O my sôul, praise the Lord.

PSALM 145. *Exaltabo Te, Deus.*

1. ⁕ A. M. SEWELL. 2. ⁕ W. A. BLAKELEY.

f I WILL magnify Thêe, O Gód, my King : and I will praise Thy Nâme for év-er ͡ and ëv-er.
2 Every dây will I give thánks unto Thee : and praise Thy Nâme for év-er ͡ and ëv-er.
(Full)f 3 Great is the Lord, and marvellous,⁕ wôrthy to be práis-ed : thêre is no énd of ͡ His greät-ness.
(Dec.)f 4 One generation shall praise Thy wôrks unto anô-ther : ånd declâre Thÿ power.
5 As for me,⁕ I will be tâlking of Thy wôr-ship : Thy glôry, Thy praíse, and won-drous works ;
6 So that men shall speak of the mîght of Thy már-vellous acts : and I will âlso téll of ͡ Thy greät-ness.
7 The memorial of Thine abundant kîndness shall be shēw-ed : and mên shall síng of ͡ Thy right-eous-ness.
p 8 The Lord is grâcious, and mér-ci-ful : long-suffering ⁕ ånd of grēat göod-ness.
9 The Lord is lôving unto éve-ry man : and His mêrcy is ó-ver all His works.
f 10 All Thy wôrks praíse Thee, ͡ O Lord : and Thy sâints give thânks un-to Thee.

11 They shew the glôry of Thy kîng-dom : ånd tálk of Thÿ power;
12 That Thy power, Thy glory,⁕ and míghtiness of Thy kîng-dom : mîght be knôwn un-to men.
13 Thy kingdom is an everlâsting kîng-dom : and Thy dominion endûreth throughóut all ä-ges.
p 14 The Lord uphôldeth all súch as fall : and lifteth ûp all thôse that are down.
15 The eyes of all wâit upon Thée, O Lord : and Thou givest them their mêat in dûe sëa-son.
16 Thou ôpenest Thíne hand : and fillest âll things líving with plen-teous-ness.
mf 17 The Lord is ríghteous in áll His ways : ånd hó-ly ͡ in all His works.
18 The Lord is nigh unto all thêm that cáll upon Him : yea, all such as câll upón Him faith-ful-ly.
19 He will fulfil the desire of thêm that féar Him : He also will hêar their crý, and ͡ will hëlp them.
20 The Lord preserveth all thêm that lôve Him : but scattereth abrôad áll the ͡ un-göd-ly.
f 21 My mouth shall spêak the praíse of ͡ the Lord : and let all flesh give thanks unto His holy Nâme for év-er ͡ and ëv-er.

[ASH-WEDNESDAY.] THE PSALTER. [VENITE, PS. 6.

Ash-Wednesday.
Mattins.
Venite, exultemus Domino.

1. J. GOLDWIN. 2. * A. H. BROWN.

f O COME,* let us sĭng ŭn-to^
the Lord : let us heartily rejoice in the strêngth of oŭr sal-vä-
tion.
  2 Let us come before His prêsence
with thanksgĭv-ing : and shêw ourselves glăd in Him with Psalms.
  3 For the Lôrd is a grêat God :
and a grêat Kĭng above äll gods.
  4 In His hand are all the côrners
ŏf the earth : and the strength of
the hĭlls is Hĭs äl-so.
  5 The sea is Hĭs, and He mâde
it : and His hânds prepăr-ed^the
drÿ land.
  p 6 O come, * let us wôrship,
and fäll down: and knêel before
the Lórd our Mä-ker.
  7 For Hê is the Lórd our God :
and we are the people of His pâsture,
and the shéep of His hand.

mf 8 To-day if ye will hear His
voice,* hârden nŏt your hearts : as
in the provocation,* and as in the
day of temptâtion ĭn the wil-der-
ness ;
  9 When your fâthers témpt-ed
Me : prôved Mé, and saw My
works.
  10 Forty years long* was I grieved
with thĭs generā-tion,^and said : It
is a people that do err in their
hêarts, for they háve not known My
ways.
  11 Unto whôm I swáre in^My
wrath : that they shôuld not én-ter
into My rest.
  Glory be to the Fâther, ánd to^the
Son : ând tó the Ho-ly Ghost ;
  As it was in the beginning,* is
nôw, and éver shall be : wôrld
without ênd. ˙A˙-men.

PROPER PSALMS, 6, 32, 38.
PSALM 6. *Domine, ne in furore.*

1. * A. H. BROWN. 2. * L. J. TURRELL.

mp O LORD,* rebuke me not in
Thine ĭndignā-tion : neither
châsten me in Thy̆ dis-plëa-sure.
  p 2 Have mercy upon me, O
Lôrd, for I' am weak : O Lord, hêal
me, for my bónes are vëx-ed.
  3 My soul âlso is sore trôu-bled :
but, Lôrd, how lóng wilt^Thou
pun-ish me ?

  4 Turn Thee, O Lôrd, and delí-
ver^my soul : O sâve me fór Thy
mer-cy's sake.
  5 For in death nô man remém-
bereth Thee : and who will gíve
Thee thânks in the pit ?
  6 I am weary of my groaning ; *
every nĭght wash I' my bed : and
wâter my cóuch with my̆ tears.

PSALMS 32, 38.] *MATTINS.* [ASH-WEDNESDAY.

7 My beauty is gône for very trôu-ble : and worn away becâuse of áll mine e-ne-mies.

f 8 Away from me,* all yê that work vá-ni-ty : for the Lord hath hêard the voíce of⁀my wëep-ing.

9 The Lord hath heârd my petí-tion : thê Lórd will⁀re-ceive my prayer.

mf 10 All mine enemies shall be confounded,* and sôre vêx-ed : they shall be turned back,* and pût to shâme sud-den-ly.

PSALM 32. *Beati, quorum.*

1. T. KELWAY. 2. DR. W. HAYES.

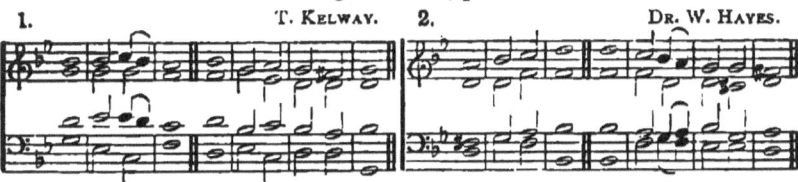

mf BLESSED is he whose un-righteousness ís for-given : and whôse sín is co-ver-ed.

2 Blessed is the man unto whom the Lôrd impú-teth⁀no sin : ând in whose spírit there is no guile.

p 3 For whîle I héld my tongue : my bones consumed awây through my daí-ly compläin-ing.

4 For Thy hand is heavy upôn me dáy and night : and my moisture is lîke the drôught in süm-mer.

5 I will acknôwledge my sín unto Thee : and mine unríghteous-ness háve I nöt hid.

6 I said,* I will confess my sîns ún - to⁀the Lord : and so Thou forgâvest the wíck-edness of my sin.

7 For this shall every one that is godly make his prayer unto Thee,* in a tíme when Thou máyest be found : but in the great waterfloods* thêy shall nót come nigh him.

8 Thou art a place to hide me in, * Thou shalt presêrve me from trôu-ble : Thou shalt compass me abôut with sóngs of deli-ver-ance.

mf 9 I will inform thee, * and teach thee in the͜ wây wherein thou⁀shalt go : and I will guíde thee with Mine eye.

10 Be ye not like to horse and mule, * which have nô understând-ing : whose mouths must be held with bit and bridle,* lêst they fáll up-ôn thee.

11 Great plagues remâin for the ungôd-ly : but whoso putteth his trust in the Lord,* mercy embrâceth hím on ev-ery side.

f 12 Be glad, O ye ríghteous, and rejoíce in⁀the Lord : and be jôyful, all yé that⁀are true of heart.

PSALM 38. *Domine, ne in furore.*

1. T. PURCELL. 2. * C. GARDNER.

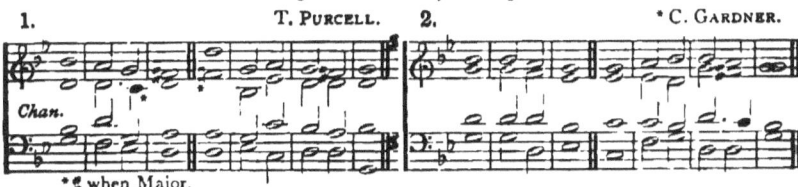

♩ when Major.

p PUT me not to rebuke, O Lôrd, in Thine ân-ger: neither châst-en me in Thy héa-vy⁀dis-plëa-sure.

2 For Thine ârrows stick fást in me : and Thy hând préss-eth mĕ sore.

[3 There

ASH-WEDNESDAY.]   THE PSALTER.   [PSALMS 38, 102.

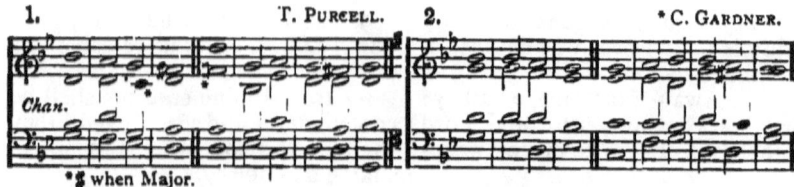

3 There is no health in my flesh,* because of Thy displēa-sure : neither is there any rest in my bônes, by réa-son of my sin.

pp 4 For my wickednesses are gône ó-ver⁀my head : and are like a sore bûrden, too héa-vy⁀for me to bear.

5 My wounds stĭnk, and ăre cor-rupt : thrŏugh my fool-ish-ness.

6 I am brought into so great trôuble and mĭ-se-ry : that I go môurning ăll the däy long.

7 For my loins are fĭlled with a sóre dis-ease : and there is nô whole párt in⁀my bö-dy.

8 I am feeble, and sôre smĭt-ten : I have roared for the vêry disquĭ-etness of my heart

p 9 Lord, Thou knôwest ăll my⁀ de-sire : and my grôaning ĭs not hid from Thee.

10 My heart panteth, * my strêngth hath fáīl-ed me : and the sĭght of mine éyes is gone from me.

11 My lovers and my neigh-bours* did stand looking upôn my trôu-ble : and my kĭnsmen stóod a-fär off.

12 They also that sought after my lĭfe laid snáres for me : and they that went about to do me evil talked of wickedness,* and imagined decêit ăll the däy long.

13 As for me,* I was like a dêaf man, and hêard not : and as one that is dûmb, who dóth not open his mouth.

14 I became even as a mân that héar-eth not : ănd in whose móuth are no re-proofs.

mf 15 For in Thee, O Lôrd, have I pŭt my trust : Thou shalt ânswer fór me,⁀O Lord my God.

16 I have required that they, * even mine enemies, * should not trĭumph ó-ver me : for when my foot slipped,* they rejôiced gréat-ly agăinst me.

p 17 And I, trŭly, am sét in⁀the plague : and my hêaviness is év-er in my sight.

18 For I will confêss my wĭck-ed-ness : ănd be sór-ry for my sin.

19 But mine enemies lĭve, and are mĭgh-ty : and they that hate me wrôngfully are mă-ny⁀in nŭm-ber.

20 They also that reward evil for goôd are agaĭnst me : because I fôllow the thĭng that göod is.

21 Forsake me nôt, O Lórd my God : bĕ not Thŏu far from me.

22 Hăste Thee to hêlp me : O Lord Gôd of mý sal-vä-tion.

Evensong.

PROPER PSALMS, 102, 130, 143.

PSALM 102. *Domine, exaudi.*

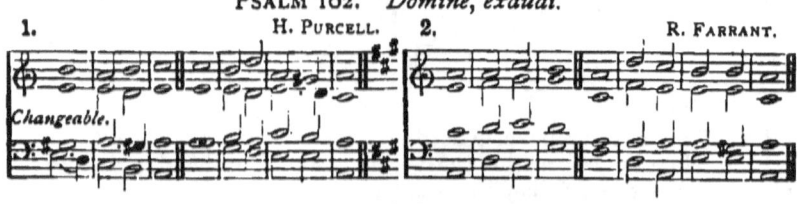

[PSALM 102.] *EVENSONG.* [ASH-WEDNESDAY.

p HĕAR my prăyer, O Lord : and lĕt my crȳing come un-to Thee.

2 Hide not Thy face from me * in the tĭme of my trŏu-ble : incline Thine ear unto me when I câll ; O hĕar me,⁀and that right soon.

pp 3 For my days are consŭmed awăy like smoke : and my bones are burnt up * ăs it wĕre a fĭre-brand.

4 My heart is smitten dôẉn, and wĭthered like grass : so that I forgĕt to eat my bread.

5 For the vôice of my grŏan-ing : my bones will scârce cleăve to mÿ flesh.

6 I am become like a pĕlican in the wĭl-der-ness : and like an ŏwl that is ĭn the dë-sert.

7 I have watched,* and am even as it wĕre a spăr-row : that sitteth alône upŏn the höuse-top.

8 Mine enemies revîle me ăll the⁀ day long : and they that are mad upon me * are swôrn togĕ-ther agäinst me.

9 For I have eaten ăshes ăs it⁀ were bread : and mĭngled my drĭnk with wëep-ing ;

10 And that because of Thine ĭndignă-tion⁀and wrath : for Thou hast tăken me ŭp, and cast me down.

11 My dăys are gône like a shā̆-dow : and I am wĭ-thered lĭke grass.

mf 12 But, Thou, O Lord, * shalt endŭre for ĕv-er : and Thy remem-brance throughout ăll gĕ-ne-rä-tions.

13 Thou shalt arise, * and have mĕrcy upon Sĭ-on : for it is time that Thou have mercy upŏn her, yĕa, the time is come.

p 14 And why ? * Thy servants thĭnk upŏn her stones : and it pitieth thĕm to sĕe her in the dust.

mf 15 The heathen shall fĕar Thy Năme, O Lord : and all the kĭngs of the eărth Thy Ma-jes-ty;

16 When the Lord shall bŭild up Sĭ-on : and whên His glŏ-ry shall ap-pear ;

17 When He turneth Him unto the prayer of the pôor dĕs-ti-tute : ănd despĭseth not their de-sire.

18 This shall be written for thôse that come ăf-ter : and the people whĭch shall be bŏrn shall praise the Lord.

19 For He hath looked dôwn from His sănc-tua-ry : out of the heâven did the Lŏrd be-hold the earth ;

20 That He might hear the mournings * of such as are ĭn captĭ-vi-ty : and deliver the chĭldren appoĭnt-ed un-to death ;

21 That they may declare the Name of the Lôrd in Sĭ-on : and His wôrship ăt Je-ru-sa-lem ;

22 When the people are gâthered togĕ-ther : and the kĭngdoms ăl-so,⁀ to serve the Lord.

p 23 He brought down my strĕngth in my joŭr-ney : ănd shŏrt-ened mÿ days.

24 But I said,* O my God,* take me not awăy in the mĭdst of⁀mine age : as for Thy years,* they endure throughout ăll gĕ-ne-rä-tions.

25 Thou, Lord, in the beginning * hast laid the foundâtion ŏf the earth : and the hêavens are the wŏrk of Thÿ hands.

26 They shall pêrish, but Thŏu shalt⁀en-dure : they all shall wax ôld as dŏth a gär-ment ;

27 And as a vesture shalt Thou change them, * and thêy shall be chăng-ed : but Thou art the sâme, and Thÿ years shall not fail.

28 The children of Thy sêrvants shall contĭ́-nue : and their sĕed shall stand făst in Thÿ sight.

[PSALM 130

PSALM 130. *De profundis.*

1. H. PURCELL. 2. *A. NEVILLE.

* These F's must be ♯ also when major

p OUT of the deep have I called unto Thée, O Lord : Lôrd hĕar mÿ voice.

2 O let Thine eărs consí-der well : thĕ voíce of my com-plaint.

3 If Thou, Lord, wilt be ex-treme * to mărk what is dóne a-miss : O Lôrd whó may abïde it ?

4 Fôr there is mér-cy⁀with Thee : thĕrefore shált Thou⁀be fĕar-ed.

5 I look for the Lord ; * my sôul doth waít for Him : ín His wórd is mÿ trust.

6 My soul flĕeth ún-to⁀the Lord : before the morning watch, * I sây, befóre the mor-ning watch.

7 O Israel, trust in the Lord,* for with the Lôrd there is mër-cy : and with Hím is plén-teous⁀re-dĕmp-tion.

8 And Hĕ shall redeem Ís-ra-el : frôm áll his sins.

PSALM 143. *Domine, exaudi.*

1. DR. BLOW. 2. *A. H. BROWN.

p HEAR my prayer, O Lord,* and consíder mý de-sire : hearken unto mĕ for Thy trúth and right-eousness' sake.

2 And enter not into jûdgment with Thy sĕr-vant : for in Thy sight shall nô man líving be jus-ti-fied.

3 For the enemy hath persecuted my soul ; * he hath smitten my lîfe dówn to⁀the ground : he hath laid me in the darkness,* as the mĕn thát have been long dead.

4 Therefore is my spirit vêxed withín me : and my heárt withín⁀me is de-so-late.

mp 5 Yet do I remember the time past ; * I mûse upon áll Thy works : yea, I exercise mysĕlf in the wórks of Thÿ hands.

6 I stretch fôrth my hánds unto Thee : my soul gâspeth unto Thée as⁀a thirs-ty land.

p 7 Hear me, O Lord, and that soon,* for my spírit wáx-eth faint : hide not Thy face from me,* lest I be like unto thêm that go dówn in-to⁀the pit.

8 O let me hear Thy loving-kindness betimes in the môrning, for in Thée is⁀my trust : shew Thou me the way that I should walk in,* for I lîft up my sôul un-to Thee.

9 Deliver me, O Lôrd, from mine é-ne-mies : for I flĉe unto Thée to hïde me.

10 Teach me to do the thing that pleaseth Thêe, for Thóu art⁀my God : let Thy loving Spirit lead me fôrth into the lánd of right-eous-ness.

mf 11 Quicken me, O Lôrd, for Thy Nâme's sake : and for Thy righteousness' sake * bríng my sóul out⁀of trôu-ble.

12 And of Thy goodness slây mine é-ne-mies : and destroy all them that vex my sôul ; for I am⁀Thy sër-vant.

Good-Friday.
Mattins.

Venite exultemus, Domino.

1. * E. TERRY.   2.   * T. MORLEY.

(Changeable.)

O COME, * let us síng ún-to⌢
the Lord : let us heartily rejoice in the strêngth of oúr sal-vä-
tion.
  2 Let us come before His prêsence
with thanksgív-ing : and shêw ourselves gláḋ in Him with Psalms.
  3 For the Lórd is a grêat God :
and a grêat Kíng above äll gods.
  4 In His hand are all the côrners
óf the earth : and the strength of
the hílls is Hís äl-so.
  5 The sea is Hís, and He máde
it : and His hánds prepár-ed⌢the
drÿ land.
  p 6 O come, * let us wôrship,
and fäll down: and knêel before
the Lórd our Mä-ker.
  7 For Hê is the Lórd our God :
and we are the people of His pâsture,
and the shéep of His hand.

mf 8 To-day if ye will hear His
voice, * hárden nót your hearts : as
in the provocation, * and as in the
day of temptâtion ín the wil-der-
ness ;
  9 When your fâthers témpt-ed
Me : prôved Mé, and saw My
works.
  10 Forty years long * was I grieved
with thís generá-tion,⌢and said : It
is a people that do err in their
hêarts, for they háve not known My
ways.
  11 Unto whôm I swáre in⌢My
wrath : that they shóuld not én-ter
into My rest.
  Glory be to the Fâther, ánd to⌢the
Son : ánd tó the Ho-ly Ghost ;
  As it was in the beginning, * is
nów, and éver shall be : wórld
without ênd. ˙A˙-men.

PROPER PSALMS, 22, 40, 54.
PSALM 22. *Deus, Deus meus.*

1.   DR. ALDRICH.   2.   * A. NEVILLE.

p **M**Y God, my God, * look upon
me ; * why hast Thôu
forsá-ken me : and art so far from
my health, * and fróm the wórds of
my com-plaint ?

  2 O my God, I cry in the day-
time, * but Thôu héar-est not : and in
the night-sêason ál-so⌢I take no rest.
  mf 3 And Thou contínuest hô-ly :
Ô Thou wór-ship⌢of Is-ra-el.

[4 Our

1. Dr. Aldrich. **2.** *A. Neville.

4 Our fathers hŏ-pĕd in Thee : they trusted in Thĕe, and Thŏu didst deli-ver them.

5 They called upon Thĕe, and were hŏl-pen : they put their trust in Thĕe, and were nŏt con-foŭnd-ed.

p 6 But as for me,* I am a wŏrm, and nŏ man : a very scorn of men,* and the oŭt-cast ŏf the pĕo-ple.

7 All they that sĕe me laŭgh me to scorn : they shoot out their lips,* and shăke their hĕads, săy-ing,

mf 8 He trusted in God,* that Hĕ would delí-ver him : let Him delí̆ver him, ĭf He will hăve him.

9 But Thou art He that took me ŏut of my mŏ-ther's womb : Thou wast my hope,* when I hanged yĕt upŏn my mo-ther's breasts.

10 I have been left unto Thee ĕver sínce I was born : Thou art my Gŏd even frŏm my mo-ther's womb.

p 11 O go not from me,* for trŏuble is hărd at hand : ănd there is nŏne to hĕlp me.

12 Many ŏxen are cŏme about me : fat bulls of Basan clŏse me ĭn on e-very side.

13 They gâpe upon me wĭth their mouths : as it were a răm̆ping and a rŏar-ing li-on.

14 I am poured out like water,* and all my bŏnes are oŭt of joint : my heart also in the midst of my bŏdy is ĕven like melt-ing wax.

15 My strength is dried up like a potsherd,* and my tongue cleaveth tŏ my gums : and Thou shalt brĭng me ín-to the dust of death.

16 For many dŏgs are cŏme about me : and the council of the wicked lăyeth sĭege a-găinst me.

17 They pierced my hands and my feet,* I may tĕll ăll my bones : they stand stăring and lŏok-ing upŏn me.

18 They part my gărments amŏng them : and cast lŏts upŏn my vĕs-ture.

pp 19 But be not Thou făr frŏm me, O Lord : Thou art my sŭccour, hăste Thee to hĕlp me.

20 Delĭver my sŏul from the sword : my dărling from the pŏw-er of the dog.

21 Săve me from the lĭ-on's mouth : Thou hast heard me also from amŏng the hŏrns of the u-ni-corns.

f 22 I will declare Thy Name ŭnto my brĕth-ren : in the midst of the congregătion wĭll I prăise Thee.

23 O praise the Lord,* yĕ that fĕar Him : magnify Him, all ye of the seed of Jacob,* and fear Him, ăll ye sĕed of Is-ra-el ;

24 For He hath not despised,* nor abhorred, the lŏw estăte of the poor : He hath not hid His face from him,* but when he călled unto Hĭm He hĕard him.

25 My praise is of Thee* in the great congregā-tion : my vows will I perform in the sĭght of thĕm that fear Him.

mf 26 The poor shall ĕat, and be să-tis-fied : they that seek after the Lord shall praise Him ;* your hĕart shall líve for ĕ-ver.

27 All the ends of the world shall remember themselves, * and be tŭrned ŭn-to the Lord : and all the kindreds of the nătions shall wŏr-ship befŭre Him.

28 For the kĭngdom ĭs the Lord's : and He is the Gŏvernour amŏng the pĕo-ple.

208

29 All sŭch as be fát upon earth : hăve eát-en,⌢and wor-ship-ped.
30 All they that go down into the dust * shall knêel befŏre Him : and nŏ man hath quíck-ened⌢his ŏwn soul.
31 My seêd shall sérve Him :
they shall be counted unto the Lôrd for a gé-ne-rä-tion.
32 They shall come, * and the heavens shall declâre His ríghteous-ness : unto a people that shall be bôrn, whóm the Lord hath made.

PSALM 40. *Expectans expectavi.*

ƒ **I** WAITED pâtiently fór the Lord : and He inclined unto mê, and heárd my cäll-ing
2 He brought me also out of the horrible pit, * oût of the míre and clay : and set my feet upon the rôck, and ór-dered⌢my gö-ings.
3 And He hath pût a new sóng in⌢my mouth : even a thânksgív-ing unto our God.
4 Mâny shall sée it,⌢and fear : and shall pût their trûst in the Lord.
5 Blessed is the man that hath sêt his hópe in⌢the Lord : and turned not unto the proud,* and to sŭch as gó a-bout with lies.
mf 6 O Lord my God,* great are the wondrous works which Thou hast done, * like as be also Thy thoughts which âre to ûs-ward : and yet there is nô man that órdereth⌢them un-to Thee.
7 If I should declâre them, and spéak of them : they should be môre than I am á-ble to ex-press.
8 Sacrifice, and meat-ôffering, Thou wóuld-est not : bût mine eárs hast⌢Thou o-pen-ed.
9 Burnt-offerings, and sacrifice for sĭn, hast Thou nót re-quir'd : thên said I,⌢ Lo, I come,
10 In the volume of the book it is written of mę,• that I should fulfil Thy will, O my God : I am
content to do it ; * yêa, Thy láw is⌢ with-in my heart.
11 I have declared Thy righteousness in the grêat congregä-tion : lo, I will not refrain my lips, O Lôrd, and thát Thou knŏw-est.
12 I have not hid Thy ríghteousness withín my heart : my talk hath been of Thy trûth, and of Thў sal-vä-tion.
13 I have not kept back Thy lôving mér-cy⌢and truth : frôm the gréat congre-gä-tion.
p 14 Withdraw not Thou Thy mêrcy frôm me,⌢O Lord : let Thy loving-kindness and Thy trûth álway⌢pre-sërve me.
15 For innumerable troubles are come about me ; * my sins have taken such hold upon me that I am not âble to lŏok up : yea, they are more in number than the hairs of my hêad, and my heárt hath fail-ed me.
16 O Lord,* let it be Thy plêasure to delí-ver me : make hâste, O Lórd, to hëlp me.
mf 17 Let them be ashamed, and confounded together, * that seek after my sôul to destróy it : let'them be driven backward, and put to rebûke, that wĭsh me ë-vil.
18 Let them be dêsolate, and rewárd-ed⌢with shame : that say unto me, * Fĭe upon thee, fĭe up-ŏn thee.

[19 Let

GOOD-FRIDAY.]   THE PSALTER.   PSALMS 54, 69.

19 Let all those that seek Thee be jôyful and glád in Thee : and let such as love Thy salvation say álway, The Lórd be praïs-ed.
p 20 As for me,* I am pôor and née-dy : bût the Lôrd careth for me
21 Thou art my hêlper and re-déem-er : make nô long tár-rying, O my God.

PSALM 54. *Deus, in nomine.*

p SAVE me, O Gôd, for Thy Náme's sake : ånd avénge me in Thy strength.
2 Hêar my práyer, O God : and hêarken unto the wórds of mÿ mouth.
3 For strangers are risen ûp a-gaînst me : and tyrants, which have not God before their eýes, sêek after my soul.
mf 4 Behold, Gôd is my hêlp-er : the Lôrd is with thém that⁀up-hold my soul.

5 He shall reward evil ûnto mine é-ne-mies : destrôy Thou thém in Thÿ truth.
6 An offering of a free heart will I give Thee,* and prâise Thy Náme, O Lord : becâuse it ís so com-forta-ble.
7 For He hath delivered me out of áll my trôu-ble : and mine eye hath seen his desîre upón mine e-ne-mies.

Evensong.

PROPER PSALMS, 69, 88.

PSALM 69. *Salvum me fac.*

p SAVE mê, Ő God : for the waters are côme in, é-ven unto my soul.
2 I stick fast in the deep mîre, where nó ground is : I am come into deep waters,* sô that the flóods run o-ver me.
3 I am weary of crýing ; my thróat is dry : my sight faileth me for wâiting so lóng up-on my God.

4 They that hate me without a cause * are môre than the haírs of ͡my head : they that are mine enemies,* and would destrôy me guílt-less, ͡are mi'gh-ty.

5 I paid them the thíngs that I né-ver took : God, Thou knowest my simpleness,* ånd my fáults are ͡ not hid from Thee.

mf 6 Let not them that trust in Thee, O Lord God of Hosts,* be ashâmed for mý cause : let not those that seek Thee be confounded through mê, O Lórd God ͡of Is-ra-el.

7 And why? * for Thy sâke have I súf-fered ͡ re-proof : shâme hath có-vered mý face.

8 I am become a stranger ûnto my brêth-ren : even an alien ûnto my mó-ther's chïl-dren.

9 For the zeal of Thine house hath êven éat-en me : and the rebukes of them that rebuked Thêe are fál-len upòn me.

10 I wept,* and chastened mysêlf with fást-ing : and thất was túrn-ed ͡ to my re-proof.

11 I put on sâckcloth ắl-so : ånd they jést-ed upòn me.

12 They that sit in the gâte speak ag´ainst me : and the drûnkards make sóngs up-òn me.

p 13 But, Lord,* I mâke my práyer unto Thee : ĭn án ac-cept-able time.

14 Hear me, O God, * in the mûltitude of Thy mêr-cy : even in the trûth of Thý sal-va-tion.

15 Take me out of the míre, that I sínk not : O let me be delivered from them that hate me,* and oût of the deˆep wä-ters.

16 Let not the water-flood drown me,* neither let the dêep swállow me up : and let not the pit shût her móuth up-òn me.

17 Hear me, O Lord,* for Thy loving-kíhdness is cóm-forta-ble : turn Thee unto me * according to the mûltitude óf Thy mêr-cies.

18 And hide nǫt Thy face from Thy servant,* for I am in trôu-ble : Ô hâste Thee, ͡and hëar me.

19 Draw nigh unto my sôul, and sâve it : O delíver me, becáuse of ͡ mine e-ne-mies.

mp 20 Thou hast known my re-proof, * my shame, and mý dishô-nour : mine âdversaries are áll in Thý sight.

p 21 Thy rebuke hath broken my heart ;* I am fûll of héa-vi-ness : I looked for some to have pity on me,* but there was no man,* neither fôund I ány to com-fort me.

22 They gâve me gáll to eat : and when I was thirsty * they gâve me vín-e-gar to drink.

mp 23 Let their table be made a snare to tâke themsélves with-al : and let the things that should have been for their wealth * be unto thêm an occá-sion ͡of fäll-ing.

24 Let their eyes be blíhded, that they sêe not : and êver bów Thou down their backs.

25 Pour out Thine indignâtion upón them : and let Thy wrâthful displéa-sure ͡take hold of them.

26 Let their hâbitátion be void : and nô man to dwêll in their tents.

27 For they persecute him whom Thôu hast smít-ten : and they talk how they may vex thêm whom Thóu hast wöund-ed.

28 Let them fall from one wícked-ness to anô-ther : and not côme ín-to ͡Thy right-eous-ness.

29 Let them be wiped out of the bôok of the lí-ving : and not be wrítten amóng the right-eous.

30 As for me,* when I am pôor and in héa-vi-ness : Thy hêlp, O Gód, shall lift me up.

f 31 I will praise the Nâme of Gód with ͡a song : and mâgnify it wíth thanks-gív-ing.

32 This álso shall pleáse the Lord : better than a bûllock thát hath horns and hoofs.

[33 The

1. Rev. W. Felton.   2. Dr. T. S. Dupuis.

33 The humble shall consíder thís, and ͡be glad : seek ye áfter Gód, and ͡your soul shall live.
34 For the Lórd héar-eth ͡the poor: and despíseth nót His pri-son-ers.
35 Let heaven and eárth práise Him: the séa, and áll that moveth there-in.

36 For God will save Sion,* and build the cíties of Jû-dah : that men may dwell there,* and háve it ín pos-sës-sion.
37 The posterity also of His sêr-vants shall inhé-rit it : and they that lóve His Náme shall dwell there-in.

PSALM 88. *Domine Deus.*

1. W. Hine.

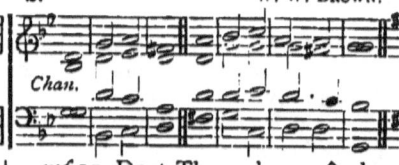

2. *W. W. Brown.

mp O LORD GOD of my salva-tion, * I have cried day and níght befóre Thee : O let my prayer enter into Thy presence,* incline Thine êar ún-to ͡my cäll-ing.
p 2 For my soul is fúll of trôu-ble : and my life drâweth nígh un-to hell.
3 I am counted as one of them that go dówn ín-to ͡the pit : and I have been éven as a mán that hath no strength.
4 Free among the dead, * like unto them that are wôunded, and líe in ͡the grave: who are out of remembrance,* and are cût awáy from Thý hand.
5 Thou hast láid me in the lów-est pit : in a pláce of dárk-ness, ͡and in the deep.
6 Thine indignation lieth hârd upón me : and Thou hast vêxed mé with all Thy storms.
7 Thou hast put away mine acquâintance fár from me : and made me to bé abhór-red öf them.
8 I am so fást in prí-son : thát I cán-not gét forth.
9 My sight faileth for véry trôu-ble : Lord, I have called daily upon Thee,* I have stretched fórth my hánds un-to Thee.

mf 10 Dost Thou shew wônders amóng the dead : or shall the dead rise ûp agaín, and praise Thee?
11 Shall Thy loving-kindness be shéwed ín the grave : or Thy fáith-fulness ín de-strüc-tion?
12 Shall Thy wondrous wôrks be knówn in ͡the dark : and thy right-eousness in the land where áll things áre for-güt-ten?
13 Unto Thêe have I crîed, O Lord : and early shall my práyer cóme be-fóre Thee.
p 14 Lord, why abhórrest Thóu my soul : and hídest Thóu Thy face from me?
15 I am in misery,* and like unto him that ís at the poínt to die : even from my youth up* Thy terrors have I súffered wíth a trou-bled mind.
16 Thy wrathful displeasure góeth óv-er me: and the féar of Théc hath ͡un-dóne me.
17 They came round about me dáily like wá-ter : and compassed mé togé-ther ͡on eve-ry side.
18 My lovers and friends hast Thou pút awáy from me : and híd mine acquaín-tance out of ͡my sight.

Lent.

Miserere.

¶ *Then shall they all kneel upon their knees, and the Priest and Clerks kneeling (in the place where they are accustomed to say the Litany), shall say this Psalm*

PSALM 51. *Miserere mei, Deus.*

1.   *A. H. BROWN.

(Minor.)   * ‖ Also when major.

p HAVE mercy upon me, O God,* âfter Thý great gŏodness : according to the multitude of Thy mêrcies dó away mine offĕn-ces.

pp 2 Wash me thrŏughly frŏm my wick-ed-ness : ând clĕanse më from my ṣin.

3 For I acknów-ledge mÿ faults : ând my sín is ever be-főre me.

4 Against Thee only have I sinned,* and dŏne this é-vil in Thy sight : that Thou mightest be justified in Thy sâying, and cléar when Thou art judg-ed.

5 Behőld, I was shá-pen^in wick-ed-ness : and in sín hath my mő-ther con-ceiv-ed me.

p 6 But lo,* Thou reqûirest trúth in^the in-ward parts : and shalt make me to ûnderstând wis-dom se-cret-ly.

7 Thou sḥalt purge me with hẏssop, and I shall be clẹan : Thou shalt wâsh me,* and I shall bë whi-ter^than snow.

8 Thou shalt make me hêar of jőy and glädness : that the bőnes which Thőu hast brok-en may re-joice.

9 Turn Thy fâce awáy from mÿ sins : ând pút out all my mïs-deeds.

10 Mâke me a clĕan heart, O God : and renêw a right spí-rit with-ín me.

11 Cast me nőt awáy from^Thy prēs-ence : and tâke not Thy hő-ly Spi-rit frőm me.

12 O give me the cőmfort of Thÿ help a-gain : and stâblish me wíth Thy frĕe Spí:-rit.

mf 13 Then shall I teach Thy wâys űn-to^the wïck-ed : and sîhners shall bé con-vert-ed un-to Thee.

p 14 Deliver me from blood-guiltiness, O God, * Thôu that árt the God of^my health : and my tőngue shall síng of Thÿ right-eous-ness.

(Major.) mf 15 Thôu shalt ő-pen^ my lips, O Lord : ând my mőuth shall shĕw Thÿ praise.

16 For Thou dẹsirest no sacrifice,* ĕlse would I give it Thee : but Thou delíghtest nőt in bürnt-of-fer-ings.

p 17 The sacrifice of Gőd is a trőu-bled spi-rit : a broken and contrite hêart, O Gőd, shalt Thŏu not de-spise.

mf 18 O be favourable and grâ-cious űn-to Sï-on : bûild Thou the wâlls of Je-ru-sa-lem.

19 Then shalt Thou be pleased with the sacrifice of righteousness,* with the burnt-őfferings ánd ob-lä-tions : then shall they..őffer young búllocks up-on Thine Al-tar.

Glőry be to the Fá-ther, and to^ the Son : ând tő thë Ho-ly Ghost ; As it was in the begínning, is nőw, and ever shall be : wőrld withőut ënd'A:-men.

PSALM 51. *Miserere mei, Deus.*

2. **A. H. Brown.*

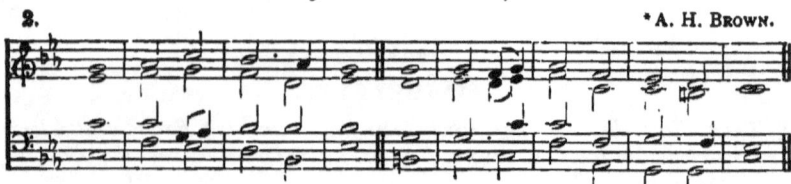

♩ HAVE mercy upon me, O God,* áfter Thý great göodness : according to the multitude of Thy mêrcies dó away mine offĕn-ces.

pp 2 Wash me thrôughly fróm my wick-ed-ness : ánd cleanse më from my ṣin.

3 For I acknów-ledge mÿ faults : ánd my sín is ever be-före me.

4 Against Thee only have I sinned,* and dône this é-vil in Thy sight : that Thou mightest be justified in Thy sâying, and cléar when Thou art judg-ed.

5 Behôld, I was shá-pen⁀in wicked-ness : and in sín hath my mö-ther con-ceiv-ed me.

p 6 But lo,* Thou reqûirest trúth in the in-ward parts : and shalt make me to ûnderstánd wis-dom se-cret-ly.

7 Thou shalt purge me with hýssop, and I shall be clęan : Thou shalt wâsh me,* and I shall bë whi-ter⁀than snow.

8 Thou shalt make me hêar of jóy and gläd-ness : that the bônes which Thóu hast brok-en may re-joice.

9 Turn Thy fâce awáy from mÿ sins : ánd pút out all my mis-deeds.

10 Mâke me a cléan heart, O God : and renêw a right spí-rit with-in me.

11 Cast me nôt awáy from⁀Thy prës-ence : and tâke not Thy hó-ly Spi-rit fröm me.

12 O give me the cômfort of Thÿ help a-gain : and stâblish me wíth Thy free Spi-rit.

mf 13 Then shall I teach Thy wáys ún-to⁀the wick-ed : and sínners shall bé con-vert-ed un-to Thee.

p 14 Deliver me from blood-guiltiness, O God,* Thôu that árt the God of⁀my health : and my tôngue shall síng of Thÿ right-eous-ness.

mf 15 Thôu shalt ó-pen⁀my lips, O Lord : ánd my móuth shall shëw Thy praise.

16 For Thou dęsirest no sacrifice,* ĕlse would I give it Thee : but Thou delíghtest nót in bürnt-of-fer-ings.

p 17 The sacrifice of Gôd is a tróu-bled spi-rit : a broken and contrite hêart, O Gód, shalt Thöu not de-spise.

mf 18 O be favourable and grâcious ún-to Sí-on : bûild Thou the wâlls of Je-ru-sa-lem.

19 Then shalt Thou be pleased with the sacrifice of righteousness, with the burnt-ôfferings ánd ob-lätions : then shall they..ôffer young búllocks up-on Thine Al-tar.

Glôry be to the Fá-ther, and to⁀ the Son : ánd tó thë Ho-ly Ghost ;

As it was in the begínning, is nów, and ever shall be : wôrld withôut ënd·A-men.

ALPHABETICAL INDEX OF CHANTS.

The Page numbers followed by a semicolon refer to the Canticles.

NAME OF COMPOSER.	DIED.	KEY.	PAGE.
ALCOCK, Dr. JOHN	1806	A	112, 126, 142, 191
———		D	59
———		D	158, 168
ALDRICH, Very Rev. H., D.D. ...	1710	A	74, 90, 131
———		A	110, 153
———		B ♭	14, 53, 84, 113
———		B ♭	56, 81, 134
———		E min.	4 ; 6, 45, 109, 207
———		F	154
———		G	89
ARNOLD, Dr. SAMUEL	1802	A	34
*ATHERSTONE, SIDNEY ...	1876	C	12 ; 1, 56, 105
———		C	129
*———	1877	E	10, 150
*———		E ♭	74
AYLWARD, Dr. T.	1801	D	84, 88, 195
AYRTON, Dr. EDMUND	1808	E ♭	15 ; 17, 123, 126 193
BACON, Rev. R. M.A.	1759	A ch.	114
*BARCROFT, LEONARD ..	1871	A	16 ; 16, 66, 170
*———		A ♭	7 ; 38, 82, 124
*———		C	13 ; 13, 39, 96
*———	1877	C	6 ; 58, 119, 188
*———		D	99, 193
*———	1877	E	2
*———		E	71, 176, 186, 190
*———		F	20, 155, 174, 189
*———		G min.	10, 44, 110
†BARNBY, JOSEPH		D	17 ; 89, 123, 178, 190, 198
†———		E	16 ; 25, 72
BARROW, J.	1789	E ch.	4, 150
BATTISHILL, JONATHAN	1801	A	75, 114, 146, 151, 190
———		D	7 ; 55, 152
———		G	118, 146, 175
BELLAMY, RICHARD, Mus. Bac. ...	1813	F	17 ; 23, 37, 72, 182
†BLAKELEY, WM. ARTHUR ...	1875	A min.	16 ; 5, 104, 210
†———		B ♭	105, 156
†———		C	18 ; 1, 179
†———		C	18 ; 54, 163, 201
BLOW, DR. JOHN	1708	E min.	11 ; 12, 46, 69, 137, 206
*BOSWORTH, THOMAS ...	1878	F	124
†BRIDGE, Dr. J. F.	1876	C	14 ; 70, 183
*BROWN, ARTHUR HENRY ...	1877	A	30, 76

Name of Composer.	Died.	Key.	Page.
Arthur Henry ...	1871	...	A	4; 30, 77, 166, 195
... ...	...	...	A	5; 32, 176
... ...	...	...	A	41, 174
... ...	1877	...	A	52, 153
... ...	1871	...	A	105
... ...	1877	...	A	129, 139, 175, 192, 196
... ...	1871	...	A	149
... ...	1877	...	A	9 (Benedicite)
... ...	1876	...	A min.	22, 206
... ...	1871	...	A min.	4; 24, 44, 184
... ...	1871	...	A ♭	158, 193
... ...	...	...	A ♭	6; 42, 127, 199
... ...	...	...	A ♭	11; 1; 65, 77
... ...	...	...	A ♭	14; 113
... ...	1875	...	B ♭	11; 26, 68
... ...	1871	...	B ♭	126
... ...	...	...	B ♭	150
... ...	...	...	B ♭	162
... ...	1877	...	B ♭ min.	14; 96
... ...	1877	...	C	8, 51
... ...	...	...	C	27, 84, 123, 151
... ...	...	...	C	38, 71, 165
... ...	1871	...	C min.	11; 12, 31, 63, 202
... ...	1877	...	C min.	214 (Miserere)
... ...	1871	...	D	3; 17, 21, 147
... ...	...	...	D	22, 74, 93, 160
... ...	...	...	D	17; 25, 27, 63, 170
... ...	1877	...	D	61
... ...	1871	...	D	7; 72, 124, 140, 189
... ...	1871	...	D	90, 134, 121, 156
... ...	1877	...	D	90, 182
... ...	1871	...	D ch.	10; 34, 154
... ...	1877	...	D ch.	16; 61, 79, 161
... ...	1877	...	D min.	45, 111, 202
... ...	...	...	D min.	69, 93
... ...	1871	...	E	9
... ...	...	...	E	14; 15, 147
... ...	1877	...	E	33, 114
... ...	1871	...	E	3; 42, 72, 101
... ...	...	...	E	107, 116
... ...	...	...	E	10; 123, 141
... ...	1871	...	E min.	17; 60, 93
... ...	1877	...	E min.	67, 109, 136
... ...	1871	...	E ♭	6, 50, 100, 138
... ...	...	...	E ♭	11, 36, 85
... ...	...	...	E ♭	5; 47, 66
... ...	1877	...	E ♭ min.	167
... ...	1871	...	F	3, 147
... ...	1877	...	F	16, 81, 189
... ...	1874	...	F	20, 164
... ...	1877	...	F	34, 120
... ...	1871	...	F	17; 34, 152
... ...	...	...	F	56
... ...	...	...	F	82, 116
... ...	1876	...	F	114
... ...	1877	...	F	160, 170

ALPHABETICAL INDEX OF CHANTS.

Name of Composer.	Died.	Key.	Page.
*Brown, Arthur Henry ...	1871	... F	164
*_____	1877	... F	9 (Benedicite)
*_____	1871	... F♯ min.	31, 134, 167
*_____	...	... G	11
*_____	1876	... G	4 : 26. 56. 179
*_____	...	... G	12 ; 55. 112, 129. 178
*_____	...	... G	59
*_____	...	... G	62
*_____	...	... G	66, 148
*_____	1877	... G	82
*_____	1871	... G	13 ; 91, 180
*_____	1877	... G	11 : 120
*_____	1871	... G	172
*_____	...	... G ch.	3 ; 107, 166. 180, 199
*_____	1877	... G ch.	213 (Miserere)
*_____	1877	... G 2	98
*Brown, Walter Wm.	1871	... B 2	41
*_____	...	... F	2, 96, 112
*_____	1871	... G ch.	5, 212
*Burnett, Cyril	1877	... B 2	58, 119. 166
*_____ Richard...	1877	... D	1 ; 49, 137
*_____	...	... F	6, 89
Byrde, W. ...	1623	G	27, 34. 42, 100
Childe, Dr. W.	1697	B 2	119, 158
†Chope, Rev. R.R. ...	1860	F	16 ; 4, 27
Cooke, Dr. Benjamin	1793	B 2	114
_____	...	F	19, 127, 179. 197
Corfe, J. ...	1820	G	107, 176. 182
*Coverdale, Oliver	1877	E	2, 7, 71, 195
*_____	1876	E min.	109
Croft, Dr. W.	1727	B min.	10 ; 49, 60, 157, 161
Dupuis, Dr. Thos. Sanderson	1796	A	55, 140
_____	...	A ch.	11 ; 52. 79, 172
_____	...	B 2	27, 75, 105, 198
_____	...	D	27, 91, 169, 189
_____	...	D min.	14 ; 46. 86, 96, 161. 210
_____	...	E min.	15 ; 2, 66, 122, 161
_____	...	E 2	32, 99, 120
_____	...	G	20
_____	...	G min.	62, 96, 134, 172
†Dyce, W. ...	...	F	14 : 91, 129, 141, 144.
†Edwards, Edwin ...	1877	G	3 : 9, 53. 131
†Elvey, Sir George. J.	...	A	36. 85, 186
†_____	...	D	37, 175
†Elvey, Dr. Stephen	...	C	89. 118
†Faning, Eaton	1877	D	113
†_____	...	F	13. 90
†_____	1877	G	26. 88
Farrant, J. ...	1598	G min.	167, 171
Farrant, R. ...	1585	A min.	63. 190
_____	...	F	144
Felton, Rev. W., Mus. Bac.	1769	E 2	10 : 45. 111, 210

ALPHABETICAL INDEX OF CHANTS.

Name of Composer.	Died.	Key.	Page.
Felton, Rev. W., Mus. Bac.	...	F	124, 140, 157
*Fisher, Charles	1877	A	3, 148, 172
*———	...	C	3; 14, 155
*———	...	D	12; 33, 151, 164, 181
*———	...	E min.	65, 81
*Foxe, James	1877	A min.	31
*———	...	C ch.	1; 145
*———	...	D	18
*———	1875	G	4
*———	1876	G	15, 65, 136
Fussel, Peter	1790	F	15, 58
†Gardner, Charles	1870	G	41, 134
†———	1876	G	5; 77, 116, 146, 187
†———	1870	G min.	17; 73, 104, 203
†Gauntlett, Dr.	1877	B♭	13 (Quicunque)
Gibbons, Dr. Christopher	1697	G	41, 103, 118, 164
Goldwin, J.	1716	G min.	96, 122, 202
Goodson, R., Mus. Bac.	1718	C	14, 30
*Graves, Edward T.	1876	E♭	10; 23, 37, 84, 194
*———	...	F	23, 158
Greene, Dr. Maurice	1755	B♭	7, 11
Hackett, J. D.	...	B♭	9, 99, 176, 196
Hayes, Dr. Philip	1797	B♭	20, 33, 101
———	...	E	127
———	...	E♭	74, 102, 154
———	...	A min.	8 (Benedicite)
Hayes, Dr. William	1777	A ch.	31, 152
———	...	D	127, 140, 194
———	...	D	142
———	...	D ch.	15; 122, 145, 186
———	...	E♭	21, 96
———	...	G min.	16; 32, 66, 134, 203
†Heap, Dr. Charles S.	1876	A min.	1; 45, 65
†Helmore, Rev. Thomas	1856	F	1; 2, 17, 52, 55
†Heywood, John	...	A♭	36, 76, 155, 172
†Hiles, Dr. Henry	...	E	53, 132, 196
†———	...	F	10; 47, 159, 175
Hindle, J. Mus. Bac.	1781	A	11; 49, 72, 99
Hine, William	1739	G	14; 11, 68, 121
———	...	G min.	172, 212
†Hopkins, E. J.	...	A	7; 56, 165
†———	...	A♭	66
†———	...	E♭	11; 26, 38, 70, 112
†Hoyte, W. S.	...	F	16; 102, 118
Humphreys, Pelham	1674	C	119, 180
———	...	D min.	4; 73, 157, 171
———	...	A	2 (Pascha)
Jones, J.	1795	B♭	16, 29
†Joule, B. St. J. B.	...	C	12 (Quicunque)
†———	...	D min.	60
†———	...	F	88, 159
Kelway, T.	1749	D	25, 139, 142

ALPHABETICAL INDEX OF CHANTS.

NAME OF COMPOSER.	DIED.	KEY.	PAGE.
KELWAY, T. ...		G	66, 141
———		G min.	5; 59, 114
———		G min.	203
KENT, JAMES...	1776	D	168
———		G ch.	76, 132, 166
KING, CHARLES, Mus. Bac.	1748	A min.	15; 6, 51, 103
———		G ch.	5; 132, 152
LAMB, B. ...	1699	F	39, 149
LANGDON, RICHARD, Mus. Bac.	1798	F	90, 149
———		G min.	1; 69, 172
LEE, W. ...	1724	D	17; 23, 56, 147
———		F	82, 104
———		G ch.	40, 111
MEDLEY, Rt. Rev. Bp.		G	16; 25, 120, 138
*MILLER, RICH. COPE	1877	D	131, 187
*———		F♯ min.	171
†MONK, Dr. EDWIN G.		A	17; 38, 54, 116, 177
†———		B♭	18, 117
†———		C	15; 21, 52, 163
†———		E♭	6; 7, 67, 77, 118
†———		F	16; 4, 100, 139
†———		G	3; 44, 56, 107
†MORLEY, THOMAS ...	1877	F ch.	5; 5, 132, 145, 207
NARES, Dr. J. ...	1783	A	3; 67, 72, 85, 134, 188
*NEVILLE, AUGUSTUS	1871	A ch.	14; 24, 69, 79, 206
*———		A♭	37, 101, 169
*———		E♭	22, 98, 157, 207
†OUSELEY, Rev. Sir F. A. G., Bart. ...		C min.	11; 11, 93
†———		E♭	7; 30, 75, 91, 170
PURCELL, DANIEL (brother of H.) ..	1717	G	2, 34, 72, 193
PURCELL, EDWARD (son of H.)	1740	D min.	11; 2, 40, 98
PURCELL, HENRY ...	1695	A ch.	15; 10, 24, 66, 204
———		A min.	68, 122, 206
———		G	29, 159, 162
——— THOMAS (uncle of H.)	1682	C min.	17; 46, 86, 156, 171
———		G	50, 138
———		G ch.	4; 46, 145, 203
†RIDLEY, WILLIAM ...	1877	A	14, 126, 168
†———		B♭	51, 89, 156, 192
†———		E♭	81, 118
*ROWLAND, GEORGE ...	1877	B♭	1, 187
*———		D	161
*———		D min.	3, 12
*RUSHBROOKE, FRED.	1877	D	56, 76
*———		D	5; 71, 177, 191
*———	1877	F	150
RUSSELL, W., Mus. Bac.	1813	C	53, 54, 142, 163
SAVAGE, W. ...	1789	C	144, 169
*SEWELL, ALFRED M.	1877	A	7, 8, 137, 190
*———		E♭	136, 201

ALPHABETICAL INDEX OF CHANTS.

Name of Composer.	Died.	Key.	Page.
*Seymour, Gerald	1871	... F	153, 177
*————	...	F♯ min.	34, 62, 86
*————	...	G ch.	121, 134, 155
†Smith, Boyton	1876	G	10; 102, 178
†Stainer, Dr. J., M.A. ...	1876	C	6 (Benedicite)
†————	...	D	1 (Venite)
†Steggall, Dr. Charles ...	...	D	15; 33, 113, 153, 160
†————	...	E	50, 117, 138
†————	...	E	75, 174
Tallis, Thomas	1585	A	73
————	...	A min.	11; 22, 40, 59, 154
————	...	A min.	17; 5, 62, 96, 209
————	...	C	9, 114, 121
————	...	F	1, 15, 70
†Taylor, Robt. Minton ...	1876	G	117, 148, 169, 183
†Terry, Edward R. ...	1876	A min.	5; 207
†————	...	B ♭	180
†————	...	C	44, 88
†————	...	E ch.	67
†————	...	E ♭	76, 168
†————	...	F	110
Tomlinson	1724	B ♭	13, 137, 146
Travers, J.	1758	E	7; 32, 117, 184
————	...	G ch.	24, 79, 209
Tucker, Rev. W.	1690	A	1, 114, 136, 195
Tudway, Dr. T.	1730	F	13; 42, 85, 172
†Turle, James	...	C	4; 16, 32, 174, 179
†————	...	F	3; 18, 89. 161
Turner, Dr. W.	1740	C	165
*Turrell, Louis John ...	1877	A	58, 163, 186
*————	...	C	15; 21, 36, 47, 177, 181
*————	...	C	6; 29, 61. 110
*————	...	C min.	210
*————	...	E	70
*————	...	F	11, 131, 165, 182
*————	...	F	15
*————	...	G	8, 118, 141
*————	...	G	6; 13, 50, 144
*————	...	G min.	12, 40, 109, 167, 202
Weldon, John	1736	G min.	1; 34, 59
*Wicks, Hubert	1871	A	86, 89, 100, 197
*————	...	C	3, 47, 101
*————	...	E	76
*————	...	F	4; 27, 55, 148
*————	...	F	72, 103
*————	...	F	15, 68
*Wilkinson, Edwin H. ...	1877	A	102, 196
*————	...	A min.	98
*————	...	A ♭	10; 159
Wise, Michael	1687	F♯ min.	63
*Wood, Edgar	1877	C	15, 103
*————	...	C♯ min.	16; 73, 111
*————	...	E ♭	27
Woodward, Dr. R. ...	1787	B ♭	8, 29

www.ingramcontent.com/pod-product-compliance
Lightning Source LLC
Chambersburg PA
CBHW020801230426
43666CB00007B/798